Revenue Sharing:
The Second Round

RICHARD P. NATHAN

CHARLES F. ADAMS, JR.

and associates

with the assistance of

André Juneau and James W. Fossett

Revenue Sharing:
The Second Round

THE BROOKINGS INSTITUTION

Washington, D.C.

Copyright © 1977 by

THE BROOKINGS INSTITUTION

1775 Massachusetts Avenue, N.W., Washington, D.C. 20036

Library of Congress Cataloging in Publication Data:

Nathan, Richard P
  Revenue sharing.

  Includes bibliographical references and index.
  1. Revenue sharing—United States. I. Adams,
Charles F., 1945–   joint author. II. Brookings
Institution, Washington, D.C. III. Title.
HJ275.N273   336.1′85   76-51884
ISBN 0-8157-5986-X
ISBN 0-8157-5985-1 pbk.

9 8 7 6 5 4 3 2 1

THE BROOKINGS INSTITUTION is an independent organization devoted to nonpartisan research, education, and publication in economics, government, foreign policy, and the social sciences generally. Its principal purposes are to aid in the development of sound public policies and to promote public understanding of issues of national importance.

The Institution was founded on December 8, 1927, to merge the activities of the Institute for Government Research, founded in 1916, the Institute of Economics, founded in 1922, and the Robert Brookings Graduate School of Economics and Government, founded in 1924.

The Board of Trustees is responsible for the general administration of the Institution, while the immediate direction of the policies, program, and staff is vested in the President, assisted by an advisory committee of the officers and staff. The by-laws of the Institution state: "It is the function of the Trustees to make possible the conduct of scientific research, and publication, under the most favorable conditions, and to safeguard the independence of the research staff in the pursuit of their studies and in the publication of the results of such studies. It is not a part of their function to determine, control, or influence the conduct of particular investigations or the conclusions reached."

The President bears final responsibility for the decision to publish a manuscript as a Brookings book. In reaching his judgment on the competence, accuracy, and objectivity of each study, the President is advised by the director of the appropriate research program and weighs the views of a panel of expert outside readers who report to him in confidence on the quality of the work. Publication of a work signifies that it is deemed a competent treatment worthy of public consideration but does not imply endorsement of conclusions or recommendations.

The Institution maintains its position of neutrality on issues of public policy in order to safeguard the intellectual freedom of the staff. Hence interpretations or conclusions in Brookings publications should be understood to be solely those of the authors and should not be attributed to the Institution, to its trustees, officers, or other staff members, or to the organizations that support its research.

To the memory of

James A. Maxwell

*in the hope that this volume
is up to his standard*

Foreword

In 1976 Congress decided that the general revenue sharing program, first enacted four years earlier as a major experiment in fiscal relations within the American federal system, should be extended through September 1980. In all likelihood, the program will endure much longer.

The distinguishing feature of general revenue sharing is that, for the first time, federal money is made available to state and local governments on a nearly unrestricted basis. Some 39,000 units receive payments. Though falling short of the "no strings" grants originally sought, the authorizing act contained a minimum of federal controls. The questions then arose: How would the money—$30.6 billion was authorized in the 1972 legislation—actually be used by the recipient governments? To what extent would expenditures be increased, taxes cut, or debt reduced? How would the recipient governments make their decisions—on whose advice and with whose participation?

Beginning with the enactment of the program in 1972, the Brookings Institution undertook to answer these questions. Financed by a series of grants from the Ford Foundation, a monitoring network of field researchers was established to make systematic observations in sixty-five state and local jurisdictions.

This is the second book summarizing the findings of the study. The first, *Monitoring Revenue Sharing,* by Richard P. Nathan, Allen D. Manvel, Susannah E. Calkins, and Associates, was published in 1975. A third and final volume is projected for publication in 1979.

In this book, the authors analyze not only the fiscal effects of revenue sharing on the sample governments (with special attention to central city finances), but also the political forces that shaped these decisions at the state and local levels. In addition, they review the national political debate of 1976, focusing on the issues raised and the modifications made in the original law.

A theme that emerged in the first volume of the series persists in this one: the diversity in both fiscal and political behavior in the recipient jurisdictions. One of the principal aims of the authors' research has been to illuminate the diversity in a way that lends a realistic perspective to the appraisal of the revenue sharing innovation. To help serve this purpose, a condensed transcript of a conference of the field associates, held at Brookings in April 1976, is included as an appendix to the text.

Richard P. Nathan, a senior fellow at the Brookings Institution and director of the general revenue sharing study from the beginning, is also directing a parallel monitoring study of the community development block grant program under a contract with the U.S. Department of Housing and Urban Development. Charles F. Adams, Jr., co-author of this volume, is a research associate in the Governmental Studies program. André Juneau, a research assistant, coded and analyzed much of the field data, and James W. Fossett, also a research assistant, contributed extensively to chapter 5. Bayle Weiner assembled the data on the history of revenue sharing for chapter 1. Allen D. Manvel, a co-author of the first volume in this series, provided valuable assistance for this volume as well.

The authors also wish to thank Thomas J. Anton, Arthur K. Mason, Robert D. Reischauer, and John Shannon for critical reviews of the manuscript. Officials of the federal government also provided assistance, notably William H. Sager of the Office of Revenue Sharing and Francis Barnett and Joel Miller of the Census Bureau. Mary M. Nathan contributed the title. Ellen Alston edited the manuscript; it was typed by Thomas T. Somuah; and the index was prepared by Florence Robinson. Gilbert Y. Steiner, as director of the Governmental Studies program, and James L. Sundquist, his successor as acting director, provided help in many ways.

As in all Brookings books, the views, opinions, and interpretations advanced here are those of the authors. They should not be ascribed to the trustees, officers, or other staff members of the Brookings Institution or to the Ford Foundation.

BRUCE K. MAC LAURY
President

February 1977
Washington, D.C.

Contents

Appendix Tables

Field Research Associates for Governmental Units Surveyed during the Second Round

Arizona: Maricopa County, Phoenix, Scottsdale, Tempe
David E. Shirley* *Professor of public administration, University of Arizona*
Willard Price *Assistant professor of public administration, University of Arizona*

Arkansas: Little Rock, North Little Rock, Pulaski County, Saline County
George E. Campbell *Attorney, Little Rock; former executive secretary, Arkansas Constitution Revision Study Commission*

California: State of California
Leslie D. Howe *Vice president, California Retailers; former state and local financial officer*

California: Carson, Los Angeles, Los Angeles County
Ruth A. Ross *Assistant professor of political science, Claremont Men's College*

Colorado: State of Colorado, Longmont
R. D. Sloan, Jr. *Associate professor of political science and director, Bureau of Governmental Research and Service, University of Colorado*

Florida: Jacksonville-Duval, Orange County, Orlando, Seminole County
John M. DeGrove *Director, Joint Center for Environmental and Urban Problems, Florida Atlantic–Florida International University*
Aileen R. Lotz *Staff consultant, Joint Center for Environment and Urban Problems*

Illinois: State of Illinois
Leroy S. Wehrle *Professor of economics, Sangamon State University; former director, Illinois Institute for Social Policy*
Robert N. Schoeplein *Associate professor of economics, University of Illinois*
John N. Lattimer *Executive director, State of Illinois Commission on Intergovernmental Cooperation*

Louisiana: State of Louisiana, Baton Rouge
Arthur R. Thiel *Research director, Public Affairs Research Council of Louisiana, Inc.*

* Deceased.

Maine: State of Maine, Bangor
Kenneth T. Palmer *Associate professor of political science, University of Maine*

Maryland: Baltimore, Baltimore County, Carroll County, Harford County
Clifton F. Vincent *Assistant professor of political science, Morgan State College*

Massachusetts: Commonwealth of Massachusetts, Holden Town, Worcester
James A. Maxwell* *Professor emeritus of economics, Clark University*

Missouri: St. Louis
Robert P. Christman *City hall reporter, St. Louis* Post-Dispatch

New Jersey: Essex County, Livingston Township, Newark, West Orange
Robert Curvin *Associate professor of political science, Brooklyn College*

New York: State of New York
Charles R. Holcomb *Publisher, The Ithaca Journal*

New York: New York City
Center for New York City Affairs, New School for Social Research (*under the direction of Henry Cohen, Dean*)

New York: Greece Town, Irondequoit Town, Monroe County, Rochester
Sarah F. Liebschutz *Assistant professor of political science, New York State University at Brockport*

North Carolina: State of North Carolina, Orange County
Deil S. Wright *Professor of political science, University of North Carolina*

Ohio: Butler County, Cincinnati, Hamilton, Hamilton County
Frederick D. Stocker *Professor of business research, Center for Business and Economic Research, Ohio State University*

Oregon: Cottage Grove, Eugene, Lane County, Springfield
Herman Kehrli *Director emeritus, Bureau of Governmental Research and Service, University of Oregon*

South Carolina: Camden, Fairfield County, Kershaw County, Winnsboro
C. Blease Graham *Assistant professor of government and research associate, Bureau of Governmental Research, University of South Carolina*

South Dakota: Minnehaha County, Rosebud Indian Tribe, Sioux Falls, Tripp County, Turner County
W. O. Farber *Chairman, Department of Government, and director, Governmental Research Bureau, University of South Dakota*

Wisconsin: Beaver Dam, Dodge County, Lowell Town, Mayville, Theresa Town
Clara Penniman *Director, Center for the Study of Public Policy and Administration, University of Wisconsin*

* Deceased.

Revenue Sharing:
The Second Round

1 *The New Act*

On October 13, 1976, President Gerald R. Ford signed into law the State and Local Fiscal Assistance Act Amendments of 1976, extending the general revenue sharing program for three and three-quarters years and providing $25.6 billion for the period of the extension legislation. The new act contained no important changes in the allocation formula, the heart of the program, although there were changes in three important areas. The civil rights provisions were significantly strengthened; new requirements for public participation, involving hearings and the publication of budget information, were included; and the auditing and accounting requirements of the act were strengthened. The origins of these changes, along with a discussion of other revisions considered and issues raised, are presented in this chapter in the context of a history of the period from the enactment of the original revenue sharing act to the signing of extension legislation.

Issues in the Ninety-third Congress

The first checks written under the State and Local Fiscal Assistance Act of 1972 were sent out December 8, 1972; the new Ninety-third Congress convened the following month. Early comments on the revenue sharing program were for the most part unfavorable. Representative Wilbur D. Mills, chairman of the House Committee on Ways and Means, said in an address to the Arkansas legislature in February 1973 that "he hoped that the program would not last beyond its allotted five years."[1] Senate Majority Leader Mike Mansfield of Montana said the revenue sharing program was not working and that he did not expect it to work in the future.[2] Sena-

1. *Revenue Sharing Bulletin* (February 1973), p. 2.
2. *New York Times*, February 27, 1973. Mansfield consistently opposed revenue-sharing legislation and was one of four senators who voted against it on final passage in 1976.

tor Adlai E. Stevenson III, Democrat of Illinois, warned against states and localities becoming overly dependent on the federal government because of revenue sharing.[3] Conservative Senator Harry F. Byrd, Jr., of Virginia complained that the federal government had no revenue to share.[4]

President Richard M. Nixon's proposed budget for fiscal 1974, announced on January 29, 1973, and recommending sharp cuts in many domestic programs, exacerbated this negative attitude toward revenue sharing. Senator George McGovern criticized the administration for using revenue sharing to displace other federal grant-in-aid funds. Although a supporter of revenue sharing in 1972, McGovern said it now appears that "what we voted for was an under-funded substitute for previous federal participation in the growth of communities across the nation."[5] In a similar vein, Walter W. Heller, who as chairman of the Council of Economic Advisors in 1964 had pressed for revenue sharing, charged that "the birth of general revenue sharing is being used to justify the homicide of selected social programs."[6]

Liberal criticism of revenue sharing was clearly dominant in this period. Others who spoke out were Democratic Representatives John A. Blatnik of Minnesota and Charles B. Rangel of New York, both of them charging that revenue sharing funds were being used to aid the "haves" and that not enough was being devoted to social needs.[7] Congresswoman Shirley Chisholm, Democrat of New York, said that although she had originally supported revenue sharing, she now believed it was not the answer; her concern, too, was that the program failed to aid the disadvantaged and minority groups.[8] Democratic Congressmen John Brademas of Indiana and Claude Pepper of Florida also criticized the revenue sharing program in this period, contending that it failed to benefit the elderly.

As the opposition became increasingly vocal, supporters of revenue sharing found it necessary to become more active. In June 1973, the U.S. Advisory Commission on Intergovernmental Relations (ACIR), a supporter of the program, released the results of a survey showing that "by a large margin, the American public approves the federal revenue sharing program. The margin of support is larger than the margin of support found

3. *Congressional Record*, daily ed., January 31, 1973, p. 1693.
4. Ibid., February 1, 1973, p. 1747.
5. Ibid., February 26, 1973, p. 3273.
6. *Revenue Sharing Bulletin* (June 1973), p. 2.
7. *Congressional Record*, daily ed., February 22, 1973, p. 987; ibid., March 1, 1973, p. 1160.
8. Ibid., February 20, 1974, p. 746.

in a similar poll conducted in May 1973 when the program was just getting underway."[9] Republican Senator Charles N. Percy of Illinois released his own survey results at a Chicago ACIR hearing in October 1973, which, in his words, indicated "overwhelming support for Federal revenue sharing."[10] Officials of the Nixon administration also stepped up their activities on behalf of revenue sharing in this first year of the program.

Nevertheless, as the second session of the Ninety-third Congress got underway in 1974, it became increasingly clear that the arena for revenue sharing extension legislation was not to be the Ninety-third Congress, as supporters had been urging. Senator Edmund S. Muskie, an advocate of revenue sharing, predicted in June of 1974 that the program would be "in for rough sledding when it comes up for renewal in the *next* Congress."[11] As election day neared, the organizations of the state and local governments, which were joined together in the so-called Big Six coalition to support revenue sharing legislation,[12] stepped up their activities. Testifying for the National League of Cities and U.S. Conference of Mayors, Mayor Moon Landrieu of New Orleans told the Senate Subcommittee on Intergovernmental Relations, "revenue sharing cannot be terminated without a devastating impact on the fiscal viability of municipal government."[13] The U.S. Conference of Mayors, at their annual convention in June 1974, adopted a resolution "supporting reenactment of the general revenue sharing program and promising to make renewal a key local issue in the Congressional campaigns."[14] In the following month, the National Association of County Officials adopted a resolution "to seek a commitment from every candidate for congressional office to support the reenactment of general revenue sharing."[15]

In this climate, a number of new revenue sharing bills were introduced in the final months of the Ninety-third Congress. Wilbur Mills, now safely

9. U.S. Advisory Commission on Intergovernmental Relations, *Changing Public Attitudes on Government and Taxes* (June 1974), p. 5.

10. *Congressional Record*, daily ed., October 18, 1973, p. 19393.

11. *Revenue Sharing*, Hearings before the Subcommittee on Intergovernmental Relations of the Senate Committee on Government Operations, 93:2 (Government Printing Office, 1974), pt. 1, p. 2 (emphasis added).

12. The Big Six included the National League of Cities, the U.S. Conference of Mayors, The National Association of County Officials, the National Governors' Conference, the International City Management Association, and the Council of State Governments.

13. Ibid., p. 525.

14. *Revenue Sharing Bulletin* (July 1974), p. 2.

15. Ibid. (August 1974), p. 2.

back in the revenue sharing camp, introduced a bill, cosponsored by Representative Hugh L. Carey, Democrat of New York, to extend the program for two years and eliminate state governments from participation. Mills's position on the exclusion of state governments was apparently the result of discussions with Mayor Abraham D. Beame of New York City; Carey's position was less clear, since he was then a candidate for the governorship of New York State. On this issue—the inclusion of state governments—Democratic presidential candidate Jimmy Carter, in both his primary and general election campaigns, took the same position as Mills and Carey. Officials of the organizations of local governments, however, supported the inclusion of state governments, and the issue never received serious consideration in congressional debate, in either the Ninety-third or the Ninety-fourth Congress. Less than a week after the introduction of the Mills bill, Senator William Brock, Republican of Tennessee, one of the most active congressional proponents of revenue sharing, introduced a bill to extend the program without change for seven years.

In October 1974, the Advisory Commission on Intergovernmental Relations met in Washington and strongly endorsed reenactment, at the same time issuing an evaluation report on revenue sharing. The commission's report concluded, "Congress should give favorable consideration to an extension of revenue sharing because the evidence to date clearly indicates that the program has strengthened our federal system in four important ways."[16] The four areas cited were: (1) redressing "fiscal imbalance"; (2) moving in "the right equalization direction"; (3) providing flexibility for federal grants; and (4) introducing progressivity into the nation's overall tax system. The Commission added that revenue sharing has "strengthened our federal system by increasing the decision-making powers of state and local governments and that its discontinuance would cause a severe shock to the state-local fiscal system."[17] While recognizing problems in the formula for distributing shared revenue, which were identified and discussed by the ACIR (in particular, "fiscal aberrations resulting from the 20 percent floor and the 145 percent ceiling on local revenue sharing allocations"), the commission urged "that the present formula be retained."[18]

In short, the climate of opinion toward revenue sharing as the Ninety-third Congress ended included: strong Ford administration and Repub-

16. Advisory Commission on Intergovernmental Relations, *General Revenue Sharing: An ACIR Re-evaluation* (October 1974), p. 39.
17. Ibid., p. 40.
18. Ibid., p. 69.

lican congressional support; a nascent campaign for reenactment on the part of organizations of state and local officials and governments; mounting criticism from within the Congress, generally from liberals, to the effect that revenue sharing failed to aid minorities, the poor, and the aged; and (as discussed later in this chapter) steadily increasing opposition from civil rights organizations.

Two important new elements also entered the picture in this period, both involving procedures for the Ninety-fourth Congress. A change in committee jurisdiction in the House of Representatives resulted in revenue sharing legislation being taken away from the Ways and Means Committee and assigned instead to the Committee on Government Operations. The switch did not bode well for revenue sharing, since Congressman Jack Brooks of Texas, chairman of the House Committee on Government Operations, had voted against revenue sharing in 1972. The second set of procedural changes adopted in 1974 that affected revenue sharing were contained in the Congressional Budget and Impoundment Control Act of 1974, which significantly limits the use of techniques for circumventing the annual appropriations process. Although a specific exception was made for the revenue sharing program through 1976, there was no assurance that the Congress would in the future countenance a multiyear appropriation for this program.[19]

Enter the Ninety-fourth Congress

The Ninety-fourth Congress, which convened January 14, 1975, did not mean a major shift in backing for revenue sharing. Of incumbents who won reelection, 69 percent had voted for revenue sharing in 1972, the same as the proportion of the Ninety-second Congress that had voted for the original revenue sharing program in 1972. Noting an increase in the number of reform-minded liberals in the new Congress, the editors of the monthly *Revenue Sharing Bulletin* predicted (correctly, as it turned out) that "revenue sharing reform provisions now under discussion—stronger civil rights enforcement, broader citizen participation, local government modernization—will receive greater attention and support."[20]

In his budget message for fiscal year 1976, President Ford strongly sup-

19. The 1972 revenue sharing act both authorized and appropriated five years of revenue-sharing funds.
20. *Revenue Sharing Bulletin* (November 1974), pp. 1, 8.

ported the revenue sharing program: "General Revenue Sharing has become an integral and important part of the Federal grants-in-aid system. This program has been highly successful providing fiscal assistance that can be applied flexibly to meet the needs of States and localities according to their priorities."[21] The President promised to submit new legislation extending the program through fiscal year 1982. His budget did not reveal the details of this legislation, although it was indicated that the funding level to be proposed would continue to include annual increments of $150 million.

This was not the first mention of revenue sharing by President Ford in transmitting his program in 1975. In his state of the union message, submitted two weeks prior to the budget message, Ford singled out two pieces of legislation he would support, which he said would be separately transmitted to the Congress—revenue sharing and the extension of the Voting Rights Act. The message as a whole concentrated on economic and energy matters, and Ford proposed an energy conservation program which in an important way affected the revenue sharing program. He requested an increase in energy taxes of $30 billion as a means of cutting the demand for fuel products and proposed that $2 billion of these funds be distributed to state and local governments "in additional revenue sharing to offset their increased energy costs."[22] Ford's proposal for higher energy taxes was rejected, and as a result this additional shared revenue was later dropped from the administration's legislative program.

On January 15, 1975, the same day as the state of the union message, Senator Brock, along with ten Republican cosponsors, introduced a bill for a permanent revenue sharing program. Going back to the original concept of the Heller-Pechman plan of 1964,[23] Brock's bill provided for the redistribution to states and localities of a fixed percentage of the federal personal income tax base. On January 23, Republican Congressmen Jack F. Kemp of New York and Albert H. Quie of Minnesota introduced a similar revenue sharing bill in the House.

21. *The Budget of the United States Government for the Fiscal Year Ending June 30, 1976*, p. 17.

22. "The State of the Union Message, January 15, 1975," in *Weekly Compilation of Presidential Documents*, vol. 11 (1975), p. 51.

23. In 1964, Walter Heller, then chairman of the Council of Economic Advisors, and economist Joseph A. Pechman of the Brookings Institution, who chaired a Johnson task force on intergovernmental finances, backed a revenue-sharing plan which President Johnson considered but did not adopt. See Richard P. Nathan, Allen D. Manvel, and Susannah E. Calkins, *Monitoring Revenue Sharing* (Brookings Institution, 1975), pp. 347–350.

Although the administration's revenue sharing bill was not submitted until April 25, 1975, the changes being considered became known outside of the administration late in December 1974. A study group on revenue sharing had been established in the spring of 1974, consisting of officials of the Domestic Council, the Treasury Department, and the Council of Economic Advisors. On December 23, 1974, this group briefed representatives of major lobbying organizations of state and local officials; a similar briefing was presented several weeks later to civil rights and social-action groups. The study group, which was headed by Treasury Under Secretary Edward C. Schmults, also included James H. Falk, associate director of the Domestic Council, Walter D. Scott, associate director of the Office of Management and Budget, and Graham Watt, director of the Office of Revenue Sharing.[24] Its proposals, which were later adopted by the administration, were the target of considerable criticism. John J. Gunther, executive director of the U.S. Conference of Mayors, complained that the administration's plan involved too slow a rate of increase in funding (at $150 million a year).[25] Others criticized the lack of formula changes, particularly the failure to do more to meet big city needs. Civil rights groups, however, were the strongest opponents of the administration plan.

CIVIL RIGHTS CRITICISM

On January 20, 1975, under the sponsorship of the Leadership Conference on Civil Rights, twenty-two organizations wrote a letter to President Ford protesting the plan being developed by the administration study group. The letter called the group's recommendations "cosmetic at best, in that they fail to deal adequately with serious problems implicit in the current revenue sharing program."[26] Describing these problems, the letter said, "Extensive grass roots investigations, conducted by reputable academic, civic, community and religious organizations, have brought to light

24. See "Ford to Recommend Few Changes in Revenue Sharing," *National Journal Reports* (January 18, 1975), p. 85.

25. Ibid., p. 86.

26. Letter to the President, January 20, 1975. Among the organizations joining in this letter were: Americans for Democratic Action, American Friends Service Committee, League of Women Voters of the United States, National Association for the Advancement of Colored People, National Association of Social Workers, National Committee Against Discrimination in Housing, National Conference of Catholic Charities, National Organization for Women, National Rural Housing Coalition, National Urban Coalition, National Urban League, and the United Methodist Church.

serious deficiencies in how well the program serves the needs of minorities, women and the poor. There is strong evidence that revenue sharing funds are being used in ways that perpetuate discrimination against minorities and women, and exclude the general public from effective participation in local spending decisions."

These criticisms were largely based on a study by the National Clearinghouse on Revenue Sharing, an organization consisting of four of the twenty-two organizations signing the letter to the President.[27] In December 1974, the clearinghouse had issued a report on revenue sharing that criticized the program on civil rights grounds and for its failure to promote citizen participation and to meet social needs.[28] A related series of reports was published by the U.S. Civil Rights Commission in February 1975. For minorities and women, the commission said, "revenue sharing accomplishes its purpose to strengthen state and local governments—but at the expense of their involvement in that process."[29]

The Civil Rights Commission called for, among other steps, more enforcement personnel and funds for the Office of Revenue Sharing—specifically for $7.5 million to employ 300 additional persons for civil rights compliance. A month later, in appropriations hearings in the House, Under Secretary of the Treasury Schmults specifically rejected the 300 figure; the department instead requested an increase of 21 persons in the compliance area, increasing the size of this unit to 51 positions.[30]

In the area of civil rights policy, the Treasury Department issued new regulations October 28, 1975, which focused on employment, broadening the scope of the program in this area, and also required that revenue sharing funds be used to ameliorate "imbalances" in the provision of services to which revenue sharing funds are allocated.[31] Civil rights organizations contended that the regulations still were inadequate, and continued to call for stronger civil rights provisions in extension legislation.

27. The four are the League of Women Voters Education Fund, the National Urban Coalition, the Center for Community Change, and the Center for National Policy Review (Catholic University).

28. National Clearinghouse on Revenue Sharing, *General Revenue Sharing in American Cities; First Impressions* (Washington: NCRS, December 1974).

29. U.S. Commission on Civil Rights, *Making Civil Rights Sense Out of Revenue Sharing Dollars*, Clearinghouse Publication no. 50 (CCR, February 1975), p. 4.

30. *Treasury, Postal Service and General Government Appropriations for Fiscal Year 1976*, Hearings before a Subcommittee of the House Committee on Appropriations, 94:1 (GPO, 1975), pt. 1, p. 271. Eleven new positions were granted for fiscal 1976.

31. *Federal Register*, vol. 40, no. 208 (October 28, 1975), pp. 50028 ff.

In November 1975, a new director was named for the Office of Revenue Sharing, Jeanna D. Tully, formerly special assistant to the director of the Office for Civil Rights, U.S. Department of Health, Education, and Welfare. Having both experience and a special interest in civil rights compliance matters, the new director indicated that she would concentrate in this field.

A number of important court cases involving civil rights compliance under the revenue sharing program were pending in this period. In one case initiated by the Office of Revenue Sharing, a portion of the revenue sharing funds for the state of Michigan were held up in a dispute concerning all-black schools in the Ferndale school district.[32] Controversy continued throughout 1975 over the widely publicized case involving the city of Chicago; under a court order, nearly $19 million per quarter in revenue sharing funds were withheld from Chicago because of discrimination in police hiring.[33]

RESEARCH STUDIES

Civil rights groups were by no means the only ones to scrutinize the revenue sharing program in this period. Indeed, few domestic programs have been so extensively studied. The National Science Foundation's RANN program (Research Applied to National Needs) allocated $2 million for this purpose. It funded a total of twenty-two studies, the major groupings being nine studies on the formula for distributing revenue sharing funds and nine on the fiscal impact and process effects of the program. Other studies were financed by the Ford and Carnegie Foundations. The findings of studies prepared under these and other auspices received considerable public attention and were the subject of a number of hearings in both houses of Congress. They considered such matters as: (1) the "fungibility" issue—that is, the difficulty of identifying the net effects of revenue sharing because of the ease with which state and local officials can transfer funds among budget categories; (2) the potential for misinformation because of the nine "priority-expenditure" categories in the act, on the basis

32. *Revenue Sharing Bulletin* (February 1975), p. 7.
33. This case, originally brought by private litigants, was resolved by a district court decision (*United States* v. *Chicago*, 395 F. Supp. 329) in February 1976. Under that decision, Chicago would be eligible to receive revenue sharing funds only if it followed a court-ordered promotion and hiring plan explicitly aimed at increasing the proportion of minority and women members of the police force. This decision was upheld by the U.S. Court of Appeals for the 7th Circuit on January 11, 1977.

of which the uses of shared revenue had to be publicly reported;[34] (3) the trade-off between new and substitution uses of shared revenue; (4) the complexities involved in defining general-purpose units of local government and in dealing with the layering of these units in the allocation of revenue sharing funds; (5) the problem of limited-function units classified as "general," as in the case of midwestern townships and New England counties; (6) the effects of the floor and ceiling provisions in the formula contained in the 1972 act in providing incentives for the retention of limited-function units and, in a number of important cases, discriminating against central cities without an overlying county government; (7) the role of state governments under revenue sharing and the relationship of federal revenue sharing to their own fiscal subventions; and (8) the general workings of the formula and its sensitivity. Several reports from the research community, including one from Brookings, called for changes in the formula for allocating revenue sharing funds.[35] The final chapter in this book deals with the impact of these and other subjects considered by researchers in the debate on legislation to extend the revenue sharing program enacted in 1976.

Among federal agencies, the General Accounting Office was also actively involved in studying the revenue sharing program. Its reports stressed, among other subjects, the difficulties involved in determining the uses of shared revenue.[36]

FORD PROPOSAL FOR RENEWAL

The administration's proposed legislation for the renewal of the revenue-sharing program, submitted to Congress April 25, 1975, reflected what was essentially a "don't rock the boat" approach. At the White House the day the bill was submitted, the President told state legislators: "Now we

34. The original act contained nine priority-expenditure categories: public safety, environmental protection, public transportation, health, recreation, libraries, social services for the aged and the poor, financial administration, and capital expenditures. It was generally agreed that these categories were a source of confusion and misinformation. See Nathan, Manvel, and Calkins, *Monitoring Revenue Sharing*, chapter 9.

35. Ibid., chapter 6.

36. At the Senate hearings on revenue sharing in 1975, Comptroller General Elmer B. Staats indicated significant reservations about the general revenue-sharing program on accountability grounds. See *General Revenue Sharing*, Hearings before the Subcommittee on Revenue Sharing of the Senate Committee on Finance, 94:1 (GPO, 1975), p. 128.

have, in my judgment, a hard battle ahead of us. But if you join with me, and we get the mayors and the county officials to join with us, we can extend this program along the lines that I'm recommending. It's not going to be easy. You will have some people who will want to change its character, reduce its money, put all kinds of limitations and strings on it. We cannot afford to have that happen."[37] The administration's bill appropriated $39.85 billion over five and three-quarters years.[38] The partial-year funding for nine months from January to September 1982 was included to conform to the new fiscal year established in the Congressional Budget and Impoundment Control Act of 1974.

The only change in the formula recommended by the President was to raise the ceiling that limited entitlements of individual cities and townships to 145 percent of the average amount of shared revenue per capita paid to municipal and township units in any particular state. This provision had been widely criticized for reducing the funds received by central city governments. The first Brookings volume on the general revenue sharing program, published in 1975, recommended the elimination of this ceiling. Pointing out that St. Louis would have gained by 78 percent in the absence of this provision, Baltimore by 51 percent, and Philadelphia by 47 percent, the report stated that "the revenue-sharing law would be greatly improved by elimination" of this provision.[39] Other research reports proposed modifying the ceiling and some recommended the adoption of a completely new allocation system designed to provide more aid to densely populated areas.

37. "The President's remarks to State Legislators Attending a Special Leadership Conference, April 25, 1975," in *Weekly Compilation of Presidential Documents*, vol. 11 (1975), p. 443.

38. This total, which allows for annual increments of $150 million, is essentially a continuation of the funding policy in the 1972 act.

39. Nathan, Manvel, and Calkins, *Monitoring Revenue Sharing*, p. 159. A number of problems would have been created by eliminating the 145 percent ceiling without at the same time making related formula revisions. Such revisions are discussed in chapter 6 of *Monitoring Revenue Sharing*, and are also considered in a subsequent report written by the staff of the Brookings revenue sharing project under a grant from the National Science Foundation. In the report to NSF, special attention was given to the concern that simply eliminating the 145 percent ceiling would raise payments for many resort communities and industrial enclaves. Tests were done on formula alternatives to reduce or avoid this problem by removing the 145 percent ceiling *only* for cities above 5,000 population and county areas above 10,000 population. See Allen D. Manvel, Jacob M. Jaffe, and Richard P. Nathan, "Revenue Sharing Formula Alternatives: Final Report" (Brookings Institution, March 15, 1976; processed).

Specifically, the Ford administration recommended raising the 145 percent ceiling by six percentage points per year over five years to 175 percent in 1982, as a means of enabling "hard-pressed jurisdictions now constrained by the per capita limitation to receive more money."[40] This change, however, was not emphasized. In describing his plan, Ford said "the basic revenue sharing formula is retained . . . (because) experience to date suggests the essential fairness of the present formula."[41]

The President's message of April 25 contained four other proposed changes. Three of these—on civil rights, citizen participation, and reporting—dealt with points raised by liberal critics of the revenue sharing program. These changes, combined with the raising of the 145 percent ceiling (also a concern of liberals), reflected a basic administration strategy of giving recognition to the liberals' position while at the same time offering proposals that were considerably less far-reaching than critics demanded. It was clear in this period that the issue of renewal was to be argued mainly in terms of the program's supporters versus its liberal critics. By this time, the conservative arguments against revenue sharing, which had been more prominent in the debate over the original act passed in 1972, were muted. Congressional liberals, however, appeared to have decided against a frontal attack; rather than opposing extension altogether, they concentrated their energies on changes related to the three so-called accountability issues noted above.

In the civil rights area, where the level of controversy was the highest, the President said his bill would "strengthen the civil rights provisions of the existing statute" by permitting the secretary of the treasury to withhold all or a portion of entitlement funds, to terminate payments, and to require repayment of shared revenue previously expended in a program of activity found to be discriminatory.

Similarly, on citizen participation, the President said his bill would "strengthen public participation in determining the use of shared revenues." The legislative provision to carry out this purpose was not very rigorous, however. It required that each recipient government assure the secretary of the treasury that "it will provide its residents with an opportunity to give their recommendations and views on the proposed expenditures of shared revenues."[42] This change, which originated with Ford's

40. "President's Message, April 25, 1975," p. 441.
41. Ibid., p. 440.
42. U.S. Department of the Treasury, "Renewal of General Revenue Sharing, 1975," p. 18.

study group, stipulated that budget hearings would satisfy the requirement, but that if such hearings were not held, "some other appropriate means of participation" would have to be indicated in an assurance to the secretary.[43]

President Ford's message also referred to a proposed change in revenue sharing to "make reporting requirements more flexible to meet varying needs." No specific revisions in the reporting system were recommended; the administration's bill simply gave increased authority to the secretary of the treasury to prescribe the form and content of reports on the uses of shared revenue required to be submitted by recipient governments.

The fourth change listed by the President related to legislative timing. To avoid a repeat of the problems anticipated by late action on revenue sharing legislation, President Ford's new bill required a report by the secretary of the treasury two years before the expiration date, designed to trigger congressional reconsideration.

Far and away the most complicated area in which revisions were proposed involved the formula for distributing revenue sharing funds. Initially, the organizations included in the Big Six coalition cooperated with the administration's "don't rock the boat" approach to the formula. But in July 1975, big-city mayors in the U.S. Conference of Mayors managed to have the conference's resolutions committee adopt a policy statement calling for "a stronger needs factor" in revenue sharing. As it turned out, their victory was short-lived. When the issue came to the floor of the conference, opposition forces, led by New Orleans Mayor Moon Landrieu, fought against the resolutions committee position, defeating it handily.

At the end of the mayor's conference, President Ford met with a delegation of one hundred mayors at the White House. Ford warned against "tinkering with the formula." He said that the revenue sharing formula is "about as equitable as you can make it. If we fool around, in my judgment you face the possibility that it [the revenue sharing program] will either not be extended on the one hand or it could be confused such that you wouldn't like it."[44]

Underlying these political maneuvers about whether and how to revise the formula was an increasing understanding of the dynamics of the allocation system. As researchers and interest groups tested various possible changes, the volatility of the formula became increasingly apparent.[45] Be-

43. *National Journal*, January 18, 1975, p. 91.
44. *Revenue Sharing Bulletin* (July 1975), p. 3.
45. See Nathan, Manvel, and Calkins, *Monitoring Revenue Sharing*, chapter 6. A number of studies funded by the National Science Foundation demonstrate this

cause of the diversity among the states in fiscal structure and political organization, seemingly small changes in the formula to deal with a particular problem could have large and often unintended consequences.

CONGRESSIONAL REACTION TO FORD PLAN

Reactions to President Ford's proposals presented few surprises. Reflecting the concern of civil rights and social action groups, Democratic Congressman Robert F. Drinan of Massachusetts was sharply critical of the President's plan and later introduced his own revenue sharing bill. Drinan's bill sought to remedy what he characterized as the serious, "but not necessarily fatal," deficiencies of the administration's bill.[46]

A canvass by the *Revenue Sharing Bulletin* in April 1975 showed a mixed reaction among members of the Subcommittee on Intergovernmental Relations of the House Committee on Government Operations. All three Republicans were registered as supporting renewal, though the chairman of the subcommittee, L. H. Fountain of North Carolina, was noncommittal in this period, as were most of the other Democratic members of the panel available for comment. In the Senate Finance Committee, the chairman of the oversight subcommittee on revenue sharing, Senator William D. Hathaway of Maine, was critical of the administration's plan. He cited as areas of particular concern "civil rights, the allocation formula among the states, and the method of funding the program itself, as well as the size of that program."[47]

---

point and show the results of tests of different formula alternatives. Under a grant from NSF, the staff of the Brookings monitoring study analyzed a range of formula alternatives, including changes in the 145 percent ceiling and the 20 percent floor, the use of county areas in the allocation system, and the tax effort and tax capacity measures factors in the original act. See Manvel, Jaffe, Nathan, "Revenue Sharing Formula Alternatives," and National Science Foundation, Research Applied to National Needs, *General Revenue Sharing: Research Utilization Project*, vol. 1: *Summaries of Formula Research* (July 1975).

46. *Congressional Record*, daily ed., June 26, 1975, p. 6277. Among its major provisions, Drinan's bill set spending at required minimal levels for the designated priority areas; required maintenance of effort; set up local citizens' advisory committees and, for states, an Office of Citizen Advocacy; revised the allocation formula generally to aid cities (raising the 145 percent ceiling to 300 percent), removing the 20 percent floor, and eliminating entitlement payments, in favor of annual appropriation; strengthened the civil rights provisions by prohibiting discrimination in *any* program or activity undertaken by a recipient government and in other ways; and provided for a five-year authorization and annual appropriations "to enhance accountability."

47. *Revenue Sharing Bulletin* (May 1975), p. 1.

Strategy for the legislative handling of revenue sharing was still fluid at this point. Should the legislation originate in the House or the Senate? With the change in committee assignments in the House, some supporters argued that since it was no longer being treated as a revenue measure (the reason for its previous assignment to the House Ways and Means Committee), it could now originate in either body. For a while, the chairman of the Senate Finance Committee, Russell B. Long of Louisiana, a revenue sharing supporter, considered initiating action in the Senate. In the end, Long held off, apparently believing there was tactical advantage in waiting for the House to act and then reacting.

Despite the argument that revenue sharing should be renewed in 1975 to avoid budget uncertainty for states and localities, it became increasingly clear in the closing days of the first session of the Ninety-fourth Congress that this would not happen. (The original act expired December 31, 1976.) The intergovernmental relations subcommittee in the House, in particular, approached its new responsibility with much care and deliberation. Staff director Delphis C. Goldberg organized two separate sets of hearings. The first examined the fiscal and economic setting of revenue sharing; the second, considering the legislation itself, did not begin until September 25, 1975. Over eighty witnesses were heard, concluding on December 2, 1975.[48]

Responsibility for the slow pace of revenue sharing renewal in the Ninety-fourth Congress was assigned to many. Some observers faulted the House Committee on Government Operations for not moving faster; others held that the interest groups involved had failed to build up enough steam behind their lobbying efforts. Another interpretation faulted the organizations of state and local officials for being too aggressive and demanding. The administration, too, came in for criticism for not applying more muscle. In any event, it came as something of a surprise to many state and local officials in mid-1975 that they were destined not to know about the form and formula—or even the continued existence—of revenue sharing until the late summer of 1976 at the earliest. The steps required by the Congressional Budget Act meant that if a bill was not enacted in 1975, it would come under the new budget process for 1976 and as a result could not be considered on the floor of either body until after May 15, 1976.

The month before the first session of the Ninety-fourth Congress ended,

48. *State and Local Fiscal Assistance Act (General Revenue Sharing),* Hearings before a Subcommittee of the House Committee on Government Operations, 94:1 (GPO, 1975).

the National Association of Counties held a "revenue sharing rally" in Washington. County officials heard speakers and met with members of Congress to urge favorable and fast action on the legislation. One of the speakers, Senator Russell Long, gave blunt advice for lobbying other members of the Congress: "If they can't help you with your most important program," said Long, "then you might not be able to help them with their most important program, re-election."[49]

NEW YORK'S FISCAL CRISIS AND COUNTERCYCLICAL AID

As the momentum built up for the renewal of revenue sharing in 1975, a major development involving state and local finances held center stage in domestic affairs and affected in important respects the revenue sharing debate—New York City's fiscal crisis. Although it was acknowledged that new revenue sharing legislation would have relatively little impact on New York's budget gap,[50] the underlying needs of New York and other large cities improved the chances for renewal by creating a mood in which fiscal problems of state and local governments were increasingly prominent.

More closely related to the New York situation was a legislative proposal introduced in the Ninety-fourth Congress to deal with the economic downturn by providing emergency financial assistance to governments with high rates of unemployment. Variously titled "countercyclical revenue sharing," "antirecession assistance," and "emergency assistance," these bills soon became linked, as far as their legislative fate was concerned, with the drive to renew revenue sharing.

The rationale for emergency payments to state and local governments was much the same as that for the original Heller-Pechman plan: instead of concentrating the federal stimulus designed to combat the 1974–75 recession in the private sector (as in the case of a tax reduction), some of the stimulus should be in the public sector in the form of emergency financial assistance to state and local governments. The prime mover behind this idea in the Congress was Senator Edmund S. Muskie.

Congressional action on this legislation did not begin until January

49. *County News*, November 24, 1975.

50. See Congressional Budget Office, *New York City's Fiscal Problem: Its Origins, Potential Repercussions, and Some Alternate Policy Responses* (CBO, October 10, 1975). New York's budget gap in the beginning of 1976 was variously estimated at $750 million to $1 billion or more. The city then received approximately $250 million annually under the general-revenue sharing program. Altogether, through June 30, 1975, it had received $1,716 million in shared revenue for this three and one-half year period.

1975 when the Senate Subcommittee on Intergovernmental Relations held hearings on the general subject of state-local financial problems. The chairman of the subcommittee, Senator Muskie, then introduced counter-cyclical assistance legislation which was passed by the Senate and added as an amendment to a House-passed emergency public works measure. The combined bill was, however, vetoed by President Ford, and his veto was sustained. But this was not the end of the road. The combined bill was revived and again passed by the Congress in June 1976; this time the President's veto was overridden. The countercyclical assistance feature of the new act authorized $1.25 billion for five quarters, beginning July 1, 1976, to state and local governments with an unemployment rate exceeding 4.5 percent for the previous calendar quarter for purposes of determining eligibility. One-third of the funds are reserved for state governments, two-thirds for local units, just as under the general revenue sharing program. Distribution is based on the excess of unemployment over 4.5 percent. Funds can be used for all "basic services," defined as any not involving capital expenditures, which presumably would be funded with the emergency public works grants contained in the same act.

REVENUE SHARING LEGISLATION IN THE SECOND SESSION, NINETY-FOURTH CONGRESS

As the second session of the Ninety-fourth Congress got underway in 1976, the focus of attention for revenue sharing legislation was the House Subcommittee on Intergovernmental Relations. Sitting as an exofficio member of the subcommittee, the chairman of the full committee, Jack Brooks, continued to oppose the legislation, although he promised that a bill would be brought to the floor for consideration. The three Republicans on the subcommittee, led by ranking minority member Frank Horton of New York, generally supported the administration position. On a number of the most critical votes in the subcommittee, the chairman, L. H. Fountain, also supported the administration, along with two and sometimes three other Democratic members of the panel. The subcommittee cleared a revenue sharing bill on April 14, 1976. While not materially changing the formula, strong civil rights and citizen participation provisions were added, along with new auditing and accounting requirements.[51] Civil rights

51. One important change was made by the subcommittee that affected the distribution system, although it was later omitted. The subcommittee added language to prevent single-purpose governmental units from receiving funds, even though according to state designations they would otherwise have been eligible for funding. This

protection, under language developed by Representative Barbara Jordan, Democrat of Texas, was extended to *all* programs and activities of recipient governments unless the recipient produced "clear and convincing evidence" that shared revenue was not used "directly or indirectly" to finance an allegedly discriminatory activity. Automatic "entitlement" funding was included at the last minute. The bill provided funding of $24.9 billion for three and three-quarters years with no annual increment.

Another important subcommittee change, also recommended by the administration, was the elimination of the so-called priority-expenditure categories. The original act specified that local governments could use shared revenue only for public safety, environmental protection, public transportation, health, recreation, libraries, social services for the poor or aged, financial administration, and ordinary capital expenditures. This requirement, it was argued, encouraged misleading budgetary practices.

Attention now turned to the full committee. To the surprise of many observers, the full committee made extensive changes. The committee reported its version of revenue sharing May 5, 1976 by a vote of 39–3, with the chairman voting in opposition. This bill contained four important changes from the subcommittee version, including a major formula change recommended by Democratic Congressman Dante Fascell of Florida. Fascell's proposal provided that the funds added annually to the program ($150 million was provided in the full committee bill, though not in the subcommittee version) be distributed on the basis of a formula keyed to a jurisdiction's percentage of population below the federally defined poverty level. Although this change would not have involved a large amount of funds, at least initially, it represented an important departure from the essentially status quo position on the allocation formula. It was estimated at the time that the major benefits of the Fascell amendment would flow to rural areas and the South.[52]

In addition to the Fascell amendment, the subcommittee bill contained: (1) a requirement for annual "governmental modernization" plans and reports by states and localities as a condition of their receiving revenue

---

change applied particularly to township governments in the Midwest, which account for one-third of all recipient governments of revenue-sharing funds, and often have only a single function (usually highways). This issue, although not reflected in the administration's proposed bill, was discussed in many research reports. The 1975 Brookings volume, for example, urged dropping the floor provision in the law and making other changes to deal with this issue. See Nathan, Manvel, and Calkins, *Monitoring Revenue Sharing*, pp. 160–62, 284ff.

52. *Revenue Sharing Bulletin* (May 1976), p. 6.

sharing funds; (2) a requirement that Davis-Bacon ("prevailing-wage") conditions apply to all construction projects funded with shared revenue;[53] and (3) a series of civil rights changes involving the power to cut off funds, the payment of attorney's fees to citizens who win civil rights suits under the act, and a provision, to which Representative Jordan objected, requiring the exhaustion of administrative remedies before having the right to sue under the act.[54] Referring to all four committee amendments, Representative Frank Horton said their purpose was to "mess it up" in order to reduce the chances of reenactment.[55]

The inclusion of the committee amendment, written by Democrat Benjamin Rosenthal of New York, requiring "governmental modernization" plans as a condition of receiving revenue sharing funds was a new element in the legislative picture in 1976. When the original revenue sharing act was adopted, a competing version written by Congressman Henry S. Reuss (Democrat of Wisconsin) proposed tying revenue sharing payments to the adoption of "reforms" of the structure and processes of state and local governments; this position was rejected in 1972. Although the issue was raised, it did not come up frequently or strongly in the consideration of extension legislation. The adoption of this provision, late in the legislative process, by the House Government Operations Committee (although less binding than the Reuss bill) was vigorously opposed by spokesmen for state and local governments.

The strategy adopted by supporters of revenue sharing at this juncture was to combine the efforts of the administration, interest groups, and congressional supporters to restore the subcommittee bill. L. H. Fountain, chairman of the subcommittee, led the effort to replace the committee version with the subcommittee's plan; a general motion to make this switch prevailed by a vote of 233–172. A separate vote was taken to eliminate the committee's Davis-Bacon amendment; again, the subcommittee position prevailed, this time by a vote of 218–174. On June 10, 1976, House bill H.R. 13367 for the renewal of revenue sharing passed by a vote of 361–35.[56]

Attention now turned to the Senate. Preoccupied with a conference on

53. The 1972 act applied the Davis-Bacon requirements only to construction projects for which more than 25 percent of the cost was paid out of revenue sharing.

54. *Revenue Sharing Bulletin* (June 1976), pp. 4–5.

55. Ibid., p. 4.

56. Voting against the bill were the chairmen of the Appropriations, Budget, and Government Operations Committees. The negative votes were cast by thirty Democrats and five Republicans.

a major tax bill, the Senate Finance Committee did not complete action until August 30, 1976. Only one day of hearings was held in the fall of 1976, the committee having already held four days of program oversight hearings in April and May 1975.[57] The committee bill, adopted by a vote of 14–0 on August 30, extended the revenue sharing program for five and three-quarters years, two years longer than the House version. It provided for an "entitlement" funding (as in the House bill), although in this case totalling $41.3 billion, beginning at an annual level of $6.85 billion for fiscal year 1977 (an increase of $200 million over the House bill). Also in contrast to the House, the Senate bill accepted the administration's recommendation that annual increments of $150 million be continued in the renewal legislation.

Contending that the federal system has been strengthened by the revenue sharing program, the Finance Committee bill, as many observers had expected, provided for few changes in the basic program. In a number of areas, its report justified this approach in terms suggesting that the objectives sought by the House amendments could be achieved by more modest changes in the law. Public hearings were to be required only where not already mandated under state and local law; the same applied to audits. In general, the committee called for flexible reporting, publication, and auditing procedures consistent with the practices and fiscal calendars of the recipient governments. The committee bill contained essentially the same approach to civil rights as in the original act. It applied the non-discrimination requirement to any program or activity that "(1) has been designated as being funded with revenue sharing funds, or (2) under all the facts and circumstances, is demonstrated to be funded in whole or in part with revenue sharing funds."[58] It was argued that this approach, combined with the elimination of the priority-expenditure categories (which both bodies favored), would mean that in most cases the nondiscrimination requirement would apply to all of the programs of the recipient governments because their allocation of these funds would be on a general or an across-the-board basis.[59] The Senate, as had the House before it, eliminated the prohibition in the 1972 act against using shared revenue for

57. *General Revenue Sharing*, Hearings before the Subcommittee on Revenue Sharing of the Senate Committee on Finance, 94:1 (GPO, 1975).

58. *Extending and Amending the State and Local Fiscal Assistance Act of 1972*, S. Rept. 94-1207, 94:2 (GPO, 1976), p. 1.

59. This approach was taken by Senator Bob Packwood (R. Ore.), a member of the Senate Finance Committee, who had originally urged more stringent civil rights standards along the lines of the House bill. See *Revenue Sharing Bulletin* (September 1976), p. 8.

matching purposes under other federal grant-in-aid programs. Although not a major issue, the criticism on this point had been that the antimatching provision was unrealistic because of the fungibility of shared revenue, and furthermore that it tended to work against allocations of shared revenue to social programs, since there are so many federal aid programs in this field. (Because of this provision, local officials often argued that shared revenue should not—or even *could* not—be allocated for other federally aided activities.)[60]

On September 14, the Senate voted 80–4 to re-enact revenue sharing.[61] A number of amendments were adopted, some of them significant, but none involving basic changes in the committee bill, as had been the case in the House. One amendment added religion, age, and handicapped status to the coverage of the nondiscrimination provision;[62] another provided for the payment of attorney's fees in civil rights suits.[63] There was also a provision for a study of the impact of revenue sharing on American federalism, to be conducted by the Advisory Commission on Intergovernmental Relations. A motion to bring revenue sharing under the annual appropriations process was defeated 62–14.

CONFERENCE COMMITTEE ACTION

Two weeks after the Senate acted, Congress completed action on revenue sharing with the adoption of a conference committee report on September 29, 1976. The Senate funding level of $6.85 billion prevailed, but without an annual increment (contained in the Senate bill but not in the House version). The House prevailed on the length of the extension period, set at three and three-quarters years. Both bodies, as noted, had eliminated the priority-expenditure categories and the prohibition against using shared revenue to match other federal grants. Both provided entitlement funding, although at the last minute a point of order sustained in the House resulted in the addition of a complex indexing provision to overcome requirements of the Congressional Budget Act of 1974.[64]

60. The Senate also added Louisiana sheriffs as eligible for direct funding equal to 15 percent of the county (parish) share.

61. Voting against were two Democrats (Mansfield and Proxmire) and two Republicans (Helms and William Scott).

62. Also in the House bill.

63. Not in the House bill; included in conference.

64. The indexing provision, which ties annual funding of revenue sharing to the growth in federal personal income tax receipts, includes a cap of $6.85 billion on total funding in any year.

On civil rights, the conference compromised between the House and Senate versions, adopting the House language that the nondiscrimination prohibition applies "to all programs and activities" of a recipient government, but limiting its coverage to the *direct* uses of shared revenue. As explained in chapter 6, the end result appears to be that if a recipient government "demonstrates by clear and convincing evidence" that shared revenue was used in a specific program area, the nondiscrimination provision does not apply to other programs or activities of that government[65]—even though these programs may be indirectly affected, as in cases where shared revenue simply substitutes for funds that would otherwise have been used for these programs. Both bodies specified a trigger mechanism for determining when the secretary of the treasury is required to begin civil rights compliance proceedings; the conference committee generally followed the Senate procedure in stipulating steps and deadlines for the suspension of shared revenue in discrimination cases.

On public participation, the House version generally prevailed. It required two hearings, one on the proposed use of funds and a second on the budget in conjunction with its adoption; the Senate bill required a budget hearing only. The conference version required two hearings, with a waiver authority given to the secretary of the treasury for cases in which such requirements are "unreasonably burdensome,"[66] or, in the case of the second hearing, where a government already provides for citizen participation in its budget process, and "a portion of such process includes a hearing on the proposed use of [revenue sharing] funds . . . in relation to its entire budget."[67]

Related to the hearing requirement, and as a part of the effort to stimulate citizen participation, both bodies continued the requirements for public reporting. The House called for planned-use and actual-use reports, both to be published in a newspaper of general circulation; the Senate provided for the publication of a planned-use report only. The conference substitute, following the Senate, required the publication of only a planned-use report and, in addition, set forth procedures for making other budget records, including a summary of the adopted budget and the proposed use of revenue sharing funds, available for public inspection.

65. *Conference Report to Accompany H.R. 13367, The State and Local Fiscal Assistance Act Amendments of 1976*, H. Rept. 94-1720, 94:2 (GPO, 1976), pp. 31–36.

66. "Unreasonably burdensome" was defined to involve costs in excess of 15 percent of the annual revenue sharing entitlement of a given jurisdiction.

67. *Conference Report*, p. 8.

As to accounting and auditing requirements, the Senate version generally prevailed. An "independent" financial and compliance audit was required at least every three years for all governments receiving $25,000 or more a year, except where "a recipient government's financial statements are audited pursuant to generally applicable state or local audit requirements."[68] The secretary of the treasury was given the authority to waive this requirement if a recipient unit demonstrates it is making "substantial progress" to establish acceptable auditing and accounting procedures.

The most important provision adopted by either body affecting the formula—the House requirement that an eligible unit must perform at least two functions—was eliminated in conference. The Senate study of intergovernmental finances was retained.

On October 13, 1976, President Ford signed the 1976 extension act in Yonkers, New York. Calling it "a people's program," Ford said "with revenue sharing, we have begun to restore the necessary balance among Federal, State and local units of Government, to restore local control over local concerns."[69]

Overall, the Ford administration's status quo position, which the affected interest groups embraced, can be said to have predominated in shaping the renewed revenue sharing program. Liberal critics of the program held back from a frontal attack, although, to the extent the program was revised, it was their ideas which were adopted. But on the principal issues—permanent funding, state and local flexibility, and the distribution formula—the renewal legislation closely resembles the 1972 act. This outcome, combined with the general lack of controversy about whether the program should be extended, supports the interpretation that once an assured flow of general assistance grants to states and localities is established, it is politically difficult to turn off the spigot. The major question now is whether a new Democratic administration, headed by a President with reservations about revenue sharing, and particularly the inclusion of state governments in the program, will alter the legislative scene when the new act comes up for renewal in the Ninety-sixth Congress in 1979–80.

68. *Conference Report*, p. 39. The changes in this section generally follow the recommendations of Comptroller General of the United States, *Revenue Sharing Act Audit Requirement Should Be Changed*, report to the Congress (July 30, 1976).
69. Press release, The White House, October 13, 1976.

2 *Fiscal Effects of Revenue Sharing*

Central to any analysis of the general revenue sharing program is the question of how shared revenue affects expenditure and revenue decisions of recipient governments. In chapter 4, this question is examined in terms of the decision-making *processes* of recipient governments; in this chapter, attention focuses on actual expenditure and revenue *outcomes*.

Theoretical Basis

THE ECONOMICS OF GENERAL REVENUE SHARING

Much of the analysis of revenue sharing has focused on the allocational results of the program. That is, how have recipient governments responded in allocating shared funds between and within the private and public sectors? Has the size of the public sector as reflected in expenditures for goods and services remained unchanged, except for a realignment in the federal-state-local expenditure components? Or has there been a realignment in the overall public-private mix, with only part of the transferred funds used to expand state and local expenditures and the remainder passed back to the private sector in the form of reduced taxes?

The theoretical arguments underlying hypotheses about the allocational impact of intergovernmental transfers are analogous to those used in consumer demand theory. Discussions in the literature typically compare behavioral responses to matching categorical grants (closed or open-ended), nonmatching categorical grants, and noncategorical grants, where differences in response patterns are related to the expected price and income effects associated with these grants.[1]

1. See for example, Wallace Oates, *Fiscal Federalism* (Harcourt Brace Jovanovich, 1972), chap. 3; James A. Wilde, "Grants-in-Aid: The Analytics of Design and

24

Using this approach, a comparison of matching categorical grants and noncategorical grants generally shows significantly higher public spending associated with the former. A matching categorical grant reduces the price of the public good for which it is intended, and this price effect, combined with the implicit income effect, serves to stimulate additional spending on that public good. The more responsive to a decline in price is demand for the particular public good, the greater will be the increment in new spending for that good. If demand is not very responsive to price changes, then the increment in new spending may be less than the size of the federal matching grant. This implies that part of the federal grant will be used to cover a portion of the program costs previously borne by the recipient government. The revenue thus freed will then be used by the recipient government for some combination of increased spending on other programs, reduced taxes and borrowing, and increased holdings of financial assets. If, on the other hand, demand is highly responsive to price changes, the increment in new spending may exceed the amount of the federal matching grant, thus implying some combination of reduced spending on other programs, increased taxes and borrowing, and reduced fund balances. In general, however, so long as demand for the particular public good is at all responsive to price changes, a matching categorical grant can be expected to result in some new spending on it.

In the case of a noncategorical grant, there is only an income effect. Given an increase in the resources available to the recipient government, the monies will be used for some combination of increased public spending, reduced taxes and borrowing, and increased fund balances. Without a price effect, there is no bias in favor of increased spending on any particular public good or service. Hence, the overall effects on public spending of a noncategorical grant can be expected to be smaller than for a matching categorical grant.

Only with the implementation of the 1972 State and Local Fiscal Assistance Act has it become possible to analyze directly the fiscal effects of a major federal noncategorical grant program. Even now it is important to recognize that generalizations about the effects of such grants are predicated on the specific set of conditions attached to the current program. In particular, the tax effort factor included in the distributional formula, the priority spending categories imposed on local governments, the pro-

Response," *National Tax Journal*, vol. 24 (June 1971), pp. 143–55; Edward M. Gramlich and Harvey Galper, "State and Local Fiscal Behavior and Federal Grant Policy," *Brookings Papers on Economic Activity, 1:1973*, pp. 15–58.

hibition against the use of shared revenue as matching funds for other federal grant programs, and the five-year life of the program all give a unique character to the 1972 general revenue sharing program and point up the wide variation that can occur under the general heading of non-categorical grants.

ALTERNATIVE METHODS OF EMPIRICAL ANALYSIS

Two broad categories of studies attempting to measure specific fiscal effects attributable to general revenue sharing funds can be distinguished: studies based on statistical analysis of published revenue and expenditure data and those based on survey data tailored specifically to analysis of the general revenue sharing program.

Under the category of statistical studies, two approaches can be taken. Longitudinal or time-series analyses attempt to ascertain the fiscal effects of revenue sharing on the basis of revenue and expenditure responses exhibited by *individual* recipient jurisdictions. But because the revenue sharing program is so young, expenditure and revenue responses can only be inferred indirectly by this method. In effect, historical spending and revenue trends are identified, and extrapolations based on these trends are made for the period of the revenue sharing grant. In the absence of other identifiable factors that may have affected the trend, differences between actual and predicted outcomes are attributed to the effect of shared revenue. Not only are there problems in testing the significance of the fiscal impact measures estimated in this way, but there are also obvious limitations to how far the results obtained for an individual jurisdiction can be generalized to other governments affected by the program.

An alternative statistical approach, involving cross-section data, derives generalizations about the effects of shared revenue from a combined sample of recipient jurisdictions, analyzed for some specific unit of time, such as one year. Because of the larger sample size and the considerable variation characterizing expenditure and revenue data used in such analyses, the independent effect of general revenue sharing funds can be measured more directly—that is, shared revenue can be specified as a separate independent variable in explaining variations in fiscal behavior by recipient governments. Moreover, the larger sample size also makes it possible to apply various statistical tests in evaluating the generalizations derived from the analyses. At the same time, however, there may be important differences in the structural, fiscal, and political characteristics of the jurisdictions included in the sample, and these differences may have an important bearing on how individual subgroups of the sample population respond to shared revenue. Without controlling for these differences, the estimated fiscal impact of revenue sharing derived from cross-section analysis may be misleading with respect to particular subgroups of recipient jurisdictions.

In the other broad category, studies based on survey data attempt to develop a data base specifically tailored to the question at hand. While having the advantage of a more tailored set of data, they also present a greater problem of reliability. This is particularly true of surveys administered to state and local officials to ascertain the real uses of shared revenues; because these funds are fungible, officials have a wide range of choices in explaining to an interviewer the "real" impact of the program on their jurisdictions. For local governments, for example, the current law requires them to *directly* allocate their shared revenue to expenditures, and, in the case of noncapital activities, only to certain priority expenditures. However, to the extent that shared revenue merely displaces own-source revenue that would otherwise have been used, the real effects of revenue sharing will be realized elsewhere—possibly as an increase in some other expenditure category or as a decrease in taxes or borrowing. To ferret out these indirect but real net effects solely on the basis of interviews with local officials is, at best, a difficult undertaking.

Smaller samples permit greater control over the consistency and quality of survey information than do larger samples. However, with smaller samples it becomes less feasible to apply statistical tests of the generalizations derived from the survey data.

THE BROOKINGS METHOD

The Brookings monitoring study is a hybrid of the statistical and survey approaches. Through a network of field associates (twenty-three of them covering sixty-five jurisdictions), a data base tailored specifically to the question of how general revenue sharing funds were used by recipient jurisdictions has been generated. The associates represent a variety of professional backgrounds, the majority coming from universities or university-related research bureaus; and none of them are officially connected to any of the jurisdictions in the sample. Each associate is well acquainted with the fiscal and political makeup of his jurisdiction, so he is in a position to provide expert judgment about the real fiscal effects of revenue sharing as well as other effects the program may have on the decision-making process and political structure of his jurisdiction. In essence, the associate reviews pertinent budget documents and uses his general knowledge of the community, combined with information provided from interviews with key decisionmakers, to answer the question: how would expenditure and revenue policies be different in the absence of general revenue sharing funds?

In order to insure maximum uniformity in the understanding of the concepts used in the analysis, the field associates attended two working conferences (held prior to the first and second rounds of field observations) at Brookings, where the report forms were reviewed item by item and uniform definitions were provided for the various fiscal and political measures used.

With the combined efforts of the field associates, it was possible to derive general inferences about behavioral responses associated with shared revenue. Moreover, with the supplementary characteristics data provided on each jurisdiction, it was possible to control for other factors (for example, local fiscal pressures and the roles played by various interest groups) in identifying general patterns of response to revenue sharing.

The approach taken in this study is an expensive one, dictating a relatively small sample size. Although the principal drawback of a small sample is that conventional statistical tests cannot be meaningfully applied to the results of the analyses, at this stage of the general revenue sharing program we believe the methodological trade-offs inherent in this study reflect the most appropriate balance of benefits and costs. As more years pass, however, it will become increasingly difficult for observers to make judgments on the fiscal implications of revenue sharing. Evidence of this is seen already in the second round of field reports where, in twenty-one of the jurisdictions, associates indicated an increase in the difficulty associated with tracking real fiscal effects. As the life span of the revenue sharing program increases, however, additional data will become available through published sources, thus making more traditional statistical approaches to measuring the fiscal impact more feasible.

In summary, we believe that the approach used in this study provides an important addition to social science research methodology. It is not a substitute for traditional statistical approaches, but rather a needed supplement, providing a means for analyzing new programs at an early stage, often the most volatile period in terms of administrative and legislative changes. Moreover, only through a network of informed field observers, which is the basis of this study, can important political and structural factors be identified and related to the fiscal impact of revenue sharing.

THE NET FISCAL EFFECT CATEGORIES

The following nine net effect categories were used in identifying the fiscal responses by recipient governments to shared revenue.

New or expanded operations: operating expenditures initiated or expanded with revenue sharing funds (excluding pay-level and benefit increases).

New capital expenditures: spending for capital projects or the purchase of equipment that, without shared revenue, would either not have occurred at all or would have occurred at least one year later.

Increased pay and benefits: the use of revenue sharing funds for pay and fringe benefit increases that would otherwise not have been authorized, either at all or at the levels approved.

Program maintenance (budget balancing): the allocation of revenue sharing funds to ongoing programs where the alternative course of action without revenue sharing would have been to cut existing programs.

Federal aid restoration: the use of revenue sharing funds to offset actual or anticipated reductions in federal grants-in-aid.

Tax reduction: the use of revenue sharing to finance ongoing programs where the net result was to free up the jurisdiction's own resources and thereby permit a reduction in tax rates.

Tax stabilization: the use of revenue sharing funds to finance ongoing programs where the result was to avoid an increase in tax rates that would otherwise have been approved.

Borrowing avoidance: substitution of shared revenue funds for borrowing that would otherwise have been undertaken.

Increased fund balances: allocation of revenue sharing funds to ongoing programs where the net effect was to increase fund balances.

The range of responses captured by these nine categories is sufficiently wide to reflect virtually any expenditure, revenue, or financial action that might be taken by recipient governments. This is not to say, however, that in all cases such actions can be easily and neatly separated from one another. This is particularly true in situations where associates had to decide between program maintenance and tax stabilization as the appropriate response category. While in some cases, knowledge about the political and economic climate of the jurisdiction made the choice apparent, there were cases where the choice was not so obvious. It should be noted in this regard that preliminary field data were subjected to close scrutiny. Ambiguities and inconsistencies were identified and, to the extent possible, resolved through followup discussions with associates.

A SUMMARY OF THE NET EFFECTS FIELD DATA

The sample of sixty-five jurisdictions for which net effects data were collected is composed of eight state governments, twenty-nine cities, twenty-one counties, six towns, and one Indian tribe. As of this writing, two rounds of field information have been collected and analyzed. The first-round information covers decisions on the uses of shared revenue made through June 30, 1973; the second round covers subsequent decisions made through June 30, 1974. Cumulative decisions made as of June 30, 1974, would coincide with actual payments received through the fourth entitlement period (fiscal year 1974) and, in some cases, with expected payments through the fifth entitlement period (fiscal year 1975). Summary data for each sample government are presented in appendix B.

In table 2-1 the net effects are summarized for the fifty-seven local and eight state jurisdictions. Net effect summaries are given for each of the two rounds of field observations and on a cumulative basis through the second round. The cumulative net effects data show uses of shared revenue by net effect category as a percent of cumulative allocations through June 30, 1974. Allocations refer to those shared revenues received or anticipated about which the recipient government has made some "quite firm" decision concerning their use. The percentage values are unweighted means, computed on the basis of the percentage distributions reported for individual jurisdictions. By averaging over the percent of total allocation assigned to each net effect category, we avoid the skewing effect that large jurisdictions would have on the summary statistics if aggregate dollar amounts were used. We are, in effect, accounting for revenue sharing decisions by the sixty-five jurisdictions rather than revenue sharing dollars *per se*.

The Allocational Impact of Revenue Sharing

Using the net effects data collected over two rounds of field observations, it is possible to piece together a picture showing how the fiscal effects of shared revenue differ among the sample jurisdictions. Of particular in-

Table 2-1. Mean Percentages of Shared Revenue Allocated by the Sample Jurisdictions, by Type of Net Fiscal Effect, Local and State

Net fiscal effect	Round 1	Round 2	Cumulative
Local governments[a]			
New spending	**56.2**	**45.9**	**51.8**
New capital	45.2	34.5	41.4
Expanded operations	10.5	10.6	9.6
Increased pay and benefits	0.5	0.8	0.8
Substitutions	**43.9**	**52.4**	**47.0**
Program maintenance	12.8	14.6	13.5
Restoration of federal aid	0.4	1.1	0.8
Tax reduction	3.8	5.0	4.4
Tax stabilization	14.1	18.3	15.3
Avoidance of borrowing	9.6	7.7	8.8
Increased fund balance	2.8	3.4	3.0
Substitution not categorized	0.4	2.3	1.2
Balance of allocation[b]	**0.1**	**1.6**	**1.2**
State governments			
New spending	**35.7**	**39.6**	**37.3**
New capital	21.1	21.0	21.0
Expanded operations	12.1	13.2	13.8
Increased pay and benefits	0.0	5.4	1.2
New spending not categorized	2.5	0.0	1.3
Substitutions	**64.3**	**58.2**	**62.5**
Program maintenance	15.3	0.0	6.7
Restoration of federal aid	3.0	13.3	7.8
Tax reduction	13.2	12.0	12.2
Tax stabilization	0.0	12.5	7.6
Avoidance of borrowing	3.3	2.5	4.0
Increased fund balance	4.5	5.4	4.6
Substitution not categorized	25.0	12.5	19.6
Balance of allocation[b]	**0.0**	**2.4**	**0.1**

Source: Field research data. Figures may not add to totals because of rounding. It should also be noted that the cumulative figures do not coincide with a simple averaging of the first- and second-round figures because of differences within jurisdictions in the amounts allocated in the two rounds.

a. In round 1, three local governments (Longmont, Hamilton Co., and Turner Co.) allocated no revenue-sharing funds and, therefore, were not included in the first round summaries. In round 2, one local government (Orlando) made no allocation and was excluded from the second round summaries.

b. Net effect not categorized as between new spending and substitution.

terest is the impact of shared revenue on the public and private sectors of recipient jurisdictions: to what extent has revenue sharing provided a stimulus to public spending by recipient governments as opposed to private spending through reductions in taxes and debt financing? It is important to recognize that the fiscal responses analyzed here refer only to initial impacts. An increase in public spending that enhances the economic climate of a community may eventually stimulate economic growth and thus the size and vitality of its private sector. Similarly, a direct stimulus to the private sector may eventually feed back as a source of growth to the local public sector through improvements and increases in the local tax base.

ALLOCATIONAL IMPACT BY TYPE OF GOVERNMENT

In Table 2-2, the expenditure and revenue responses reported by the field associates are summarized for the four types of government (state, county, city, and township) by public and private sector impact. The summaries are based on the cumulative net effect responses reported through the second round of field observations.[2] The public and private sector impacts are each divided into two subgroups, based on whether the reported response denoted an explicit action or the avoidance of an action that would otherwise have occurred. Accordingly, expenditure actions affecting the public sector are classified as *new spending* (the sum of new capital uses, expanded operations, and increased pay and benefits) and *maintained spending* (the sum of program maintenance and federal aid restoration). Similarly, revenue actions affecting the private sector are classified as *tax reduction* and *revenue stabilization* (the sum of tax stabilization and avoidance of borrowing). Increases in fund balances do not fit the expenditure or revenue classifications and, therefore, are excluded from the analysis in this section.[3]

2. One of the benefits of having two rounds of data is that the disparities in the rates at which revenue sharing funds were allocated in the first round are reduced significantly when the net effects data are cumulated over two rounds. For the first round, the average percent of shared revenue allocated for the sixty-five jurisdictions was 96, with a standard deviation of 49 percentage points. On a cumulative basis, the average is 83 percent, with a significantly lower standard deviation of 23 percentage points. Even on a cumulative basis, one jurisdiction, Turner County, Wisconsin, was reported to have allocated only 8.4 percent of its shared-revenue entitlements, actual and expected, through entitlement period 5. Because of this atypical behavior, this jurisdiction is not included in the summary analyses that follow. Also excluded are Illinois and Rosebud Indian Tribe. In both rounds, the Illinois associate was unsuccessful in tracking shared-revenue allocations beyond ruling out new spending uses. Rosebud is excluded because of its unique characteristics, which do not lend themselves to inclusion in any of the subgroups examined in this section.

3. For the four types of governments in our sample, the average percent of cumulative allocations accounted for by increased fund balances was as follows: states, 5.3 percent; cities, 3.9 percent; counties, 2.4 percent; and towns, 1.6 percent.

Table 2-2. Cumulative Public and Private Sector Impacts of Shared Revenue Allocations, by Type of Government, through June 30, 1974

| | *Unweighted mean percentages of shared revenue allocated* | | | | | |
| | *Public sector* | | | *Private sector* | | |
Type of government	*New spending*	*Main- tained spending*	*Total*	*Tax reduction*	*Revenue stabili- zation*	*Total*
States (*n* = 7)	42.6	16.6	59.2	13.9	13.2	27.1
Counties (*n* = 20)	55.1	5.1	60.2	8.1	26.3	34.4
Cities (*n* = 29)	44.5	21.1	65.6	1.4	26.1	27.5
Towns (*n* = 6)	69.5	6.3	75.8	7.5	15.0	22.5

Source: Field research data.

For all four types of government, the direct impact of shared-revenue uses on the public sector exceeds the direct impact on the private sector. However, the table shows that the degree of difference in sector impact and the composition of the expenditure and revenue responses varies significantly both between state and local governments and among local governments.

For the seven state governments, nearly 60 percent of shared-revenue uses were reported as having a direct impact on public spending, and over two-thirds of that impact was realized through explicit new spending actions, as opposed to the avoidance of spending cutbacks.[4] The 27.1 percent of shared revenue allocations reported as having a direct impact on the private sector are about evenly split between explicit actions to cut taxes and the avoidance of discretionary revenue increases that would otherwise have occurred. It should be noted that approximately 9 percent of the allocations by these states (not including increases in fund balances) could not be categorized in terms of expenditure or revenue impact. Hence, the figures in table 2-2 understate the total expenditure and revenue impacts, but not to the extent of significantly changing the overall allocational pattern shown.

4. The reader is reminded that the percentage figures for any group of jurisdictions in our sample are unweighted means, based on the percent distribution of allocated revenues within individual jurisdictions and not on the distribution of total shared revenues represented by our sample. Again, we are accounting for revenue sharing *decisions*, not revenue sharing *dollars*.

For the twenty county governments, the total impact of shared revenue allocations on the public sector is not significantly different from that shown for state governments. Most of the public spending impact reported for county governments was accounted for by new spending as opposed to avoidance of cutbacks. While new capital expenditures accounted for the largest share of new spending actions by counties, new or expanded operation uses were significant, accounting for nearly 13 percent of total allocations. This is below the 16 percent reported for states, but the highest proportion of the three types of local governments.

As for the private sector impact, it can be seen that for counties, a higher proportion is accounted for by revenue stabilization measures than by explicit tax cuts. Borrowing avoidance was the principal revenue stabilization action taken by counties, averaging 17.4 percent of cumulative shared revenue uses compared to 8.9 percent for tax stabilization; this proportion is considerably higher than for any of the other three government classifications.

Nearly two-thirds of shared-revenue uses reported for the twenty-nine cities went to public spending, with a relatively high proportion accounted for by spending maintenance. As was the case for all three types of local governments, virtually all of the shared revenue used to avoid spending cutbacks by city governments fell under the heading of program maintenance as opposed to federal aid restoration.[5] Uses of shared revenue to reduce taxes were negligible among city governments, and the 26.1 percent of total uses reported as revenue stabilization was primarily associated with tax stabilization uses. As is indicated later in this section, the emphasis on program maintenance and tax stabilization uses by city governments is highly correlated with the higher levels of fiscal pressure faced by these governments.

The six town governments in the sample were reported to have used nearly 70 percent of their shared-revenue allocations for new spending, and nearly all of this spending was in the form of new capital spending. As a result, the public sector impact of revenue sharing is particularly significant among town governments in the sample, accounting for an average of over three-quarters of cumulative shared-revenue allocations for this group.

5. The relatively high percentage of maintained spending reported for state governments was about evenly split between program maintenance (7.7 percent) and federal aid restoration (8.9 percent).

Table 2-3. Cumulative Public and Private Sector Impacts of Shared Revenue Allocations, by Population of Local Government, through June 30, 1974

	Unweighted mean percentages of shared revenue allocated					
	Public sector			*Private sector*		
Population of government	*New spending*	*Maintained spending*	*Total*	*Tax reduction*	*Revenue stabilization*	*Total*
Under 50,000 (*n* = 17)	62.1	10.2	72.3	1.6	20.7	22.3
50,000–99,999 (*n* = 15)	62.6	13.9	76.5	7.0	12.2	19.2
100,000–500,000 (*n* = 11)	38.1	15.3	53.4	3.4	40.0	43.4
Over 500,000 (*n* = 12)	32.6	17.0	49.6	6.6	33.1	39.7

Source: Field research data.

ALLOCATIONAL IMPACT BY SIZE OF GOVERNMENT

Within local government classifications, considerable differences exist in the size and scope of individual governments. In order to examine the relationship between size of government and uses of shared revenue, the fifty-five local governments were grouped according to size of population: under 50,000; between 50,000 and 100,000; between 100,000 and 500,000; and over 500,000. Table 2-3 summarizes the net effects data for each group according to public and private sector impact.

As the table clearly shows, the impact of shared revenue on the public sector drops dramatically for jurisdictions above 100,000 in population—from around 75 percent of total uses for jurisdictions of under 100,000 to around 50 percent for those over 100,000. The difference is accounted for primarily by new spending, and, in particular, new spending on capital projects. Corresponding to the drop in public spending, a significantly higher percentage of shared-revenue uses by larger jurisdictions have a direct effect on the private sector, primarily by way of tax stabilization and borrowing avoidance actions.

This marked difference in the use of shared revenue (particularly the role of capital spending) is related in part to the scope of functional activities for which different-sized jurisdictions are responsible. Smaller jurisdictions are more likely to have less wide-ranging responsibilities in the provision of public goods and services, and those activities for which smaller jurisdictions do have direct responsibility tend to be more capital intensive. Using the proportion of local government general expenditures accounted for by capital outlays as a measure of capital intensity, local government activities can be grouped according to capital intensity as follows: welfare programs—virtually no capital input; education, public safety, sanitation, health, and corrections—between 5 percent and 11 percent of general expenditures accounted for by capital outlays; highway and sewerage programs—up to two-thirds of general expenditures accounted for by capital outlays.[6]

When, on a national basis, municipal governments are grouped according to population size, a clear pattern emerges showing a decline in the proportion of total expenditures accounted for by the most capital-intensive activities as population size increases. In 1971–72, the sum of highway and sewerage activities accounted for about one-fourth of total general expenditures for cities and towns of between 10,000 and 25,000 in population, and declined to less than 10 percent for cities and towns of over 100,000 in population. A similar pattern emerges for county governments: in 1971–72, one-fourth of general expenditures were accounted for by highway activities for counties with populations between 10,000 and 25,000, declining to about 8 percent for counties of over 100,000. In general, because the activities for which smaller local governments are directly responsible tend to be more capital intensive, it is not surprising to find these governments using a higher proportion of their shared revenue for capital expenditures.

Another factor that may partly explain the difference in net effect patterns between large and small city and town governments concerns attitudes toward the general revenue sharing program. Intergovernmental transfers have historically played a less important role in the budgets of smaller city and town governments as compared to larger and more urban municipalities. Nationally, state and federal transfers accounted for approximately 23 percent of total general revenues for cities and towns of under 100,000 population in 1971–72; for municipalities over 100,000, the figure increases to over 37 percent.[7] Correspondingly, property taxes

6. These measures of capital intensity are based on local government expenditure data for 1971–72 summarized in U.S. Bureau of the Census, *1972 Census of Governments*, vol. 4, no. 5: *Compendium of Government Finances* (GPO, 1973), table 10. The expenditure and revenue detail that follows for size of local governments is based on data found in *1972 Census of Governments*, vol. 4, no. 4: *Finances of Municipal and Township Governments*, table 17; and vol. 4, no. 3: *Finances of County Governments*, table 11.

7. For county governments, intergovernmental transfers accounted for approximately 43 percent of general revenues in 1971–72, with no significant difference between small and large counties.

plus special assessments and current charges have been much more important to smaller cities and towns. In 1971–72, revenue from these highly predictable and controllable sources of revenue accounted for approximately 61 percent of total general revenue for municipalities of under 100,000 population, compared to approximately 44 percent for municipalities over 100,000. Given this difference in the historical composition of revenue flows, it is not unreasonable to expect smaller jurisdictions to be more reluctant to begin new operating programs, or to alter existing revenue flows, in response to a new source of funds over which they have less control and about which there is greater uncertainty.

Information provided by our field associates sheds some light on the relationship between size of jurisdiction and attitudes about revenue sharing funds. Associates were asked to characterize the influence of the five-year life of the 1972 revenue sharing program on the planned uses of shared revenue reported by their jurisdictions. The degree of influence was rated on a scale of 0 to 4, 0 indicating no influence and 4 indicating significant influence. For seventeen of the twenty-three cities and towns with populations of under 100,000, associates rated the influence of the five-year limit at 2 or higher, compared to only three of the twelve cities with populations of over 100,000. This reported difference in sensitivity to the five-year limit suggests that attitudes about shared revenue do play a role in determining how these funds are used, and it is consistent with the relatively high proportion of one-shot capital projects reported for smaller jurisdictions.

It should be noted that between the first and second rounds of field observations there was a decline in the number of cases in which the five-year limit was reported to have had an influence on decisions about the use of shared revenue. As reported in *Monitoring Revenue Sharing,* 67 percent of the sample jurisdictions in round one were characterized as being at least somewhat influenced by this feature of the program; in 40 percent of these cases, the degree of influence was reported as significant as opposed to some or moderate. For round two, the comparable figures are 55 percent and 33 percent, respectively. Hence, it would appear that while uncertainty about the future of the revenue sharing program continues to be an important issue, especially among smaller towns and cities, greater familiarity with the program may have served to mitigate the constraining effect that this uncertainty has had on some recipient governments in deciding the uses of shared revenue.

That larger and more urban local governments have been more willing to integrate shared revenue into their ongoing expenditure and revenue flows may in part be due to the fact that they have greater familiarity with intergovernmental transfers. In some cases, however, these governments may be acting out of necessity. As shown in table 2-3, maintenance of spending and revenue stabilization uses account for over 50 percent of total shared revenue uses by the two groups with populations of over 100,000. This response pattern is at least partly a reflection of the greater fiscal pressure conditions faced by many of these jurisdictions.[8]

ALLOCATIONAL IMPACT BY DEGREE OF FISCAL PRESSURE

The associates in each round were asked to characterize the degree of fiscal pressure existing in their jurisdictions. In evaluating fiscal pressure, the associates were instructed to consider current circumstances in relation to past fiscal trends, focusing particularly on such factors as rising and uncontrollable costs, recently imposed new taxes or changes in existing tax sources, tax delinquency, short-term borrowing, reactions to proposed bond issues, and public employee pay-rate controversies. Four categories of fiscal pressure were used: extreme, moderate, light, and none. Combining the fiscal pressure conditions for both rounds, ten jurisdictions were judged to have been under no fiscal pressure in either round, twenty-six were judged, on balance, to have experienced light pressure for the two rounds, twenty moderate, and six extreme fiscal pressure.[9] Grouping the net effects data on the basis of these fiscal pressure characterizations, table 3-4 summarizes the public and private sector impacts for each group.

The most striking observation about the response patterns shown in the table is the similarity between the ten jurisdictions characterized as having no fiscal pressure and the six cities characterized as experiencing extreme pressure. For both groups, the use of shared revenue provided more stimulus to the private sector than to the public sector.[10] Total pri-

8. Of the jurisdictions with populations under 100,000, 60 percent were characterized by our associates as experiencing either no or only light fiscal pressure, with the balance characterized as facing moderate fiscal pressure. Of the over–100,000 jurisdictions, 52 percent were characterized as facing either no or only light fiscal pressure, 22 percent moderate pressure, and 26 percent extreme fiscal pressure.

9. All six jurisdictions in the extreme group are city governments (Baltimore, Newark, New York City, Rochester, St. Louis, and Worcester).

10. It should be noted that for the ten least hard-pressed jurisdictions 6.6 percent of cumulative shared-revenue allocations could not be traced to specific expenditure and revenue categories. For the six hard-pressed cities, this percentage increases to 11.8 percent. Hence, the total private and public sector impacts are understated for both groups, but not to the extent of significantly altering the overall allocational patterns shown in table 2-4.

Table 2-4. Cumulative Public and Private Sector Impacts of Shared Revenue Allocations, by Fiscal Pressure Conditions, through June 30, 1974

| | *Unweighted mean percentages of shared revenue allocated* | | | | | |
| | *Public sector* | | | *Private sector* | | |
Fiscal pressure category[a]	*New spending*	*Maintained spending*	*Total*	*Tax reduction*	*Revenue stabilization*	*Total*
None	35.2	6.9	42.1	9.1	39.5	48.6
(*n* = 10)						
Light	68.8	9.8	78.6	2.1	15.9	18.0
(*n* = 26)						
Moderate	46.3	20.7	67.0	8.9	16.7	25.6
(*n* = 20)						
Extreme	7.2	22.0	29.2	3.4	54.7	58.1
(*n* = 6)						

Source: Field research data.

a. The cumulative fiscal pressure characterizations are based on an averaging of the fiscal pressure ratings for the first and second rounds of field observations. In cases where the average fell between two rating levels, the higher of the two individual ratings was used.

vate-sector impact for the ten least hard-pressed jurisdictions (including four counties, two states, two cities, and two towns) accounts for 48.6 percent of cumulative allocations, compared to a 42.1 percent public-sector impact. For the six cities under extreme fiscal pressure, the difference in sector impact is even more pronounced, with 58.1 percent of shared-revenue allocations directly affecting the private sector, compared to 29.2 percent affecting the public sector.

The nature of the impact on public and private sectors does vary between these two groups, however. New spending, while low for both groups, is particularly low for the six hard-pressed cities, accounting for only 7.2 percent of total allocations. At the same time, spending to maintain existing programs accounts for 22 percent of shared-revenue uses by these cities, the highest percentage of the four groups. For the ten least hard-pressed jurisdictions, the public-sector impact is provided primarily through new spending uses, and most of this is accounted for by capital expenditures, as opposed to new or expanded operations. The 6.9 percent maintenance of spending shown for these jurisdictions is nearly all accounted for by federal aid restoration uses by one state government (Colorado).

The significant impact on the private sector reported for both groups is provided primarily through tax stabilization and borrowing-avoidance measures. In the case of the six hard-pressed cities, tax stabilization dominates, accounting for nearly 52 percent of cumulative allocations, compared to less than 3 percent for borrowing avoidance. For the ten least hard-pressed jurisdictions, tax stabilization accounts for 28.2 percent of cumulative allocations and borrowing avoidance for 11.3 percent.

Despite the marked similarity in the overall impact of revenue sharing on the public and private sectors, the implications of revenue sharing for these two groups of governments are quite different. For the ten sample jurisdictions with no fiscal pressure, shared revenue provides a means of sustaining that situation: while, on average, slightly more than one-third of their allocated shared revenue went to new spending, the largest proportion was aimed at avoiding whatever potential fiscal pressure might arise in financing ongoing and planned activities. In contrast, revenue sharing plays a much more critical role for those jurisdictions currently faced with extreme fiscal pressure. Existing programs would have to be cut (possibly even further than they have been) without this outside assistance, and even greater fiscal pressure would occur in the form of higher taxes in the absence of revenue sharing. For these jurisdictions, new spending uses are inconsequential.

Newark, New Jersey is one of the six city governments included in the extreme fiscal pressure group. In congressional testimony, Newark's Mayor Kenneth A. Gibson described the important role of revenue sharing in helping hard-pressed cities break the cycle of fiscal erosion. Noting the rising demand for services faced by his city and a 20 percent decline in rateables over the past decade, Mayor Gibson observed that

the higher we are forced to raise taxes to provide services, the more businesses and homeowners are forced to leave. This means fewer jobs, greater demands on city services, and fewer rateables to provide them. If we were to cut down on the delivery of services, the result would be the same. More businesses and homeowners would be forced to leave.

. . . [G]eneral revenue sharing is the only form of federal assistance that enables urban governments to break this cycle. It is the only federal program that permits us to maintain basic services without destroying the rateable base upon which the future social and economic prosperity of our cities depend.[11]

Turning now to the two groups characterized as experiencing light and moderate fiscal pressure, it can be seen in table 2-4 that shared revenue had a significantly greater impact on the public sectors of these two groups than was the case for the two extreme groups. For the twenty-six jurisdic-

11. Testimony of Mayor Kenneth A. Gibson before the Subcommittee on Intergovernmental Relations of the House Committee on Government Operations, October 8, 1975.

tions characterized as facing light fiscal pressure (including three states, twelve counties, nine cities, and two towns), 78.6 percent of shared-revenue allocations directly affected the public sector, primarily through new spending. While capital expenditures were the dominant new spending use, new or expanded operations accounted for 14 percent of cumulative allocations by this group. Revenue-stabilization measures accounted for most of the private sector impact, with borrowing avoidance accounting for nearly 14 percent of cumulative allocations.

For the twenty governments facing moderate fiscal pressure (including two states, four counties, twelve cities, and two towns), two-thirds of cumulative shared-revenue allocations were used for public spending. Of that amount, a relatively large proportion is accounted for by actions to maintain previous spending levels. Over all four groups of governments, a clear pattern emerges showing the increasing importance of shared revenue as a means of maintaining existing programs as the level of fiscal pressure increases.

ALLOCATIONAL EFFECTS SUMMARIZED

To summarize the findings in this section, the following general observations can be made:

1. Revenue sharing has had an impact on both the public and private sectors of recipient jurisdictions, and, in general, the impact on public spending accounts for a larger proportion of shared-revenue uses.

2. Across different types of recipient governments, shared revenue has provided greater public-sector stimulus for city and, particularly, township governments than for state and county governments. However, among local governments, a relatively high proportion of the spending stimulus for city governments is associated with maintenance of existing program levels, accounting for approximately one-fifth of cumulative shared-revenue uses by these governments.

3. Among smaller local governments, public spending accounts for a significantly larger proportion of shared-revenue uses than is the case for larger urban governments. This difference is accounted for primarily by the use of shared revenue for new capital projects, and is explained partly by differences in the scope of activities for which local governments are responsible and partly by differences in attitude toward revenue sharing.

4. As the level of fiscal pressure faced by recipient governments in-

creases, a higher proportion of shared revenue is used to maintain existing programs. On balance, however, greater private stimulus is provided
in particularly hard-pressed jurisdictions. In this respect, jurisdictions at
either end of the fiscal pressure spectrum tend to be alike. However, for
jurisdictions facing little fiscal pressure, this strategy simply helps them to
maintain their favorable fiscal climate. For those jurisdictions experiencing a particularly unfavorable fiscal climate, the use of shared revenue
to help stabilize taxes is a way of slowing the rate of fiscal deterioration.

Analysis of Individual Net Effect Categories

In examining each of the net fiscal effect categories, particular attention
is given to the information provided by our field associates in explaining
the circumstances that affected their decisions to allocate a significant portion of shared revenue to individual net effect categories. The effects of
various legislative provisions of the 1972 revenue sharing act on decisions
about how to use revenue sharing funds are also examined.

NEW CAPITAL SPENDING

Capital spending has accounted for a larger proportion of shared-revenue uses than any other net effect category. For the sixty-five sample jurisdictions, an average of 40 percent of cumulative shared-revenue allocations were assigned to this category, with the proportion varying from a
low of 21 percent for the eight state governments in the sample to a high
of 67 percent for the six township governments.

For the townships, new capital spending reported in the second-round
field data occurred primarily in two program areas, environmental protection (water, sewerage, and sanitation projects) and transportation
(street, road, and highway projects). The field associate for Lowell and
Theresa Townships (Wisconsin) reported in both rounds of field observations that new capital spending on road construction and maintenance
equipment accounted for all shared-revenue uses by these two rural jurisdictions. This reflects the limited scope of activities performed by these
governments. As the associate describes the situation: "Towns in rural
Wisconsin are largely responsible for administering various taxes for themselves, school districts, counties and the state, and for maintaining town
roads."

In Livingston Township, New Jersey, nearly three-quarters of cumulative shared-revenue uses were allocated to new capital spending. Characterized by the associate as a "prosperous community with no significant low-income population," Livingston directed its new capital spending to recreational and environmental protection projects. In summarizing the situation in Livingston Township, the associate noted that "it is clear that Livingston had no pressing need to use the funds for meeting operating expenses, nor any great need or interest to undertake social programs; politically concrete, lasting capital projects would appeal most to the citizens of Livingston."

North Carolina and Louisiana stand out as the only state governments in the sample that used significant proportions of their shared revenue for capital projects, using 74 percent and 92 percent, respectively, of cumulative allocations. In North Carolina, a state described by our associate in his second report as enjoying "excellent fiscal health," capital allocations went to a variety of programs, most notably higher education, corrections, recreation, and health. In Louisiana, road construction accounted for all the capital allocations reported in the two rounds of field observations. The associate in Louisiana reported that by making these capital projects possible revenue sharing may have had a negative impact on the pressure that had been building in the state for better planning by the state highway department. As explained by the associate, "for many years, politics rather than planning has been the main criteria in determining construction projects with the result that many of the most heavily traveled roads are in the poorest condition. Opposition has been building up against any proposals to increase highway taxes or to authorize bond issues for highway construction, but the availability of federal revenue sharing funds has blunted some of the efforts to have a planned highway construction program."

For the twenty-one county governments, new capital spending accounted for an average of 42 percent of cumulative shared-revenue uses through June 1974. Information provided by the associates in the second round of field observations shows that transportation and public building projects ranked first, followed by public safety and education, as the areas most affected by new capital uses of revenue sharing by counties.[12] For the twenty-nine cities, capital spending accounted for an average of 36 percent of cumulative shared-revenue allocations. Public transportation was the

12. See the last section of this chapter for a more detailed accounting of the programmatic impact of expenditure uses of shared revenue.

Table 2-5. Twelve Sample Cities in Which New Capital Allocations Dropped by Twenty Percentage Points or More between the First and Second Rounds of Field Observations

City	Percentage point drop in new capital allocations	Net effect category showing a significant increase from first to second round
Sioux Falls, S.Dak.	−67.5	Tax stabilization/ borrowing avoidance
Baton Rouge, La.	−61.2	Borrowing avoidance
Phoenix, Ariz.	−60.0	New or expanded operations
Jacksonville, Fla.	−50.0	Program maintenance
Carson, Calif.	−48.3	Program maintenance
North Little Rock, Ark.	−44.7	Increased pay and benefits
St. Louis, Mo.	−32.4	Program maintenance
Springfield, Mass.	−30.0	Program maintenance
Hamilton, Ohio	−29.1	*
Cottage Grove, Oreg.	−28.5	Tax reduction
Scottsdale, Ariz.	−25.0	Tax stabilization
Eugene, Oreg.	−21.6	Program maintenance

Source: Field research data.
* No one category shows a significant increase.

program area most significantly affected by capital uses of shared revenue, followed by public safety, environmental protection, and public housing projects, each receiving about equal weight.

A decline in capital allocations by cities. A comparison of first- and second-round net effects data revealed that the percent of shared-revenue allocations accounted for by capital spending dropped significantly for city governments, from an average of 44 percent to 25 percent.[13] Of the twenty-seven cities that allocated shared revenue in both rounds, a drop of twenty percentage points or more in new capital allocations was reported in twelve cases, and in no case was any significant increase in capital allocations reported between the first and second rounds. The twelve cities are listed in table 2-5, along with the percentage point drop in new capital allocations between the first and second rounds. In most cases, the drop in new capital allocation was accompanied by a correspondingly significant increase in another individual net effect category; these categories are also shown.

As the table shows, in only two cases was the decline in capital alloca-

13. County and town governments showed no such significant change. There were a few cases where capital spending declined, but these declines were offset by increased capital spending reported for other jurisdictions.

tions matched by an increase in one of the other new spending categories—new or expanded operations in Phoenix, and increased pay and benefits in North Little Rock. For the other ten cities, the decline in capital allocations was accompanied by an increase in revenue stabilization, tax reduction, or program maintenance uses. In Baton Rouge and Sioux Falls, borrowing avoidance increased, implying that between the first and second rounds the rate of acceleration of new capital spending generated by revenue sharing slowed, and an increasing share of revenue sharing funds was being used to offset at least some of the borrowing that would otherwise have been needed to finance these projects.

In seven cities the drop in capital allocations was accompanied by an increase in program maintenance or tax stabilization uses. Three of these cities were characterized as being under moderate or extreme fiscal pressure in both rounds of field observations, and in two other cases fiscal pressure was reported to have increased between the first and second rounds. In explaining the switch from new capital spending to program maintenance, the associate in St. Louis quoted Mayor John Poelker as follows: "General federal revenue sharing certainly has been very welcome, but steep rises in costs for personnel and materials and equipment have lessened its impact on city services. Like most cities throughout the nation, the first year of revenue sharing was used mostly for long delayed public improvements. But thereafter, this money was integrated into the regular budget because of sharply increased operating costs. In short, it has enabled us to keep our head above water. Ironically, the failure of the national government to find an effective means of curbing inflation has greatly lessened the effect of revenue sharing."

Five-year limit. Because the 1972 revenue sharing program extended over a period of only five years, there was some speculation that nonrecurring capital projects would be the dominant use of revenue sharing funds. Rather than adopt new operating programs or expand existing ones, which in both cases would have to be cut or financed by tax increases if the revenue sharing program was not renewed in 1976, governments might tend to favor one-shot capital projects. As noted earlier, this feature of the program appears to have had a greater effect on smaller recipient governments, and its overall influence seems to have lessened somewhat between the first and second rounds of field observations. The switch from capital projects to program maintenance and tax stabilization uses by some city governments suggests that increasing demands on own-source revenues to finance existing services may have made it less feasible to follow a strategy of keeping revenue sharing monies entirely separate from on-going revenue and expenditure flows.

Evidence of such a change in attitude was provided by the associates monitoring the cities of Scottsdale, Arizona, and Springfield, Oregon, two of the twelve cities reporting a significant drop in new capital allocations. The associate for Springfield reported a significant increase in program maintenance uses in round two corresponding to the decline in new capital spending. He noted that higher costs due to inflation had made it necessary to increase the use of revenue sharing for operating expenditures and that "overall, revenue sharing funds significantly aided in avoiding a serious financial strain for the city." With regard to the five-year limit, the associate observed that "some city officials, and especially the Springfield city manager, have expressed great concern about the five-year duration of the revenue sharing program and have sought to devote as much of these funds as possible to nonrecurring items. However, the five-year limit probably was less of a constraint this year than earlier, since budget officials were faced with the choice of using more revenue sharing money for operating expenses or reducing certain operations. The five-year limit was still a very important consideration."

The associate for Scottsdale reported that rising operating costs (attributed in this case to both inflation and extremely rapid population growth) explained the decline in the proportion of revenue sharing allocations used for capital projects and the corresponding increase in tax stabilization uses between the first and second rounds. While city officials were reluctant to integrate shared revenue into the operating budget because of the uncertainty generated by the five-year life of the program, they were, according to the associate, even more reluctant to raise property taxes to the extent that would have been required had shared revenue not been used to finance a portion of ongoing operations.

Impact of the prevailing-wage requirement. Another legislative provision of the revenue sharing act is the requirement that prevailing wage rates as defined by the Davis-Bacon Act be paid in cases where more than 25 percent of the cost of a capital project is financed by shared revenue. This provision would be expected to have a constraining influence on the uses of shared revenue for capital projects in places where it is possible to employ labor at wage rates below Davis-Bacon standards. Alternatively, jurisdictions may attempt to spread revenue sharing funds so that revenue sharing accounts for less than 25 percent of the financing of each project. This latter tactic was reported in *Monitoring Revenue Sharing* for Holden Township (Massachusetts) and the State of North Carolina.

In the second-round field reports, associates reported only five cases where the Davis-Bacon provision appeared to have some influence on local decisions. In Longmont, Colorado, the associate indicated that the city's finance director felt that the provision might create problems in getting local contractors to bid on projects. In Livingston Township, New Jersey, the associate noted that the town's business manager felt that small capital projects (such as the four tennis courts previously financed by revenue sharing funds) would not be financed by revenue sharing in the future because such projects could be undertaken at lower costs by non-union contractors. In general, however, it does not appear that the Davis-Bacon provision has been a major factor in decisions about uses of shared revenue for capital projects.[14]

NEW OR EXPANDED OPERATIONS

For the sixty-five sample jurisdictions, new or expanded operations accounted for an average of 10 percent of cumulative shared-revenue uses through June 1974. Allocations were reported in this category for four of the eight states, resulting in an average cumulative allocation of 16 percent for state governments. New or expanded operations averaged nearly 13 percent of cumulative allocations for counties, compared to only 7 percent for cities. For the six townships in the sample, uses of shared revenue for new or expanded operations were insignificant.

The specific program areas affected by these allocations varied by type of government. For states, health and education services and, to a lesser extent, social services were the areas most affected by new or expanded operating uses of shared revenue in round two. For counties, public safety, transportation, and social services were about equally affected, followed by recreation. Most of the impact from the limited allocations of shared revenue to new or expanded operations by cities in round two occurred in the area of public safety programs.

In twelve jurisdictions, 20 percent or more of cumulative shared-revenue allocations were reported as new or expanded operation uses. These twelve jurisdictions are listed in table 2-6, along with the percent of cumulative allocations accounted for by new or expanded operations, type of government, and fiscal pressure conditions.

14. At one point in the debate on the 1976 renewal legislation, the House Government Operations Committee proposed to apply Davis-Bacon to all capital projects involving shared revenue, regardless of the proportion, but this proposal was eliminated from the final House bill.

Table 2-6. Twelve Sample Jurisdictions in Which 20 Percent or More of Cumulative Shared Revenue Allocations Were Reported as New or Expanded Operation Uses

Jurisdiction	Type of government	Percent of allocation to new or expanded operations	Fiscal pressure conditions[a]
Maine	State	71.5	Light
Rosebud, S.Dak.	Indian Tribe	66.4	Extreme
Pulaski, Ark.	County	60.4	Light
Eugene, Oreg.	City	33.7	Moderate
Phoenix, Ariz.	City	33.2	Light
Kershaw, S.C.	County	32.3	Light
Fairfield, S.C.	County	27.2	Moderate
Los Angeles County, Calif.	County	24.2	Moderate
Camden, S.C.	City	21.8	Light
Orange, N.C.	County	21.8	Moderate
Monroe, N.Y.	County	21.1	Light
Dodge, Wis.	County	20.7	Moderate

Source: Field research data.
a. See table 2-4, note a.

County governments show the greatest tendency to use shared revenue to expand existing operating programs or begin new ones. Within this group, Pulaski County (Arkansas) stands out; over 60 percent of its cumulative shared-revenue allocations were reported as new or expanded operating uses. Public safety and road maintenance account for the majority of these allocations, but the associate for Pulaski also reported that a significant effect of general revenue sharing was the impetus provided to expand the scope of county services, particularly in the areas of recreation and health. According to the associate, "the use of [revenue sharing] funds for recreational areas in [low-income and predominately black] communities which have previously had no access to such facilities is viewed by the county as a major accomplishment."

Two-thirds of the revenue sharing allocations reported for Rosebud Indian Tribe (South Dakota) were assigned to new or expanded operations. These allocations were distributed among a variety of program areas, most importantly public safety, environmental protection, health, social services, and financial administration. Historically, Rosebud has depended almost entirely on federal transfers for its operating revenue. Hence, unlike most other jurisdictions in the sample, revenue sharing did not have a particularly significant impact on the tribe's budget process or the pattern of expenditure decisions that resulted. It should be noted that a change in tribal administration delayed final budget approval as of the second-round field observations, so most of the reported impact of revenue sharing funds relates only to first-round information.

The one state in the sample that made a significant commitment to new or expanded operations out of shared revenue is Maine. The associate reported that nearly all of the shared-revenue allocations assigned to this net effects category went to education in the form of state aid to local school districts. The state of Maine decided at the beginning of the revenue sharing program to use shared revenue as a means of meeting its goal of increasing the state's share of local school costs from one-third to one-half. While the additional state subsidy for education was judged by the Maine associate to represent an expanded state role in public education that resulted in higher levels of total spending for public education statewide, there was also some tax-reduction impact realized among local school districts. This secondary impact is examined later in this chapter.

In California, revenue sharing was also used to provide additional state aid to local districts. However, the California associate judged the primary net fiscal impact to be one of tax reduction in the form of lower school property taxes, with no significant impact on the level of statewide educational spending.

Although the distinction between these two cases may seem somewhat ambiguous, an examination of statewide local school expenditure patterns for the two states supports the judgments of our associates. In Maine, per capita expenditures for local education increased by 32 percent between fiscal years 1972 and 1974. This is over twice the average rate of increase for the United States. In California, per capita expenditures for local schools increased by 14 percent, just under the average for all states.[15] A general point to be drawn from these two cases is that, while tracking the net effects of revenue sharing is difficult for every type of recipient government, cases like California and Maine, which pass through significant portions of their entitlements to local governments, can be especially difficult to track.

Eugene, Oregon, is one of the three cities for which a significant proportion of shared-revenue allocations went to new or expanded operations, principally public safety, recreation, and social services. In a letter to the Eugene associate, the assistant city manager characterized the new spending in these areas as "of lower operational priority." He said the basic

15. U.S. Department of Commerce, *Governmental Finances* (GPO, various years).

decision rule underlying revenue sharing uses by the city was to avoid making essential services dependent on shared revenue and to use these funds only to finance projects that could be cut back in the event that the revenue sharing program ended. Commenting on the official explanation of the funding of new operations in Eugene, the associate noted that it fails to reflect the influence of various interest groups on decisions about shared-revenue uses, particularly with respect to new spending on recreational services.

The role of social action groups. This observation by the Eugene associate raises a more general question about the influence of interest groups in determining the uses of revenue sharing funds. Because, in general, new or expanded operating programs can be expected to have a more direct and immediate effect on people than is true of most capital projects, the relationship between reported activity by social action groups and new or expanded operating uses of shared revenue is of particular interest.

When asked about activity by interest groups regarding revenue sharing uses, seven associates reported significant activity by various social action groups, sixteen reported some activity, and thirty-nine no activity. Among the types of groups mentioned were various ethnic organizations, the United Way Organization, library associations, senior citizen groups, day care organizations, and associations serving retarded people. When the net fiscal effects data for the sixty-five jurisdictions are related to this information on social action group involvement, there is some evidence that these groups have had an impact on the uses of shared revenue. For example, of the twelve jurisdictions reporting over 20 percent of cumulative allocations to new or expanded operations, one-half reported some degree of activity by social action groups. For the other jurisdictions in the sample, less than one-third reported such activity.

A comparison of new capital and new operating uses of shared revenue provides a further indication of the impact of social action groups. For the jurisdictions reporting no group involvement, capital allocations accounted for an average of 42 percent of cumulative allocations, compared to 8 percent for new operating uses. For the jurisdictions reporting at least some involvement by such groups, capital uses averaged 36 percent and new operations 13 percent of cumulative allocations. While these differences are not especially pronounced, they do suggest that social action groups have had some effect on the level of new operating uses of shared revenue, and this outcome appears to reflect a trade-off between new capital and new operating uses.

INCREASED PAY AND BENEFITS

In only four jurisdictions was shared revenue reported to have played any appreciable role in determining pay and benefit increases. In one of them, St. Louis, a significant impact was reported in the first round of field observations but not in the second. In the other three (North Carolina, North Little Rock, Arkansas, and Hamilton, Ohio) the effect of shared revenue on salary increases was reported only in the second round. In North Carolina, the associate reported that the availability of revenue sharing made possible a salary increase for state employees amounting to 7½ percent rather than the 5 percent that had originally been planned. For the two cities, police and fire personnel were both mentioned as the groups directly affected. According to the associate for Hamilton, "the police and fire departments continue to be very influential, not only in the allocation of revenue sharing money but in the normal budget process itself. They have argued, apparently quite effectively, that revenue sharing money definitely eases the city's fiscal position and warrants increased salaries for their members." At the national level, the International Association of Fire Fighters was active in its support of the general revenue sharing program and has made concerted efforts with its local affiliates to press for wage and salary increases out of shared revenue. The North Little Rock associate reported that "pressure by the organization for the city firemen was to some degree influenced by its national organization. A representative of the national organization assisted in negotiations with the city during a work slowdown on the part of the firemen. There was no direct mention of revenue sharing allocations as far as the claims by the firemen were concerned, but they clearly were aware of its substantial use in funding the city budget and the fact that there were some funds as yet unallocated."

In addition to the four jurisdictions noted above, revenue sharing was reported to have played some role in salary negotiations in nine others. The fact that revenue sharing allocations were not assigned to the increased pay and benefits category in these cases means that in the judgment of the associate these funds did not play a crucial role in determining final settlements. As the associate in California observed, "there have been major salary increases recently and shared revenue lessened the state's ability to plead fiscal hardship in attempting to resist employees' demands. However, it is doubtful that revenue sharing materially affected the raises actually granted."

PROGRAM MAINTENANCE

Uses of shared revenue to avoid cutbacks in existing services accounted for an average of nearly 13 percent of cumulative allocations for the sixty-five sample jurisdictions. As seen earlier, program maintenance uses have been particularly important for city governments in the sample, averaging over one-fifth of cumulative allocations; public safety, followed by transportation and recreation, were the program areas most significantly affected in round two. For states, towns, and counties, the proportion of shared-revenue allocations accounted for by program maintenance uses drops significantly, to a range of between 4 percent and 8 percent.

Table 2-7 shows the fourteen jurisdictions for which 20 percent or more of shared-revenue allocations were reported as program maintenance, along with the percent of allocation to this category, type of government, and fiscal pressure conditions. Of the ten cities listed in the table, Cincinnati, Ohio, stands out for having used nearly 90 percent of its cumulative shared-revenue allocations for program maintenance. The situation in Cincinnati was described by the associate in his second-round report as follows: "The fiscal climate of the city is such that if it had not been for revenue sharing, cuts would have had to be made in city services. It is extremely unlikely that taxes would have been increased, as the city income tax (2 percent) is already the highest in the state and the property tax levy is, for all practical purposes, off limits to any increase." The specific areas for which revenue sharing provided the means of maintaining existing services in Cincinnati covered a wide range, including police protection, sewerage treatment facilities, road maintenance, and health and recreational services.

In the second-round report, the associate in the city of Jacksonville, Florida, assigned all of that city's allocations to program maintenance. It will be recalled that Jacksonville was one of the cities discussed earlier in which a significant drop in capital uses occurred between the first and second rounds. As reported by the associate, the fiscal situation in Jacksonville changed abruptly between the first and second rounds, from relatively light to between moderate and extreme. This sharp turnaround was directly related to the impact of the energy crisis on the operating budget of the city-owned electric utility. Because of a six-fold increase in the price of oil to the wholly oil-based utility, the expected transfer in operating profits from the utility to the general fund was reduced by $10 million. Faced with this unexpected shortfall in operating revenues, the city froze a large

Table 2-7. Fourteen Sample Jurisdictions in Which 20 Percent or More of Cumulative Shared Revenue Allocations Were Reported as Program Maintenance

Jurisdiction	Type of government	Percent of allocation to program maintenance	Fiscal pressure conditions[a]
Cincinnati, Ohio	City	89.1	Moderate
St. Louis, Mo.	City	71.0	Extreme
Los Angeles, Calif.	City	60.8	Moderate
Carson, Calif.	City	57.2	Light
Eugene, Oreg.	City	49.6	Moderate
Springfield, Oreg.	City	46.5	Moderate
Jacksonville, Fla.	City	45.2	Moderate
Worcester, Mass.	City	42.4	Extreme
Massachusetts	State	39.5	Moderate
Hamilton, Ohio	City	37.4	Moderate
Holden, Mass.	Town	34.0	Light
North Little Rock, Ark.	City	32.7	Light
Saline, Ark.	County	23.7	Light
Kershaw, S.C.	County	23.2	Light

Source: Field research data.
a. See table 2-4, note a.

number of capital projects for which revenue sharing had been tentatively allocated and shifted these funds entirely to maintaining current operations. In summarizing the net effects discussion in his second report, the associate noted that "a drastically worsened fiscal situation brought about by the great increases in fuel oil costs has been met by an equally drastic reordering of federal revenue sharing priorities."

Program maintenance is one of the more perplexing net effect categories to pinpoint and analyze. Unlike new capital or operating uses, program maintenance amounts to a nonevent—the avoidance of a cutback in services that, in the absence of revenue sharing, would have occurred. The tax stabilization category poses a similarly difficult problem: a tax cut can be documented, but the avoidance of a tax increase is a nonevent. Moreover, for a jurisdiction facing moderate or extreme fiscal pressure, the field associate must frequently decide between these two nonevents; would this government have cut back services in order to balance its budget, or would it have raised taxes? While the implications of these two actions for the private versus public sector impact are clear, it is frequently quite difficult to make this distinction. To a considerable degree, the associate's knowledge of the fiscal and political history of a jurisdiction provides the key for making such judgments, but circumstances may change over time so as to alter the picture substantially.

The Massachusetts associate, for example, reported in round one that all of the shared revenue had been used to "reduce outstanding bills owed by the state to local governments." In effect, revenue sharing made it possible for the state to meet its prior commitments to assist local governments, particularly school districts. By the second round, however, the situation had changed. The costs of financing a growing state debt had become a matter of increasing public concern; according to the associate, higher taxes were inevitable, and without revenue sharing to help service part of the growing debt (as mandated by state law), they would have risen even higher. Hence, in the second round, the associate reported that revenue sharing was being used to hold down the rate of increase in state taxes.

FEDERAL AID RESTORATION

This net effect category can be viewed as a special case of program maintenance, referring specifically to the use of shared revenue to maintain programs that have experienced a cutback in federal funding. In both the first and second rounds of field reports, associates reported very little activity in this area. Only one jurisdiction, Colorado, was reported to have assigned a significant percent of its allocated shared revenue to federal aid restoration—nearly three-fifths of cumulative allocations through June 1974. The Colorado legislature, in its 1974–75 appropriations bill, explicitly earmarked revenue sharing funds for maintaining spending in those areas that might be affected by a cutback in categorical grant funding. According to the Colorado associate, the impact of this law was expected to affect a number of program areas, including education, library, and health services. But the program area most significantly affected was aid to local governments for capital projects related to sewerage treatment facilities. In the 1974–75 appropriation report of the Colorado legislature, a $24 million gap was reported between congressional appropriations for capital grants for environmental projects in Colorado and expected releases of funds by the administration. In order to proceed on schedule with the state's water and sewerage treatment program, and avoid the projected additional costs if the program were delayed, a decision was made to allocate nearly $18 million in revenue sharing monies to this program.

A deliberate strategy, such as that adopted in Colorado, to coordinate general revenue sharing with other federal grant programs is bound to be difficult to implement precisely. At the very least, such planning calls for a high degree of flexibility in the budget process, an ability to predict likely revenue flows from various federal grant programs for the budget year, and an ability to accommodate unanticipated shifts in these revenue flows that occur during the budget year.

Recent developments in categorical grant funding. The interaction between general revenue sharing and other federal grant-in-aid programs to state and local governments is, at best, difficult to gauge precisely. An examination of outlays of federal grants (other than general revenue sharing, public assistance, and food stamps) to state and local governments from fiscal 1973 through fiscal 1975 shows that, in aggregate terms, these outlays increased each year.[16] However, as can be seen in table 2-8, year-to-year growth rates have been very uneven, ranging from a low of 6.6 percent in fiscal 1973 to 20.8 percent in fiscal 1975. Moreover, actual outlays do not reflect efforts to slow the growth in appropriations for many programs, or efforts to slow the rate at which appropriated funds were subsequently obligated.

An examination of individual grant programs reveals even greater year-to-year fluctuations in growth rates. Social service grants, mostly to state governments for providing services to persons on welfare, declined significantly in fiscal 1973 and 1974, primarily because of legislative changes in determining the allocation of such funds among the states and changes in administrative regulations for determining eligibility for assistance.[17]

Erratic growth patterns can also be seen in grants affecting other major program areas such as education, community development, and manpower training. In the case of community development and manpower, the situation is complicated by consolidations of previous categorical grants into block grant programs. The Community Development Block Grant program consolidated a number of separate categorical grants administered

16. Public assistance and food stamp grants are excluded because changes in functional responsibility that occurred from 1973 to 1975 resulted in the federal government's assuming a greater share of direct responsibility in providing assistance in both these areas.

17. Social service grants to states were switched to a closed-ended formula program as part of the State and Local Fiscal Assistance Act of 1972. The ceiling amount was set at $2.5 billion, and the effect of the population-based formula varied significantly among the states in terms of actual and potential gains and losses in funds received under the revised program. The immediate effect of the tightened regulations governing eligibility was to significantly reduce total outlays to well below the $2.5 billion ceiling. For a comprehensive analysis of the changes occurring in the social services grant program, see Martha Derthick, *Uncontrollable Spending for Social Services Grants* (Brookings Institution, 1975).

Table 2-8. **Annual Growth Rate in Federal Grants to State and Local Governments, Fiscal 1973–75**
Percent

Type of grant	1973	1974	1975
All grants (excluding general revenue sharing, public assistance, and food stamps)	6.6	8.5	20.8
Social services	−12.2	−8.8	39.2
Elementary and secondary education	3.4	−8.5	36.6
Manpower training	−14.6	15.2	120.2
Community development[a]	−2.5	3.5	6.2

Source: *Special Analysis, Budget of the United States Government* (selected years).
a. Includes all community development grant outlays administered by the Department of Housing and Urban Development except housing assistance.

by the Department of Housing and Urban Development (most importantly urban renewal and model cities); the Comprehensive Employment Training Act involved a similar consolidation of separate categorical programs administered by the Department of Labor. As in the case of the social services grant program, these consolidations meant a switch to formula-based allocations to states and localities. Hence, the impact on individual jurisdictions in terms of funding-level changes varies according to differences in participation rates in the previous categorical programs.[18]

In general, efforts to impound funds to programs for which Congress has appropriated money, efforts to cut back or limit the growth in new appropriations, and the restructuring of grant programs in major functional areas have made it difficult for states and localities to plan ahead in anticipating the role of federal grants in their budgets. Hence, many of these governments may simply have been discouraged from making direct linkages between revenue sharing funds and changes occurring within categorical grant programs.

18. It should be noted that the information in table 2-8 relates only to outlays, which are not necessarily a good measure of current levels of activity within individual grant programs. This is particularly true of grants affecting capital projects such as environmental and community development programs. In the case of Environmental Protection Agency grants for water and sewerage treatment projects, for example, outlays increased over the period of observation, but to a large extent these outlays reflect obligations incurred in previous years. On the other hand, the uneven growth in outlays to community development projects reflects the switch to CDBG funding and understates the actual level of activity occurring in this area. The significant amount of funding that has been committed to this program will show up as outlays in later years, when projects proceed to various stages of completion.

The impact of the antimatching provision. There has been speculation that the prohibition against the use of revenue sharing monies as matching funds for federal categorical grant programs may further deter recipient governments from using shared revenue in programs affected by federal matching grants, even as permitted supplements to grant-related expenditures. Some support for this notion is provided from the sample jurisdictions. For example, the associate for Fairfield County, South Carolina, described the prevailing attitude as opposed to the use of shared revenue in areas affected by categorical grants "so that we don't get all tied up in red tape." The Los Angeles associate reported that "questions were raised that LEAA (Law Enforcement Assistance Administration) monies might be lost if allocations of revenue sharing funds to the police budget reduced the general fund effort." Altogether, some sensitivity to the nonmatching provision in deciding on the uses of shared revenue was reported for eleven of the jurisdictions. The combination of uncertainty about actual levels of funding for various categorical grant programs and the potential conflicts that might arise from the antimatching provision if shared revenue is used to restore anticipated shortfalls in categorical aid may have further discouraged recipient governments from developing a concerted strategy in this area.

TAX REDUCTION

Over the two rounds of field observations, revenue sharing was reported to have played a direct role in decisions to reduce taxes in fourteen sample jurisdictions. Uses of shared revenue to reduce taxes implies that jurisdictions were able to substitute shared revenue to finance ongoing operations and thus reduce the need for own-source tax revenues. Typically, revenue sharing was only one of several factors associated with a decision to cut taxes; related factors were increases in yields from other nontax revenue sources and improving fund balances.

In nine jurisdictions, 10 percent or more of cumulative shared-revenue allocations were accounted for by tax reduction uses. These nine cases are shown in table 2-9, along with the percent of cumulative allocations assigned to the tax reduction category, type of jurisdiction, and fiscal pressure condition. In California, which had the largest percentage for any sample jurisdiction, tax cuts accounted for approximately 87 percent of total shared revenue uses. The associate for California explained the situation as follows: "The availability of revenue sharing has enabled the state

Table 2-9. Nine Sample Jurisdictions in Which 10 Percent or More of Cumulative Shared Revenue Allocations Were Reported as Tax Reduction Uses

Jurisdiction	Type of government	Percent of allocation to tax reduction	Fiscal pressure conditions[a]
California	State	86.9	Moderate
Dodge, Wis.	County	59.0	Moderate
Baltimore, Md.	County	47.8	None
Greece, N.Y.	Town	36.4	None
Cottage Grove, Oreg.	City	19.3	Moderate
Newark, N.J.	City	19.0	Extreme
Harford, Md.	County	18.6	Light
Los Angeles, Calif.	County	13.4	Moderate
Monroe, N.Y.	County	13.2	Light

Source: Field research data.
a. See table 2-4, note a.

to maintain its 1972 commitment to increased local school support on an ongoing basis without dipping into its normal surplus. Without revenue sharing, there is every reason to believe that there would not have been the increased support to local schools to finance property tax reductions. In addition, the one-time state tax cuts in 1973–74 would have been less than the $700 million enacted."

For four of the eight local governments shown in table 2-9 (Los Angeles, Baltimore, and Harford Counties and the city of Newark), the decision to reduce taxes was reported initially in the first-round reports. As discussed in *Monitoring Revenue Sharing,* Newark is a particularly interesting case because it is a city under extreme fiscal pressure. In his second-round report, the Newark associate again emphasized that "the critical function of revenue sharing since it started is that it has allowed Newark to hold down and reduce for the first time in recent years its extremely high property tax rate which has bound the city in a vicious cycle of decline."

In analyzing the use of shared revenue to cut taxes, the question arises as to whether revenue sharing might be used to cut taxes temporarily (perhaps to gain a political advantage during an election) only to have them accelerate in subsequent periods. For the sample jurisdictions reporting significant tax reduction uses in the first round, this would not appear to have been the case. In three of the four cases, field information provided in round two indicated that revenue sharing was continuing to play an important role in helping to hold the line on taxes. In the fourth case, Harford County, Maryland, the situation was less clear. County taxes were reduced even further during the second round of field observations, but, in the opinion of the field associate, these subsequent cuts would have occurred anyway and the cuts made in the previous period would have been maintained even without revenue sharing. Two factors that went into this judgment were the county election, which coincided with the second-round field observations, and the fact that actions to cut taxes were rather widespread among local governments in Maryland. On balance, the associate concluded that if revenue sharing had not been available to Harford County, the most likely result in the second round would have been a cutback in various capital improvement projects.

The four local governments that initiated tax cuts in the second round were the town of Greece and Monroe County (New York), the city of Cottage Grove (Oregon), and Dodge County (Wisconsin). The Rochester-area associate reported that approximately one-half of the revenue sharing allocations covered in the second round were used to cut taxes in the town of Greece. She described the circumstances leading to the decision to cut taxes as follows: "Despite the fact that the 1974 operating budget for Greece was almost 24 percent greater than for 1973, there was a decrease of 15 cents in the property tax rate. The explanation involves three factors: continuing growth in assessed valuation, increased shared revenues from the state, and general revenue sharing. At the time the 1974 budget was adopted the town supervisor specifically cited general revenue sharing as a major factor allowing the reduced tax rate."

A similar situation was reported for Monroe County, which used approximately one-half of its allocated shared revenue to help finance a 10 percent reduction in the county tax rate in 1974. Neither of these two jurisdictions was characterized as facing moderate or extreme fiscal pressure, and the surpluses generated by general revenue sharing and other favorable fiscal trends gave rise to a combination of tax reduction and increased spending uses of shared revenue. In effect, general revenue sharing represented a pleasant windfall to these jurisdictions, allowing them to continue operating in a very favorable fiscal climate.

The city of Cottage Grove, Oregon, was also judged to have used approximately one-half of its shared-revenue allocations to cut taxes during the second round of field observations. The circumstances leading to the tax cut were, however, quite different from those reported for the two New York jurisdictions. The city was characterized by the Oregon associate as being under moderate to extreme fiscal pressure. The mayor had pushed hard to have revenue sharing monies used for various capital projects and expanded operations, but to do this, a tax increase would have been needed to maintain existing service levels. On four occasions, the voters of Cottage Grove rejected the additional levy, and the earmarked shared revenue was integrated into the operating budget to finance ongoing operations. As a result, rather than an additional levy, the city's property tax rate was reduced.

The tax effort factor. The fact that a jurisdiction's revenue sharing entitlements depend in part on the relative tax effort it makes suggests that there might be some bias against using revenue sharing funds to cut taxes. The associates were asked in the second-round field observations to report any evidence that this provision of the distribution formula had such an impact. Such evidence was reported in only four cases: Rochester, New York, Butler County, Ohio, Springfield, Oregon, and Dodge County, Wisconsin.

The associate for Rochester reported that to circumvent the state-imposed limit on property taxation for general-purpose and educational operating expenditures, the city had considered the use of special charges (which are excluded from the computation of the relative tax effort factor used in the revenue sharing formula) for financing the fire bureau, a major component of the city's operating budget. This tactic was not adopted, however, and the negative effect on revenue sharing entitlements for the city was cited as the reason. In Dodge County, a tax cut was made, but only after carefully calculating the potential loss of shared-revenue payments to the county. In Butler County, the tax effort provision was a factor not in the decision whether to cut taxes, but in whether to raise them. The associate for Butler reported that in seeking a tax increase, the county intended to stress the implications of the proposed tax increase for revenue sharing entitlements to the county.

In the city of Springfield, the mayor commented on the consequences of the city's low tax effort (relative to neighboring jurisdictions) and observed, "unfortunately, a relatively low tax effort is not a bargain. Not only does it reduce the amount of property tax revenue available, but, additionally, under the provisions of the State and Local Fiscal Assistance Act of 1972, a low tax effort also reduces the amount of federal revenue sharing the city can expect to receive." The *Springfield News* reinforced this point in an editorial, observing that the declining entitlement of the city was a direct consequence of the declining tax effort in Springfield relative to that of neighboring cities, which were realizing a corresponding increase in their entitlements.[19]

19. "Low Tax Support Strikes New Blow," *Springfield News*, March 11, 1974.

Table 2-10. Fourteen Sample Jurisdictions in Which 20 Percent or More of Cumulative Shared Revenue Allocations Were Reported as Tax Stabilization Uses

Jurisdiction	Type of government	Percent of allocation to tax stabilization	Fiscal pressure conditions[a]
Rochester, N.Y.	City	100.0	Extreme
Mayville, Wis.	City	100.0	Moderate
Essex, N.J.	County	96.3	None
West Orange, N.J.	City	91.5	None
Newark, N.J.	City	81.0	Extreme
Massachusetts	State	60.5	Moderate
Baltimore, Md.	City	58.2	Extreme
Beaver Dam, Wis.	City	52.5	Moderate
New York City	City	37.3	Extreme
Bangor, Me.	City	35.8	Moderate
Worcester, Mass.	City	35.0	Extreme
Baltimore County, Md.	County	34.5	None
Livingston, N.J.	Township	27.5	None
Scottsdale, Ariz.	City	22.8	None

Source: Field research data.
a. See table 2-4, note a.

TAX STABILIZATION

In the case of the tax stabilization net effect category, the availability of revenue sharing monies is judged to have made it possible for a jurisdiction to avoid or limit an increase in local taxes rather than providing the means for an actual tax cut. Of the two net effect categories relating to tax policy, associates reported considerably more tax stabilization activity; on average, over 14 percent of cumulative shared-revenue allocations were reported as tax stabilization uses for the sixty-five sample jurisdictions. By type of jurisdiction, a significantly higher proportion of cumulative allocations were reported as tax stabilization for cities (averaging over 22 percent) than for states, counties, and townships (whose average allocations ranged from 7 percent to 9 percent).

Tax stabilization uses were reported as particularly significant in fourteen jurisdictions (shown in table 2-10), in each case accounting for 20 percent or more of cumulative allocations through June 1974. The pattern of tax stabilization uses in relation to fiscal pressure conditions shown in table 2-9 is consistent with the observation made earlier in this chapter: both for jurisdictions under no fiscal pressure and for those under extreme

fiscal pressure, revenue sharing has had a greater impact on revenue policies than on expenditure policies. The result is that for both groups, revenue sharing has, on balance, provided greater stimulus to the private
sector. However, the implications of these similar allocational imports are
quite different for the two groups. For the least hard-pressed jurisdictions,
revenue sharing has provided a means of sustaining a favorable fiscal climate; for jurisdictions under extreme fiscal pressure, revenue sharing has
provided a means of helping to slow the deterioration of their fiscal
environments.

The different circumstances underlying the tax stabilization uses of
shared revenue by these two groups of sample jurisdictions are clearly
reflected in the field observations of our associates. Essex County, New
Jersey, is an example of a prosperous government that was reported to
have used nearly all of its shared-revenue allocations over two rounds for
stabilizing taxes. In his second-round report, the associate for Essex described the fiscal climate of the county as follows: "The county's fiscal
situation remains very sound. The contrast between the extremes of wealth
and poverty in its different localities continues, but the county as a whole
is still a vital economic center in New Jersey." With respect to the role of
revenue sharing in the county's budget, the associate reported that "as was
the case last year, revenue sharing funds have been used to hold down
taxes and have not been targeted on any particular program area in the
budget. Without revenue sharing, the tax rate would have to have been
raised to cover the bulk of the $13 million budget increase for welfare,
correctional and hospital facilities, and educational services. On balance,
however, revenue sharing, while helping to keep taxes down, has not been
essential to the county's overall prosperity."

At the other end of the fiscal pressure spectrum are five cities with
populations of over 100,000, each characterized as under extreme fiscal
pressure and reported to have used a significant proportion of shared revenue to help stabilize taxes. In explaining the fiscal situation in Rochester,
New York, the associate noted that "high debt-service costs, little growth
in assessed valuation, and higher wages and benefits for city employees
continue to create a situation of extreme fiscal pressure for the city of
Rochester." Reporting that cuts had been made in "nonessential" services
such as recreation, the associate concluded that without revenue sharing,
it is very likely that property taxes would have been raised even more
substantially than they were. A former Rochester city official observed
that "revenue sharing is simply money to help hold the line to meet higher

costs which inflation and increased personnel, services, and facilities force on us. This is going to be a continuing problem for a city stuck with a real property tax, such as we are, as the major source of local revenue. . . ."

BORROWING AVOIDANCE

Over the two rounds of field observations, seventeen sample jurisdictions were reported to have used some portion of shared revenue as a means of avoiding borrowing. In all cases, borrowing avoidance was directly related to capital projects; this implies that in the absence of revenue sharing these capital projects would have been undertaken, although a greater portion of the costs of these projects would have been met through borrowing. While the borrowing avoidance and new capital spending categories are closely related, the net effect implications are quite different. The new capital spending category refers to a decision to undertake a project; in the absence of revenue sharing, the project would not have been undertaken for at least another year. In the case of borrowing avoidance, revenue sharing affects only to the manner of financing and not the decision to proceed with the capital project.

On a cumulative basis, borrowing avoidance was reported to have accounted for 20 percent or more of shared revenue allocations in eight sample jurisdictions, listed in table 2-11. All of these experienced relatively light or no fiscal pressure. Again, for these jurisdictions revenue sharing did not play a critical role in deciding whether or not to undertake the projects, but rather, in deciding the means by which they would be financed.

The case of Orange County, Florida, offers a good example of the use of shared revenue to avoid borrowing. As of June 1974, borrowing avoidance was reported to have accounted for nearly all of the cumulative shared-revenue allocations by the county. As reported in *Monitoring Revenue Sharing,* the county had received voter approval and was preparing to issue bonds to finance its capital improvements program when revenue sharing was enacted. A decision was made to use revenue sharing to finance the program on a pay-as-you-go basis rather than follow through on the bond sale. This strategy continued to be followed in round two.

Significant borrowing avoidance uses were also reported in round one for Butler County, Ohio, and Minnehaha County, South Dakota; a significant portion of Butler County's round-two allocations were also reported as borrowing avoidance. In both jurisdictions, associates reported

Table 2-11. Eight Sample Jurisdictions in Which 20 Percent or More of Cumulative Shared Revenue Allocations Were Reported as Borrowing Avoidance Uses

Jurisdiction	Type of government	Percent of allocation to borrowing avoidance	Fiscal pressure conditions[a]
Butler, Ohio	County	94.7	Light
Orange, Fla.	County	93.8	None
Minnehaha, S. Dak.	County	57.9	Light
Maricopa, Ariz.	County	50.8	Light
Monroe, N.Y.	County	34.7	Light
Baton Rouge, La.	City	36.5	Light
Irondequoit, N.Y.	Township	26.4	Light
Maine	State	24.9	Light

Source: Field research data.
a. See table 2-4, note a.

that the various capital projects would have been undertaken without revenue sharing and that only the method of financing was affected. Significant borrowing avoidance was reported in round two for the city of Baton Rouge, Louisiana. According to the associate, "federal revenue sharing provides local officials with the opportunity to undertake certain projects without the need for getting voter approval for a bond issue. Many of the projects financed from revenue sharing funds are not high priority and may not have received public support. Perhaps the rationale of the local officials is to use the revenue sharing funds for projects which might not get voter approval and to submit to voters only those projects which are urgently needed."

Of the various sample jurisdictions making significant use of shared revenue to avoid borrowing, Baton Rouge was the only case in which revenue sharing may have been used by officials as a way around a possibly unpopular bond referendum. To the extent that the borrowing avoidance in Baton Rouge was related to capital projects that might not have received voter approval, revenue sharing can be said to have made it possible for the city to undertake these projects. Accordingly, borrowing avoidance may be more correctly interpreted as only a nominal net effect in Baton Rouge, with the real net effect more appropriately categorized as new capital spending. In general, however, the field information over two rounds suggests that borrowing avoidance uses have primarily reflected decisions by jurisdictions under relatively little fiscal pressure on how to finance capital projects that would have been undertaken even without revenue sharing funds.

INCREASED FUND BALANCES

The final net effect category covers shared revenue used to increase the fund balances of the recipient government. The implication here is that shared revenue has simply been substituted for own-source revenue in funding the operations of the government and has not, in any real sense, affected existing revenue or expenditure flows. In effect, revenue sharing has added to the recipient government's available surplus.

As is true of the other net effect categories, increased fund balance uses represent the net effect of a deliberate action taken by the recipient government in deciding how to use revenue sharing funds. Accordingly, the increased fund balance category does not reflect funds remaining in an individual government's trust fund or separate bank account in which revenue sharing payments are initially deposited.[20] Even when a government does allocate shared revenue so as to effectively increase its fund balance, this fiscal effect may be only an intermediate or temporary one. The additional surplus may eventually show up in revenue or expenditure flows, perhaps providing the means of avoiding a future tax increase or of funding a new operating or capital program. In general, therefore, the fiscal implications of shared revenue used to increase fund balances are less clear than the other net effect categories.

Increased fund balances accounted for 10 percent or more of cumulative shared revenue allocations in seven of the sample jurisdictions, which are listed in table 2-12. In three jurisdictions—New York State, Dodge County, Wisconsin, and Baltimore County, Maryland—increased fund balance uses of shared revenue were found only in round one. As reported in *Monitoring Revenue Sharing,* the decision by New York State to increase fund balances was attributed at the time to an anticipated tax cut, which subsequently took place when the 2½ percent income tax surtax was suspended in 1973 and 1974.

The city of Bangor, Maine, was reported to have used approximately one-third of its shared-revenue allocations in both rounds to increase fund balances. In his second-round report, the associate for Bangor noted that "the main strategy behind the use of revenue sharing in Bangor continues

20. The 1972 revenue sharing act requires recipient governments to "obligate or appropriate" revenue sharing funds, including interest earned on these funds, within twenty-four months from the end of the entitlement period in which they are received. Requests to extend this time period may be made to the Office of Revenue Sharing.

Table 2-12. Seven Sample Jurisdictions in Which 10 Percent or More of Cumulative Shared Revenue Allocations Were Reported as Increased Fund Balances

Jurisdiction	Type of government	Percent of allocation to increased fund balances	Fiscal pressure conditions[a]
Beaver Dam, Wis.	City	47.5	Moderate
Bangor, Me.	City	32.7	Moderate
New York State	State	22.8	Light
Dodge, Wis.	County	20.3	Moderate
Little Rock, Ark.	City	19.5	Moderate
Baltimore County, Md.	County	17.7	None
California	State	13.1	Moderate

Source: Field research data.
a. See table 2-4, note a.

to be one of improving fund balances. The city budgeted $491,000 in surplus for 1974, an amount that it would clearly not have been able to provide in the absence of revenue sharing funds."

The other three jurisdictions reporting 10 percent or more of cumulative shared-revenue allocations as increased fund balances are the cities of Little Rock, Arkansas, and Beaver Dam, Wisconsin, and the State of California. In these three jurisdictions, increased fund balance uses were reported only in round two of the field observations. In general, the information provided after two rounds of field reports continues to support the observation made in *Monitoring Revenue Sharing* that recipient governments are not simply holding onto shared revenue as a means of building up fiscal reserves. Rather, these funds are having a direct effect on revenue and expenditure decisions of recipient governments by providing the means for maintaining existing revenue and expenditure patterns or the means for reducing taxes or increasing expenditures.

The Impact of Expenditure Uses of Shared Revenue

In addition to the net effects data discussed in the preceding two sections of this chapter, associates reported in round two on the program areas that were affected by expenditure uses of shared revenue.[21] Where

21. Information on program impact was also provided in the first round of field observations, but because the round-two data provide a more complete accounting of expenditure uses, only they are discussed here.

the net effects data showed allocations to the new capital, new or expanded operations, program maintenance, and federal aid restoration,[22] associates were asked to break those expenditures down into nine specific program areas: public safety, environmental protection, public transportation, health, recreation, libraries, social services, education, and other. Within particular program areas, further breakdowns were reported by type of function—for instance, under public safety, police and fire protection were reported separately.[23]

With this added information, it is possible to use the field data to examine the allocational impact of revenue sharing not only on the public versus the private sectors, but also within the public sector of recipient jurisdictions. Following a summary of the field data, two issues are given special attention, both of which have received considerable publicity. The first concerns how the uses of shared revenue have affected the disadvantaged; the second concerns discrepancies between what are judged by the field associates to be real programmatic impacts and those officially reported to the Treasury Department's Office of Revenue Sharing. The section concludes with a general discussion of the fungibility issue associated with federal grant programs.

SUMMARY OF THE PROGRAMMATIC IMPACT OF REVENUE SHARING

Table 2-13 summarizes the second-round field information relating to program areas affected by revenue sharing expenditures. For each type of sample government, the unweighted mean percentages of shared revenue allocations to specific program areas are shown in the first nine rows;

22. The other net effect expenditure category, increased pay and benefits, was not broken down by program area. (As noted earlier, very little activity had been reported under this category.)
23. The program areas specified in the reporting form used by the Brookings field associates overlap to a considerable extent with the priority spending categories designated in the 1972 State and Local Fiscal Assistance Act and used in the actual-use reports administered by the Treasury Department's Office of Revenue Sharing. However, the reader should note that, as in the case of the earlier discussion of the net effects data, the impact of shared revenue on various program areas reported by the field associates represent their judgments of *real* effects, which will not necessarily coincide with "official" designations reported by recipient governments. As is discussed later in this chapter, it is quite clear that actual-use data often reflect only accounting transactions, i.e., where revenue sharing simply substitutes for sources of revenue that otherwise would have been used in a program area, and not the real impact of revenue sharing funds.

Table 2-13. Percent of Total Shared Revenue Allocations to Various Programs, by Type of Sample Jurisdiction, Second-Round Field Observations[a]

Program	Type of government[b]			
	States (n = 7)	Counties (n = 21)	Cities (n = 27)	Townships (n = 6)
Public safety	2.7	8.4	16.6	2.2
Environmental protection	9.2	3.6	7.9	23.2
Public transportation	16.1	14.4	11.7	25.4
Health	6.4	3.4	1.2	0
Recreation	1.3	3.6	6.5	4.5
Library	1.3	2.5	0.9	0.5
Social services	2.5	3.3	3.3	0
Education	7.4	4.7	0	0
Other	3.8	10.9	5.8	13.8
Balance not allocated to a specific program	3.5	5.8	5.7	0
All programs	54.2	60.6	59.8	69.6

Source: Field research data.

a. Figures are unweighted mean percentages. Last row total is equal to the sum of the proportions of shared revenue allocations in round two accounted for by the following four net effect categories: new capital, new or expanded operations, program maintenance, and federal aid restoration.

b. The city of Orlando, Florida, allocated no revenue-sharing money in round two of the field observations and was excluded from the computations. New York City and Illinois were also excluded because associates in these two jurisdictions were unable to track shared-revenue allocations in round two to specific net effect categories.

the total of these expenditure uses of shared revenue plus portions not traced to specific program areas is shown in the last row.

As discussed earlier, township governments exhibited the greatest propensity to use revenue sharing funds for expenditure purposes; in round two of the field observations, nearly 70 percent of shared-revenue allocations by these governments was accounted for by expenditure uses, primarily new capital spending. For states, counties, and cities, the proportion of shared-revenue allocations in round two accounted for by the four net effect expenditure categories ranges from 54 to 61 percent. Nearly one-half of the expenditure allocations reported for cities in round two was accounted for by program maintenance uses.

For the seven state governments, public transportation ranks first, accounting for an average of 16 percent of total shared-revenue allocations in round two. Environmental protection, health, and education account for between 6 and 10 percent each of shared-revenue allocations, while relatively little activity is indicated for the other program areas.

Two points about state expenditures should be noted. First, a significant portion of the states' shared-revenue funds was channeled through local governments in the form of state aid; of the seven states included in this analysis, all but Louisiana were reported to have used at least some of their shared revenue for such aid over the two rounds of field observations. Aid to public education was the predominant form of aid, although in Colorado such aid affected a number of program areas. The second point, closely related to the first, is that the 7.4 percent shown for education in table 2-13 understates the actual magnitude of state uses of shared revenue in this area. In California, for example, nearly 80 percent of the shared revenue allocated by the state in round two was reported by the field associate as having been used to reduce taxes, but this tax cut was implemented in the form of aid to local school districts as a means of reducing dependence on local property taxes to finance education. Hence, the tax reduction use of shared revenue in California is indirectly aid to public education.

The data for Maine also understate the impact of state uses of revenue sharing for education. In its biennial budget for 1973–75, the state appropriated its shared revenue for the first five entitlement periods for local school aid. Because of the reporting format used in this study (for each observation period, allocations of both actually received and anticipated shared revenue were reported), the impact of revenue sharing on education in Maine was recorded in the first-round data and is not reflected in the data for the second round. However, if the percentage of allocation for education reported in round one is applied to round two, approximately one-fifth of the shared-revenue allocations by state governments would be related to education. And if the tax stabilization use of shared revenue by California in round two is also included, the education-related proportion of shared revenue allocations by state governments in the sample would increase to an average of nearly 30 percent.

For the twenty-one county governments in the sample, public transportation (roads, highways, and mass transit subsidies) was the program area most significantly affected by expenditure uses of revenue sharing in round two. Following public transportation is the category "other," accounting for an average of nearly 11 percent of the allocations. Among the programs identified under other, financial administration and public buildings were the two areas most frequently cited for all three types of local governments in the sample. Public safety ranks third among expenditure uses of revenue sharing by counties, followed by education. All spending by county governments for education was related to capital projects.

Among cities, public safety (including police, fire, and correctional services) was the program area most frequently cited, accounting for an average of approximately 17 percent of shared-revenue allocations in round two. Public transportation ranked second, followed by environmental protection (sewerage, sanitation, and water supply). Compared to the other three types of governments in the sample, the use of shared revenue for recreational services was highest among cities, accounting for 6.5 percent of allocations.

For the six township governments in the sample, environmental protection and public transportation account for nearly 50 percent, on average, of shared-revenue allocations in round two. Expenditures classified as "other" also were a significant proportion of expenditure uses.

Among smaller-sized local governments in the sample generally, greater emphasis was found on transportation and environmental protection programs. For the thirty-two local governments under 100,000 in population, these two program areas accounted for an average of 31 percent of shared-revenue allocations in round two, compared to approximately 9 percent for the twenty-two local jurisdictions over 100,000. This greater concentration of shared-revenue in these two capital-intensive program areas is consistent with observations made earlier about the relationship between size of local government and the net fiscal effects pattern associated with general revenue sharing. The composition of program areas for which these governments are directly responsible are more heavily concentrated in capital-intensive areas such as highway and sewerage construction and maintenance.

THE SOCIAL IMPACT OF REVENUE SHARING

Among the most vocal critics of revenue sharing are those who argue that the program fails to help the disadvantaged. Indeed, as the history of the program treated in chapter 1 reveals, this has been one of the most—if not *the* most—controversial issue in revenue sharing since 1972. Most of the public debate has focused on the social-service uses of revenue sharing as reported in planned- and actual-use reports to the U.S. Treasury. (Social services for the aged and poor is one of the nine priority-expenditure categories contained in the 1972 act.)

Our second-round field data indicate that recipient governments have, in fact, put relatively little emphasis on social-service programs. Included under this heading are such activities as legal aid, job training and placement, counselling, and housing assistance. In general, these services are aimed at the aged, low-income groups, and other categories of disadvantaged persons. As shown in table 2-12, for states, counties, and cities, only between 2 and 4 percent of shared-revenue allocations in round two were traced by the field associates to expenditures for these types of services. For township governments, no shared-revenue expenditures were reported for this program area.

Apart from direct expenditures for social-service programs, however, it is possible that benefits from revenue sharing funds may accrue to the disadvantaged in other ways. Expenditures on health, recreation, and education, for example, may not be directly aimed at the disadvantaged, but can nevertheless provide important benefits to this group. To construct a more complete picture of the effects of revenue sharing on the disadvantaged, the field associates were asked to report, on the basis of the two rounds of field observations, the extent to which revenue sharing was used directly in social program areas or in other ways that provided benefits to the disadvantaged, defined for these purposes as low-income groups and minorities. The specific question posed to the field associates was as follow: "On the basis of your observations for the entire period of the revenue sharing program to date, please summarize your views as to whether, how, and to what extent the availability of shared revenue to this government has been used in social program areas or, in terms of its net effects, has benefited low-income groups and racial minorities. Please identify any specific programs (either newly established or maintained by revenue sharing) which you believe may result in social benefits."

Using this open-ended question, aimed at a general rather than a detailed assessment, it is not possible to arrive at a precise accounting of the benefits of revenue sharing to the disadvantaged. In some cases, the associates indicated that the question did not seem relevant, either because of the absence of an identifiable disadvantaged group within the jurisdiction or because of the limited role of the jurisdiction (particularly townships and smaller county governments) in providing services to the disadvantaged. Of the sixty-five sample jurisdictions, only seven were identified as having used revenue sharing funds in a way that provided significant benefits to the disadvantaged, either because the proportion of allocations affecting the disadvantaged was relatively large or because, in the opinion of the associate, revenue sharing played an important role in providing the means for an expanded role by the jurisdiction in areas that affected the disadvantaged. The seven include two states, Maine and Colorado, and five local governments: the cities of Phoenix (Arizona) and Eugene (Oregon), and Pulaski County (Arkansas), Los Angeles County (California), and Lane County (Oregon).

Before reviewing these seven cases, it should be noted that in many of the other sample jurisdictions associates reported that at least some benefits from revenue sharing accrued to the disadvantaged, either directly through specific programs or indirectly through expenditure or revenue policies that provide important benefits for these groups. The cities of Little Rock and North Little Rock (Arkansas), Baton Rouge (Louisiana), Hamilton (Ohio), Bangor (Maine), Worcester (Massachusetts), and Springfield (Oregon) and the counties of Orange (North Carolina), Fairfield (South Carolina), Monroe (New York), Seminole and Orange (Florida), and Minnehaha (South Dakota) are among those sample jurisdictions where associates reported some shared funds spent on programs that benefit the disadvantaged. The areas mentioned included health, housing, and recreation, public safety, and employment services. Public transportation (primarily bus subsidies) was frequently given as an example of a service not aimed at any particular income group which nevertheless was of particular benefit to the disadvantaged. In most of these cases, benefits to the disadvantaged derived from some combination of new or expanded operations and program maintenance. However, some new capital uses, such as improvements to health and criminal justice facilities, were identified as having an effect on the disadvantaged.

To these jurisdictions should probably be added the cities of Cincinnati, Ohio, and St. Louis, Missouri. Each has a relatively large low-income population, and in both cases program maintenance was the primary use of revenue sharing. Although no new spending out of revenue sharing was reported for either city in the second-round field observations, the associates indicated that revenue sharing had important implications for the disadvantaged. The St. Louis associate explained the situation as follows: "To my knowledge, the city has not used revenue sharing to provide specific benefits to low-income groups or racial minorities. However, the city operates two acute-care hospitals, a nursing home for senior citizens, a hospital for the chronically ill, neighborhood health clinics, recreation programs, neighborhood improvement programs, and summer youth programs which primarily benefit the poor. Nearly all of the city's shared revenue has been used to maintain these and other existing programs, and without revenue sharing, service cuts would have been made in many of them. Hence, revenue sharing has had an important impact on the disadvantaged population of St. Louis."

We turn now to the seven jurisdictions in which revenue sharing uses were reported by the field associates to have had a significant impact on the disadvantaged. The two state governments in the group offer an interesting contrast. In Maine, the additional state aid to local school districts made possible by revenue sharing was judged by the associate to have had a particularly important effect on low- and middle-income groups. According to the associate, "the new educational finance law tries to equalize educational opportunities by providing equal dollars for equal tax effort. As a consequence of the law, property taxes for education were reduced for about 60 percent of the state's population. Another 29 percent of the population had a tax increase of less than 10 percent, while for the remaining 11 percent of population, property taxes increased by more than 10 percent. Many of the communities in which taxes increased are relatively well off, and the school tax rate was below average. The persons most likely to gain under the new law are the middle-to-low-income citizens. The law clearly has some redistributive effect."

In Colorado, the impact on the disadvantaged was realized through various expenditure uses of shared revenue. As reported earlier, Colorado used all of its shared revenue to replace actual and anticipated cuts in federal categorical grants. Although aid to localities to help finance sewerage treatment projects was the program area most affected, nearly one-quarter of the state's allocated shared revenue in round two was used for programs that the associate reported are of primary benefit to the disadvantaged—community mental health centers, employment services, day care, rent subsidies, and family planning services.

Phoenix, Arizona stands out among the five local governments in which a significant impact from revenue sharing on the disadvantaged was reported. The associate described the situation as follows: "The city had begun to expand its social-welfare activities prior to revenue sharing, but with the advent of the program it moved more rapidly into this field. A portion of its funds were used to replace lost federal funding, but new programs were also launched. These included a new senior citizen center, an expanded inner-city recreation center, support for social and welfare programs for off-reservation Indians, and a new program of self-help counselling. The city is also using revenue sharing to expand public transportation, which is of primary advantage to lower-income groups. Approximately 15 percent of the city's 1974–75 revenue sharing monies can be traced to new programs which provide significant benefits to low-income groups."

In Los Angeles County, benefits to the disadvantaged from revenue sharing were traced to two primary areas, grants to community action agencies and a mass transit subsidy. New expenditures to improve juvenile justice procedures and facilities, probation counselling, and narcotics programs were also cited by the associate as uses of shared revenue that affected the disadvantaged. In Pulaski County, Arkansas, revenue sharing was said to have provided the means for an expanded county role in the social-service area, particularly for recreation and health services. The associate also cited a contribution to the public transit system and capital improvements to the county hospital and juvenile hall as examples of shared-revenue uses providing important benefits to low-income residents. The city of Eugene and Lane County, Oregon, operated together in using portions of their shared revenue to finance a joint social-service program. The associate described this as "the most significant program developed in the Lane County area as a result of federal revenue sharing."

Although the seven jurisdictions identified as providing significant benefits to the disadvantaged from revenue sharing are quite diverse, they do have some common characteristics. As a group, they cluster in the light to moderate range of fiscal pressure, and none was characterized as being under extreme fiscal pressure in either the first or second round of field observations. Except for Eugene, which operated jointly with Lane County in the social-service area, the local governments in this group are in the over 100,000 population group. Total uses of shared revenue for new or expanded operations were relatively high for these five local jurisdictions, averaging 36 percent of second-round shared-revenue allocations, compared to approximately 11 percent for all local governments in the sample. The combination of no extreme fiscal pressure and larger population size may contribute to the greater willingness of these jurisdictions to use revenue sharing for new or expanded operating programs, as opposed to stabilizing taxes, maintaining existing programs, or adopting a more conservative strategy of using revenue sharing to finance one-shot capital projects.

Another common characteristic is that activity on the part of social-action organizations related to revenue sharing was reported for each of these local jurisdictions. In Phoenix, for example, the associate reported that "a number of minorities had viable organizations prior to revenue sharing and were beginning to make themselves felt politically. Mexican-Americans, Indians, and the aged are all able to exercise considerable political clout and were active participants in the public hearings on revenue sharing." The Los Angeles associate reported that "broad-based community interest groups have had a significant impact on decisions about revenue sharing."

In all, twenty-two of the sample jurisdictions were reported by the associates to have used shared revenue in ways that benefited the poor and minorities—in seven of these cases to a significant extent. This is approximately one-third of the sample units. It is clear that the social impact of revenue sharing, while hard to gauge, cannot be judged simply by reference to specific social-service uses of revenue-sharing funds such as those reported to the U.S. Office of Revenue Sharing. The incomplete, and potentially misleading, nature of these official reports is explored in the next section of this chapter.

A CRITICAL ASSESSMENT OF ORS ACTUAL-USE DATA

All governments that receive general revenue sharing funds are required to submit to the Treasury Department's Office of Revenue Sharing an actual-use report, showing how these funds have been used in each entitlement period. Recipient governments must distinguish in these reports between shared revenue used for capital projects and that used for operating and maintenance expenditures, and under these two broad categories the functional areas must be indicated. Expenditures of shared revenue for operating and maintenance uses by local governments are restricted to the following "priority expenditure" categories: public safety, environmental protection, public transportation, health, recreation, libraries, social services for the poor or aged, and financial administration. No restrictions are placed on local governments regarding functional areas in which shared revenue may be used for capital projects. For state governments, there are no program restrictions for either operating or capital uses of shared revenue.

The published summaries of the actual-use reports issued by ORS provide a variety of tabulations showing the program areas for which revenue sharing funds have been designated. But these official designations do not necessarily reflect the real impact of revenue sharing. If shared revenue simply substitutes for funds that otherwise would have been used to finance a particular program or project, then the real impact of revenue sharing will be felt elsewhere, possibly as additional spending in other non-designated program areas or a reduction in taxes. The format of the ORS actual-use report itself suggests that discrepancies can exist between the officially reported designations of shared revenue to specific programs and the real fiscal impact of those funds. State and local governments are asked to check various boxes indicating whether, as a result of revenue sharing, own-source revenues (either taxes or borrowing) are lower than would have been the case in the absence of revenue sharing. Clearly, shared revenue cannot promote additional spending (or maintain spending levels that would otherwise have been reduced) by the full amount of a jurisdiction's revenue sharing entitlement and, at the same time, provide the means for reducing taxes or debt financing. Moreover, in reporting the use of revenue sharing for entitlement period 5, ORS cautions the reader about the limits of the actual-use data: "The Use Reports for Entitlement Period 5 . . . summarize direct expenditures of general revenue sharing funds only. An analysis of the broader consequences or ultimate impact of general revenue sharing monies on services at the state and local levels of American government is beyond the scope of this report."[24]

Despite these limitations of the ORS data, a number of studies have used them to show the "real" programmatic impact of revenue sharing. All these studies reveal a significant impact from revenue sharing on public safety programs at the local level. Actual-use report data have, from the beginning of the revenue sharing program, consistently shown public safety as accounting for a greater portion of shared-revenue expenditures than any other local government function; in entitlement period 5 the ORS shows public safety accounting for an average of thirty-six cents of every revenue sharing dollar spent by local governments. But again, these figures represent official designations of the use of shared revenue for public safety and do not necessarily reflect new or additional spending in this area. Conclusions about the programmatic impact of revenue sharing (that is, identifying programs that would not have been funded or would have been funded at a lower level in the absence of revenue sharing) based on actual-use reports can thus be very misleading, overstating the impact on some programs and understating it for others. Furthermore, the consequences of such interpretations can have serious implications for other federal grant programs. For example, the strong propensity to use revenue sharing

24. Department of the Treasury, Office of Revenue Sharing, *Reported Uses of General Revenue Sharing Funds 1974–75: A Tabulation and Analysis of Data from Actual Use Report 5* (ORS, February 1976), p. vii.

for public safety programs that appears in the ORS data has raised questions about the need for the law enforcement block grant program, administered by the Law Enforcement Assistance Administration of the Department of Justice. But if official data reflect only accounting decisions and not actual new spending on public safety and law enforcement, then the apparent overlap between the two federal grant programs is exaggerated. Recipient governments have simply substituted shared revenue for their own funds that would otherwise have been spent for public safety. If, on the other hand, actual-use data showing shared revenue spent on public safety does reflect new spending, then one can conclude that the role of federal aid in state and local expenditures for public safety is significantly greater than the amounts reflected by the LEAA block grant program. The essential question, in short, is whether these revenue sharing allocations are, in fact, adding to local spending for public safety.

Thus, the net fiscal effects of revenue sharing dollars in relation to other federal aid programs can become a question of significant policy consequence. When this question was raised in reference to the law enforcement block grant program, the National Institute of Law Enforcement and Criminal Justice of the U.S. Department of Justice requested that the Brookings revenue sharing field data be subjected to a special review to compare these findings with ORS actual-use data pertaining to public safety. The principal finding of this special study was that "officially reported expenditures of shared revenue compiled by the Treasury Department's Office of Revenue Sharing were six times greater than *new spending* for law enforcement out of revenue sharing in the Brookings field research in 1973 and four times greater in 1974."[25]

These results are based on information for fifty-two of the local governments included in the Brookings sample. For these jurisdictions, ORS actual-use information for entitlement period 4 (covering officially reported expenditures of shared revenue from July 1, 1973, through June 30, 1974) shows that, on an unweighted mean basis, approximately 34 percent of shared-revenue expenditures were attributed to public safety uses. Using a set of nationally determined weights that permit the law enforcement component of public safety to be separated, law enforcement pro-

25. Richard P. Nathan, Dan Crippen, and André Juneau, *Where Have All the Dollars Gone? Implications of General Revenue Sharing for the Law Enforcement Assistance Administration* (U.S. Department of Justice, Law Enforcement Assistance Administration, National Institute of Law Enforcement and Criminal Justice, 1976), p. 1.

grams alone were officially designated as accounting for 25 percent of total shared-revenue expenditures, on average, by these jurisdictions.

Using the Brookings field data for the second-round observations (covering allocations and firm commitments of shared revenue made between July 1, 1973, and June 30, 1974), new spending on public safety averaged approximately 8 percent on an unweighted mean basis; new spending on law enforcement (included as a separate functional category in the reporting form used by the field associates) accounted for an average of approximately 6 percent of shared-revenue allocations.[26]

The differences revealed by this special study of the programmatic impact of revenue sharing clearly indicate that revenue sharing funds have not gone for new public safety and law enforcement programs in anything like the amounts suggested by the ORS actual-use data. This is not to say that the Treasury data are wrong, only that public safety and law enforcement are areas in which official designations for general revenue sharing uses reflect especially high substitution effects as opposed to new spending effects.

THE FUNGIBILITY ISSUE

Any attempt to explain the role of different federal grants in determining expenditure decisions of recipient governments must carefully consider the fungible nature of these funds.

26. The Brookings field data used in this comparative analysis reflect only new spending on public safety and law enforcement out of revenue-sharing funds. New spending in this case refers to the sum of allocations to new and expanded operations and new capital use reported by the associates. Program maintenance uses affecting public safety and law enforcement programs are not included. While program maintenance uses do not, by definition, expand the size or scope of local government activities in these program areas, they are not simply accounting uses of shared revenue: program maintenance implies that spending in a program area is higher than it would have been in the absence of revenue sharing. If program maintenance uses were added to new spending, the average percent of shared-revenue allocations accounted for by public safety would increase from 8 percent to approximately 12 percent. A similar adjustment to the law enforcement component of public safety causes the average percent of shared-revenue allocations in round two accounted for by law enforcement uses to increase from 6 percent to approximately 9 percent. But even with this upward adjustment, the differences between ORS designations to public safety and law enforcement and allocations reported by the Brookings field associates are still significant; in both cases nearly three-to-one for 1974. (Because the program maintenance net effect category was not broken down by functional category in the first-round field observations, comparable adjustments cannot be made to the field data for that period.)

All forms of federal aid to states and localities are fungible. No matter how ingenious the conditions placed on the use of grant monies, recipient governments can and do exercise considerable discretion in determining their allocation. Noncategorical grants, such as general revenue sharing, are used to stimulate both the public and private sectors of recipient jurisdictions, and the pattern of allocational impact—both between the public and private sectors and within the public sector—varies widely across state and local governments, "priority expenditure" categories notwithstanding. The allocational impact of categorical grants is ultimately determined by the preferences that recipient governments have for the particular public goods and services at which such grants are aimed; for these types of grants, fungibility is also a very real issue.

The question then becomes how this common feature of fungibility operates through the general revenue sharing program in comparison to other forms of federal grants. Researchers have come at this question from a number of different perspectives.[27] Various studies in specific functional areas—for example, public-service employment and education—have attempted to gauge the substitution effects of federal grants. An evaluation of the 1971 public service employment program estimated that roughly half the funds appropriated in 1971 for public service employment had substitution effects, rather than creating new jobs.[28] Another recent study by a political scientist on education programs examined the substitution effects of federal grants-in-aid for education and found that "powerful local factors overshadow the effect of the [national] legislative and executive controls."[29]

27. A large number of articles on this subject—Edward M. Gramlich describes it as an "outpouring"—have appeared in the *National Tax Journal*. This literature is summarized by Gramlich in "The Effects of Federal Grants on State-Local Expenditures: A Review of the Econometric Literature," in National Tax Association, *Proceedings of the Sixty Second Annual Conference on Taxation* (NTA, 1970), pp. 563–93.

28. National Planning Association, "An Evaluation of the Economic Impact Project of the Public Employment Program" (May 1974; processed).

29. David O. Porter, with David C. Warner and Teddie W. Porter, *The Politics of Budgeting Federal Aid: Resource Mobilization by Local School Districts*, Sage Professional Paper in Administrative and Policy Studies, 03-003 (Indiana University, 1973). Porter describes the typical behavior of school administrators as follows: "They promote their own priorities by using those revenues with the greatest number of restrictions first, saving those with the fewest restrictions until last—i.e., a sort of propensity to conserve all-purpose revenues. This procedure allows the administrator to adapt the restrictions placed on revenues to his or her own priorities and demands, rather than allowing resource suppliers to impose their priorities. An ad-

The methodologies and data used in these studies are highly divergent, but several general points about the likely impact of federal grants in terms of substitution versus new spending effects can be made: (1) the older a grant, the greater will be its substitution or displacement effects; (2) project grants can be expected to have greater new-spending effects than formula grants; (3) the higher the matching ratio, the greater will be the ratio of substitution to new-spending effects; (4) grants made to special-purpose jurisdictions (such as school districts and housing and urban renewal districts) will have greater new-spending effects than grants made to general-purpose units of state and local government; and (5) overall, the broader the permissible uses and the fewer the restrictions on federal grants, the greater will be their substitution effects.

In this framework, one would expect general revenue sharing on the average to have lesser new-spending effects and, accordingly, greater substitution effects than most other types of federal grants. But, again, the point to be stressed is that other forms of fiscal subvention will also produce a combination of substitution and new-spending effects.

The fungibility issue associated with general revenue sharing and the serious limitations inherent in the ORS actual use data were not lost on those responsible for the 1976 renewal legislation. The House Government Operations Committee proposed that the priority-expenditure categories for local government be eliminated, and this change was included in the final version of the 1976 renewal legislation. The committee also recommended that planned-use reports by recipient governments specify whether revenue sharing is to be used for new or expanded operations, for maintaining existing programs, or for stabilizing or reducing taxes, and that documentation be provided showing the relationship of revenue sharing funds to relevant functional items in the recipient government's budget. This proposal was incorporated in the House bill but was eliminated in conference. In chapter 6, we examine in more detail how Congress dealt with the fungibility issue in the renewal process and, in this regard, raise questions about certain revisions made to the program. These questions notwithstanding, it is significant that fungibility was recognized as a major issue in the consideration of the renewal legislation.

---

ministrator has more flexibility when he obligates his more restricted funds for items in his regular program and reserves general purpose funds for activities which cannot be funded through special grants or programs." Although Porter finds that federal grants for education often are not used for their intended purposes, it should be noted that federal funds provided directly to individual school districts often end up increasing aggregate spending on education.

3 Revenue Sharing and Central Cities

A subject covered in this volume, but not in the first volume in this series, is the effect of revenue sharing on central city finances, surely a timely subject. On the domestic front, the recent period has been marked by what many have referred to as a crisis of the cities. Many mayors have lobbied for emergency assistance from the federal government, claiming that the combination of recession and inflation make such aid essential. The nation's largest city faced a financial emergency; according to columnist William Safire, New York, "the big apple," was in "a big pickle."[1] What light can a study of the revenue sharing program throw on this subject? In the Brookings sample for the study of general revenue sharing there are fifteen cities that according to the Office of Management and Budget, qualify as primary central cities of standard metropolitan statistical areas (SMSAs). As a preliminary step, it is useful to get a broad idea of how the revenue sharing program in general affects large, densely populated urban areas and their finances.

The Revenue Sharing Formula and Urban Areas

The "urban focus" in the revenue sharing program must be considered to include both urban counties and large cities. As reported in *Monitoring Revenue Sharing,* per capita entitlements to local governments in the largest and most densely populated counties (including county governments themselves) generally exceed the national average.

Under the formula contained in the original act and the extension legislation passed in 1976, it is both the very largest and the smallest county

1. William Safire, "The Big Apple in a Big Pickle," *New York Times,* May 19, 1975.

81

Table 3-1. Index of Local Shared Revenue per Capita for County Areas,
by Population Size and Population Density, 1972

			Population, 1970	
County classification	Number	Index (U.S. = 100)	Millions	Percent of U.S.
Population, 1970 (thousands)				
Over 1,000	20	112	44.9	22.1
500–1,000	54	97	37.2	18.3
250–500	72	94	25.2	12.4
100–250	198	93	31.2	15.4
50–100	332	91	23.1	11.4
25–50	569	96	19.9	9.8
10–25	1,014	106	16.6	8.2
Under 10	859	118	5.1	2.5
Population per square mile, 1970				
Over 3,000	33	125	32.3	15.9
1,000–3,000	72	93	43.1	21.2
500–1,000	61	92	21.6	10.6
100–500	417	89	51.6	25.4
50–100	516	95	21.5	10.6
20–50	1,007	107	22.9	11.3
10–20	441	113	6.0	2.9
Under 10	571	122	5.1	2.1

Sources: Calculated from Treasury Department data; classification of county areas based on U.S. Bureau of the Census, County and City Data Book (GPO, 1972) table 2.

areas that benefit most from revenue sharing. The index shown in table 3-1 follows this pattern for 1972; data for other years would give the same picture. The relationships change, however, when shared revenue is examined in relation to the revenue raised for nonschool purposes by the recipient governments: the larger and more densely populated a county area, the smaller its shared revenue as a percentage of its own revenue. This pattern is shown in table 3-2, in which revenue sharing for 1972 is compared to nonschool taxes in fiscal 1971.

When the focus is shifted to the largest central cities, as opposed to county areas, the revenue sharing advantage per capita was even greater. In 1972 the nation's twenty-five largest cities (ranging in size from New York, 7,895,000 to Denver, 515,000) received 36 percent more in shared revenue per capita than the nationwide average for all local governments. Nineteen of these cities are SMSA central cities which can be analyzed in relation to their suburbs (defined here as the balance of the SMSA). Column 7 of table 3-3 shows that in all nineteen of these cases revenue

Table 3-2. Index of Local Shared Revenue for 1972 per $100 in Local Nonschool Taxes, 1970–71, by County Areas

County classification	Index (U.S. = 100)
Population, 1970 (thousands)	
Over 1,000	66
500–1,000	79
250–500	105
100–250	122
50–100	155
25–50	191
10–25	213
Under 10	185
Population per square mile, 1970	
Over 3,000	67
1,000–3,000	73
500–1,000	99
100–500	127
50–100	171
20–50	186
10–20	183
Under 10	168

Sources: Same as table 3-1.

sharing tends to reduce fiscal disparities between city and suburb.[2] This analysis is based on the assumption that shared revenue paid to county governments benefits cities within the county proportionate to their population; for example, if a city has 30 percent of the county's population, 30 percent of the county's shared revenue is attributed to the city under this assumption.

One possible interpretation of these findings is that the pattern of incidence is an appropriate one because very large and densely populated urban areas, especially central cities, have the greatest public service costs and needs, whereas smaller urban areas tend to have an inverse relationship between size and various indicators of urban need. According to a recent study, "the per capita cost of local public services increase as the population of the metropolitan area increases."[3] One can also argue that poor rural areas should be given preference under revenue sharing. This

2. Omitted from the table are Honolulu and Jacksonville, which constitute their entire SMSAs, as well as four other cities—Houston, Dallas, San Antonio, and Phoenix—for which the data needed to estimate the city's portion of the tax revenue of overlying local governments were not available.

3. Thomas Muller, *Growing and Declining Urban Areas: A Fiscal Comparison* (The Urban Institute, 1975), p. 21.

Table 3-3. Shared Revenue for 1972 and Local Tax Revenue in Fiscal 1970–71, for the Central Cities and Outlying Portions of Nineteen Selected SMSAs

| | Per capita local tax revenue, 1970–71 (dollars) | | Shared revenue, 1972, as percent of local tax revenue, 1970–71 | | Ratio of city area to balance of SMSA | | |
| | | | | | Per capita local tax revenue, 1970–71 | Shared revenue per capita | Shared revenue as percent of local tax revenue |
SMSA	City area (1)	Balance of SMSA (2)	City area (3)	Balance of SMSA (4)	(5)	(6)	(7)
Median	...	...	7.9	5.3	1.28	1.97	1.45
New York							
City[a]	413.26	414.68	6.6	2.9	1.00	2.25	2.26
Chicago	270.11	228.31	7.9	4.5	1.18	2.07	1.75
Low Angeles	399.11	320.27	5.9	5.4	1.25	1.36	1.09
Phila-							
delphia[a,b]	266.14	207.18	8.6	4.3	1.28	2.58	2.01
Detroit	269.57	247.35	10.7	4.9	1.09	2.39	2.19
Baltimore[a]	237.98	209.11	11.1	7.8	1.14	1.62	1.42
Cleveland	296.87	271.26	8.4	4.0	1.09	2.29	2.10
Indianapolis[a]	230.84	170.35	6.8	5.3	1.36	1.72	1.27
Milwaukee	308.69	241.94	9.5	5.7	1.28	2.12	1.66
San Francisco[a]	589.14	353.18	4.2	4.2	1.67	1.69	1.01
San Diego	251.29	239.00	7.0	5.5	1.05	1.34	1.27
Boston[a]	375.88	306.25	7.2	5.6	1.23	1.58	1.29
Memphis[b]	198.67	122.78	12.9	8.3	1.62	2.53	1.56
St. Louis[a,b]	287.94	211.99	7.1	5.0	1.36	1.90	1.40
New Orleans[a]	159.72	93.70	18.1	16.9	1.70	1.82	1.07
Columbus	206.44	169.70	7.5	4.7	1.22	1.92	1.58
Seattle	250.15	176.85	8.3	5.8	1.41	2.05	1.45
Pittsburgh	275.56	181.01	11.0	8.5	1.52	1.97	1.29
Denver[a]	318.37	201.30	7.2	4.9	1.58	2.32	1.47

Sources: Shared revenue and population, calculated from Treasury Department data; tax data, from U.S. Bureau of the Census, *Local Government Finances in Selected Metropolitan Areas and Large Counties: 1970–71* (GPO, 1972), table 1. Tax amounts include a proration of the tax revenue of governments overlying the primary cities.

a. City-area data pertain to the entire central country.

b. "Balance of SMSA" amounts shown for the Philadelphia, Memphis, and St. Louis areas exclude the portions of those SMSAs outside the primary states.

is, in fact, the pattern we find—big cities, large urban areas, and poor rural areas receive the largest amounts of aid per capita. With regard to cities, the issue generally has been whether the relative advantage for distressed central cities in the nation's largest urban areas or, for that matter, for rural poverty areas, should be even greater. In this chapter, focused on central cities, we examine their conditions more closely.

Conditions of Central Cities

There is wide variation in the economic and social conditions of central cities. Many large cities in the South and West are new, relatively well-off, geographically spread-out cities; a number of them have made significant structural changes (annexations and mergers) to broaden their economic base. It is the older cities in the Northeast and North Central regions of the country that are most likely to face what can be referred to as "urban crisis" conditions. This regional concentration of poverty-impacted, politically isolated core cities stems in large measure from a freezing of boundaries in the latter part of the nineteenth century for cities that were relatively large by then-current standards, but are now surrounded by much larger suburban hinterlands.

Census data can be used to demonstrate these points.[4] Table 3-4 presents comparative data on central cities and and their suburbs for fifty-five of the nation's largest metropolitan areas.[5] The first column shows a composite index expressing city-suburban relationships for six measures from the 1970 census: (1) unemployment (percent of civilian labor force unemployed); (2) dependency (persons under eighteen or over sixty-four as a percent of total population); (3) education (percent of persons twenty-five or older with less than a twelfth-grade education); (4) income level (per capita income); (5) crowded housing (percent of occupied housing units with more than one person per room); and (6) poverty (percent of families below 125 percent of the low-income level).

City-suburban ratios were calculated for each measure. For per capita income, where a higher amount is a desirable characteristic, the suburban amount in each instance was divided by the city-area amount. For each of the other five items involving undesirable characteristics, the city-area

4. Analysis based on an article by the principal authors of this volume, "Understanding Central City Hardship," *Political Science Quarterly*, vol. 91 (Spring 1976), pp. 47–62.

5. Eleven SMSAs with populations over 500,000 were omitted from this analysis for the following reasons: (1) Washington, D.C., because of its uniqueness as a combined state and local government; (2) Honolulu and Jacksonville, because their consolidated city-county governments comprise entire SMSAs; (3) San Antonio, Memphis, and Nashville, because the population of the central city is more than three-quarters of that of the SMSA; and (4) five other areas where the most populous central city has less than 18 percent of the total SMSA population—Albany-Schenectady-Troy, Anaheim–Santa Ana–Garden Grove, New Brunswick–Perth Amboy–Sayerville, Paterson-Clifton-Passaic, and Riverside–San Bernardino–Ontario.

Table 3-4. Index of Central City Disadvantage Relative to Balance of SMSA, and Selected Data, for Fifty-five SMSAs

Primary central city of SMSA	Central city "hardship index"[a]	Region[b]	SMSA population, 1970 Total (thousands)	Percent in central city	Percent in central county
Newark	422	NE	1,857	20.6	50.1
Cleveland	331	NC	2,064	36.4	83.4
Hartford[c]	317	NE	664	23.8	([d])
Baltimore[d]	256	NE	2,071	43.7	43.7
Chicago	245	NC	6,975	48.2	78.7
St. Louis[d]	231	NC	2,363	26.3	26.3
Atlanta	226	S	1,390	35.8	43.7
Rochester	215	NE	883	33.6	80.7
Gary	213	NC	633	27.7	86.2
Dayton	211	NC	850	28.6	71.3
New York[d]	211	NE	11,572	68.2	68.2
Detroit	210	NC	4,200	36.0	63.5
Richmond[d]	209	S	518	48.2	48.2
Philadelphia[d]	205	NE	4,818	40.4	40.4
Boston	198	NE	2,754	23.3	26.7
Milwaukee	195	NC	1,404	51.1	75.1
Buffalo	189	NE	1,349	34.3	82.5
San Jose	181	W	1,065	41.9	100.0
Youngstown	180	NC	536	26.1	56.6
Columbus	173	NC	916	58.9	90.9
Miami	172	S	1,268	26.4	100.0
New Orleans[d]	168	S	1,046	56.7	56.7
Louisville	165	S	827	43.7	84.1
Akron	152	NC	679	40.5	81.5
Kansas City, Mo.	152	NC	1,254	40.5	52.2
Springfield, Mass.[c]	152	NE	530	30.9	86.6
Fort Worth	149	S	762	51.6	94.0
Cincinnati	148	NC	1,385	32.7	66.7
Pittsburgh	146	NE	2,401	21.7	66.8
Denver[d]	143	W	1,228	41.9	41.9
Sacramento	135	W	801	31.8	78.9
Minneapolis	131	NC	1,814	24.0	52.9
Birmingham	131	S	739	40.7	87.2
Jersey City	129	NE	609	42.8	100.0
Oklahoma City	128	S	641	57.2	82.2
Indianapolis[d]	124	NC	1,110	67.1	71.8
Providence[c]	121	NE	913	19.6	63.6
Grand Rapids	119	NC	539	36.6	76.2
Toledo	116	NC	693	55.4	69.9
Tampa	107	S	1,013	27.4	48.4
Los Angeles	105	W	7,036	40.0	100.0
San Francisco[d]	105	W	3,110	23.0	23.0
Syracuse	103	NE	637	31.0	74.3
Allentown	100	NE	544	20.1	47.0
Portland, Oregon	100	W	1,009	37.8	55.2
Omaha	98	NC	540	64.3	72.1
Dallas	97	S	1,556	54.3	85.3
Houston	93	S	1,985	62.1	87.8
Phoenix	85	W	968	60.1	100.0
Norfolk[d]	82	S	681	45.2	45.2
Salt Lake City	80	W	558	31.5	82.2
San Diego	77	W	1,358	51.3	100.0
Seattle	67	W	1,422	37.3	81.3
Ft. Lauderdale	64	S	620	22.5	100.0
Greensboro	43	S	604	23.9	47.8

Sources: Central city disadvantage index, calculated as described in the text from data in U.S. Bureau of the Census, *County and City Data Book, 1972* (1973), tables 2, 3, 6; county areas and population, from U.S. Bureau of the Census, *1972 Census of Governments*, vol. 1: *Governmental Organization* (1973).

a. See definition in text.
b. NE = Northeast, NC = North Central, S = South, W = West.
c. New England SMSA, comprising city and township areas, rather than entire counties.
d. Combined city-county.

value was divided by the suburban value. The resulting ratios were standardized to give equal weight to each of the six comparative measures.[6] These standardized ratios were then summed to derive composite index numbers, which in turn were adjusted to a base level of 100. An index figure of over 100 denotes that the primary central city is disadvantaged in relation to the balance of its SMSA; the higher the figure the greater the disadvantage. A figure under 100 denotes that the central city is better off than its suburbs in terms of the six measures when each is given equal weight.[7]

Central Cities in the Brookings Sample

Eight of the central cities in the Brookings revenue sharing sample are included in table 3-4—Baltimore, Cincinnati, Los Angeles, Newark, New York, Phoenix, Rochester, and St. Louis. Five are above 200 on this "hardship index," denoting especially marked city-suburban disparities. Jacksonville, included in the sample, also exceeded 500,000 in SMSA population in 1970, but is not included in table 3-4 because it is a consolidated city-county that lacks any outlying suburban area in its SMSA for comparative purposes. The Brookings revenue sharing sample also includes six cities located in SMSAs below 500,000 population in 1970: Orlando, Florida; Worcester, Massachusetts; Little Rock, Arkansas; Baton Rouge, Louisiana; Eugene, Oregon; and Sioux Falls, South Dakota.

As demonstrated here, an essential subject for an understanding of the conditions of central cities is their political structure. Does the central city have an overlying county government? If so, is it responsible for major governmental services provided to central city residents? Is the central city a consolidated government (like Jacksonville), accounting for all, or most,

6. This was done by distributing from 0 to 100 the values of the ratios for each of the six measures listed, using the following formula: $X = a \ (Y - Ymin)$ where $a = 100/(Ymax - Ymin)$; $X =$ the standardized city-suburb ratio to be computed; $Y =$ each city's ratio; $Ymax =$ the maximum value of Y; and $Ymin =$ the minimum value of Y.

7. It should be noted that eight of the eighteen cities that show up most favorably are in metropolitan areas having more than one central city: Greensboro, Ft. Lauderdale, Seattle, Norfolk, Allentown, San Francisco, Los Angeles, and Tampa. In those instances, the balance of SMSA figures entering into the index calculation refer to a more urbanized suburbia than is usually the case. Of the other forty cities listed, only three (Minneapolis, Springfield, and Gary) are in SMSAs with more than a single central city.

of the population of the metropolitan area? Or is it a combined city-county limited to the inner city, as in the case of St. Louis or Baltimore among the sample cities? What is the state's role? Do regionwide special districts provide important services for central city residents?

Of the fifteen central cities in the Brookings revenue sharing sample, two—Jacksonville and Baton Rouge—are areawide governments. At the other end of the spectrum, Newark's population is the most isolated, accounting for only a fifth of the total population of its SMSA. The central cities in the Brookings sample are ranked in table 3-5 according to their share of total SMSA population.

In this chapter, the revenue sharing experience of central cities in the sample is reviewed first for the ten central cities with overlying counties and then for the remaining five which are either consolidated governments or combined city-counties.

In addition to the material presented in this chapter, appendix A, which presents excerpts from the transcript of the final conference of the Brookings field research associates, contains a discussion of the differential impact of shared revenue on five central cities and their suburbs. The discussion of these cases is presented from the viewpoint of the associates and reflects an additional eighteen months of experience under the revenue sharing program (covering the period from July 1, 1974 to December 31, 1975); it serves both to expand and update the record, and at the same time to provide an insight into the methodology used in this study.

ANALYSIS FOR CENTRAL CITIES WITH AN
OVERLYING COUNTY GOVERNMENT

We begin the assessment of revenue sharing for central cities with an overlying county by looking at the role of the county government, specifically at the comparison of per capita revenue from own sources for the county government with the same figure for its central city.[8] On this basis, Los Angeles County is shown to have the strongest relative role among the ten urban counties considered. Per capita general revenue from its own sources for Los Angeles County in 1972–73 was 78 percent of that for the

8. Census data on general revenue from own sources for 1972–73 were not available at the time of this writing for four counties: Minnehaha, South Dakota; Pulaski, Arkansas; Lane, Oregon; and Worcester, Massachusetts. For these counties, 1971–72 data were used. Data are from U.S. Census Bureau annual publications on city and SMSA finances.

Table 3-5. Central Cities in the Brookings Sample Ranked by Percentage of SMSA Population

City	City percentage of SMSA population	City population, 1970 (thousands)
Jacksonville	100.0	528.9
Baton Rouge	95.3	271.9
Sioux Falls	76.1	72.5
New York	68.2	7,894.9
Phoenix	60.1	581.6
Worcester	51.2	176.6
Baltimore	43.7	905.8
Little Rock	41.0	132.5
Los Angeles	40.0	2,809.8
Eugene	35.8	76.3
Rochester	33.6	296.2
Cincinnati	32.7	452.6
St. Louis	26.3	622.2
Orlando	23.1	99.0
Newark	20.6	382.4

Source: U.S. Bureau of the Census, *County and City Data Book, 1972,* tables 3, 6.

city of Los Angeles. One other overlying county in the sample, Monroe County, New York, was above 50 percent in these terms. Monroe County's per capita revenue from own sources in 1972–73 was 61 percent of that for Rochester, the central city. It should be noted that both California and New York are states with a tradition of strong county government.

At the other end of the spectrum, the per capita revenue from own sources of Worcester County, Massachusetts, was only 4 percent of that for its central city in fiscal 1973. Massachusetts, typical of New England, stands out as a weak-county state. Four other overlying county governments in the sample have a relatively limited role, as indicated by the fact that they were below 25 percent in terms of the county's own-source revenue compared to that for the central city: Minnehaha, South Dakota (overlying the city of Sioux Falls), had 24 percent; Pulaski County, Arkansas (overlying the city of Little Rock), 14 percent; Hamilton County, Ohio (overlying the city of Cincinnati), 12 percent; and Lane County, Oregon (overlying the city of Eugene), 11 percent. The three remaining counties are in the middle range: Maricopa County, Arizona (overlying the city of Phoenix), with 44 percent; Essex County, New Jersey (overlying the city of Newark), 32 percent; and Orange County, Florida (overlying the city of Orlando), 28 percent.

One major reason for differences in the relative role of county governments is the importance of welfare expenditures. As of mid-1974, county governments in California and New York were required to pay a portion of the nonfederal costs of state welfare benefits, which helps to explain their high standing as shown above. Two other states among the ten in this group (New Jersey and Ohio) also require local governments to share in welfare costs. Among these four states, the county share of welfare spending is highest in New York, at 50 percent of the nonfederal share (also highest in the nation).

The organization of public schools is another important factor for understanding differences in the role of county governments in relation to central cities. Three of the central cities with overlying counties in the Brookings sample (Newark, Rochester, and Worcester) have dependent school districts, so the revenue collected for schools is counted in the city's total. If own-source revenue for schools is omitted from consideration, the revenue role of the overlying county government would increase. In Newark, for example, if the city's school taxes and charges are omitted, county own-source general revenue on a per capita basis rises from 32 percent of that for the city to 52 percent.

Another significant difference among urban counties is the extent of their unincorporated area. A recent study by the National Association of Counties showed that the unincorporated area of urban counties tends to be greatest in the South and West.[9] (The study also found that counties with the largest proportion of unincorporated area "tend to have a greater degree of direct legal authority to perform community development and related activities."[10])

The assumption up to this point has been that central cities are affected by the general revenue sharing payments made to their overlying county government on a basis *equal* to their proportion of the county's population. We must now ask how good this assumption is. One way to test it is to look at the property tax base. Property taxes dominate at the local level; they accounted for nearly two-thirds of the general revenue from own sources of local governments in fiscal 1974 and for 80 percent of their taxes.[11] The important city-county relationship for purposes of analyzing

9. *Community Development Capabilities Study* (Department of Housing and Urban Development, Office of Policy Development and Research, June 1975; processed), p. II-4. The data are based on seventy-eight responses out of a total national sample of eighty-five urban counties.

10. Ibid., p. II-5.

11. U.S. Bureau of the Census, *Governmental Finances in 1973–74* (GPO, 1975), table 17. Like any generalization about American local government, there

**Table 3-6. Central Cities in the Brookings Sample Ranked by
City-County Assessed Valuation Ratio**[a]

City	Central city population as a percentage of county population, 1970	City assessed valuation as a percentage of county assessed valuation, 1971	Assessed valuation percentage divided by population percentage × 100
Little Rock, Ark.	46.1	58.5	127
Eugene, Oreg.	35.7	36.8	103
Los Angeles, Calif.	39.9	40.2	101
Rochester, N.Y.	41.6	40.4	97
Orlando, Fla.	28.7	26.3	92
Cincinnati, Ohio	48.9	43.9	90
Sioux Falls, S.Dak.	76.1	67.7	89
Worcester, Mass.	27.7	19.8	71
Newark, N.J.	41.1	22.9	56

Source: U.S. Bureau of the Census, *1972 Census of Governments*, vol. 2, table 4.
a. Comparable census data on city assessed property valuation were not available for Phoenix, Arizona.

the impact of revenue sharing would thus be the central city's share of the taxable property base of its overlying county as compared to its share of county population. Table 3-6 ranks nine of the ten central cities in the Brookings sample with overlying county governments on the basis of the following ratio: central city assessed valuation ÷ county assessed valuation/central city population ÷ county population × 100.

To illustrate what this ratio means for revenue sharing, assume that a given urban county is found to have used all of its shared revenue to reduce or stabilize its property tax. If the central city's proportion of the overlying county's property tax base is smaller than its share of county population—as shown by a value less than 100 in the third column of table 3-6—its residents presumably will receive less benefit from this tax relief out of shared revenue than residents of the county who live outside of the central city. Assuming that all county shared revenue of the ten counties in table 3-6 was used for tax reduction or stabilization purposes, the residents of Little Rock would gain the most, those of Newark the least.

On the expenditure side of the ledger, the effects on the central city of spending out of revenue sharing funds by overlying county governments

---

are, of course, important exceptions. Among the Arizona local units in the sample, for instance, sales tax revenue exceeds that from property taxes. Property taxes tend to be much less important in the South than in other regions; they tend to be highest in the Northeast.

are much harder to assess because of the variation in the responsibilities of different local governments.[12] But the field research data for this study enable us to obtain at least a preliminary indication.

FIELD DATA

In collecting the field research data for fiscal 1974, each associate for a central city was asked to assess the proportion of benefits from the overlying county's shared revenue that accrue to city residents.[13] Was it more, less, or about the same, compared to the central city's proportion of total county population? Only for Los Angeles County were the benefits of shared revenue to central city residents judged to be greater than those to county residents. Three central cities (Little Rock, Newark, and Rochester) were said to have received lower per capita benefits from revenue sharing than their overlying county; for the remaining five cases, the central city and overlying county were judged to have benefited equally on a per capita basis from revenue sharing.

Not only does Los Angeles County stand out among these nine cases, but its central-city residents were also found to be essentially as well off in social and economic terms as residents of the rest of the Los Angeles SMSA. (Los Angeles has a city-suburb disparity rating of 105 in table 3-4.) The principal reason for the greater benefit to Los Angeles city residents out of shared revenue allocated by Los Angeles County in fiscal 1974 was the assignment of nearly one-third of the county's shared revenue to two purposes: a subsidy for bus riders (some two-thirds of it affecting city residents) and special payments to community social-service groups, the clear majority of which were for groups within the city of Los Angeles. The latter arrangement has especially interesting implications for city-county relations.

In California county governments administer welfare benefits and social-service programs, and they pay approximately one-third of the non-

12. A recent study by the Bureau of the Census on the finances of five central cities and a selected "satellite city" for each attempted to evaluate differences in expenditures by major function, taking into account spending by all levels of government. Of the cities in the Brookings sample, only Los Angeles is included in this study, and in this case, the satellite city (Burbank) is not in the Brookings revenue-sharing sample. See "Composite Finances in Selected City Areas," A special Survey Sponsored by the U.S. Department of Housing and Urban Development (Bureau of the Census, Governments Division, August 1974; processed).

13. Nine central cities and paired overlying counties are included in the sample as described above.

federal share of these costs. When requests by community groups for social-service funding out of shared revenue were made to Los Angeles city officials, these points were judiciously noted by the city's chief administrative officer. He pointed out that Los Angeles County had established special procedures for budgeting shared revenue "in a manner which facilitates consideration of requests from a significant number of private groups." The city, he noted, need not follow suit: "In fact, a significant City-County difference is that the County has a broad welfare responsibility. Thus, although any private group is free to apply to the City for funds and to appear at the Council's public hearings on the budget, there is no apparent reason for the City to diverge from its standard budgetary procedures in considering requests."[14] A recent study indicates that, like Los Angeles County, a number of other county governments in California used revenue sharing as an impetus to greater citizen involvement in decisionmaking and priority setting for welfare and social service activities.[15]

It is interesting to compare Los Angeles to Rochester, New York, even though in the latter case city residents were said to have benefited less in 1974 from shared revenue than residents of the outlying county area. City officials in Rochester were much less circumspect about the role of the overlying county government under revenue sharing. The associate reported that revenue sharing resulted in "a new focus" on the role of county government. "This interest seems to have been stimulated locally by officials of the City of Rochester, where, of course, the disadvantaged are concentrated." City officials testified at a county hearing on the allocation of shared revenue, urging a grant from these funds to the Rochester model cities program. (These hearings were called after citizens' groups complained about the lack of such meetings.) The efforts of the city officials, however, were for naught. The county attorney advised, and the county legislature concurred, that the county could not make direct payments to the model cities program. The associate estimated that the county government actually did use about 10 percent of its revenue sharing funds to benefit low-income and minority city residents through a subsidy to the bus system, a summer youth employment program (mainly for inner-city

14. C. Erwin Piper, "Report from City Administrative Officer to the Los Angeles City Council Finance Committee on Criteria for the Objective Evaluation of General Revenue Sharing Funds for Programs Serving the Poor and Elderly" (May 22, 1974; processed), p. 4.

15. Paul Terrell, "Planning, Participation and the Purchase of Service: The Social Impact of General Revenue Sharing in Seven Communities" (University of Southern California, November 1975; processed).

youth), and improved probation services. But she reported that the chief beneficiaries of the county revenue sharing allocations were (1) "middle-income property owners because of property tax stabilization" and (2) county residents generally "in that the parks and roads slated to be improved are located outside the city."

Although Rochester is not customarily thought of as a core city with particularly serious social and economic problems, it does have many of these characteristics. It ranks eighth among the fifty-five central cities in table 3-4 in terms of the degree of relative hardship of the central city compared to its suburbs. The city's population, which accounted for approximately 40 percent of that of the county in 1970, declined by 7 percent from 1960 to 1970. The city was classified as experiencing "extreme" fiscal pressure in both periods of the Brookings field research. The associate described Rochester in 1973 as "an old city, whose fiscal resources are strained."

Besides Rochester, two other central cities in the sample with overlying counties were found to have been aided less than proportionately from county shared revenue in 1974. The fact that Newark, New Jersey, is in this group is of special importance. Newark, among central cities in the nation, stands out as especially hard pressed: it has the highest socioeconomic hardship ratio comparing city to suburbs in table 3-4. The associate for Newark described the city as "under severe financial strain because of its heavy service needs, shrinking tax base, and skyrocketing taxes."[16] Newark and Essex County are the only central city and overlying county in the sample to have used all of their shared revenue for tax relief in both periods of the field research. If the city and outlying county area shared equally in per capita terms in the tax base of Essex County, a likely conclusion would be that county government tax relief out of shared revenue would have the same impact proportionately in Newark as in the rest of Essex County. But this was not the case. Newark's share of the population of Essex County in 1970 was 41.1 percent, but its share of county assessed valuation for property taxes in 1972 was only 22.9 percent. Thus, column 3 of table 3-6 shows Newark's share of Essex County's assessed valuation as 56 percent of what it would be if there were parity between the two areas.[17]

This substantial shortfall in Newark's relative share of the tax base of

16. According to the associate, the mayor of Newark, Kenneth A. Gibson, commented recently, "Wherever cities are going, Newark will get there first."

17. Relations between Newark and Essex County are discussed in appendix A, pp. 187–89.

its overlying county raises the larger question of the extent to which this pattern is typical for central cities. On the basis of data for a random (one-in-ten) sample of forty-four large central cities, Newark's situation is not typical. Table 3-7 shows city-county assessed value ratios; table 3-8 summarizes these data.[18] Thirty-five of the cities in table 3-7 are primary central cities of SMSAs. Using the same approach as in the analysis for Newark, most of these cities would be expected to benefit from county tax relief out of revenue sharing on a basis reasonably in line with their share of county population; a few would do better than this, and a larger number worse. Of the thirty-five primary SMSA cities considered, four (Albany, Scranton, Colorado Springs, and Lansing) would benefit on this basis by at least 10 percent more from a curtailment of county taxes than is indicated merely by their proportion of county population. But benefits for a dozen cities on this basis would be at least 10 percent less than their population proportions would suggest, including Pittsburgh, Detroit, San Jose, Cincinnati, Tampa, Jersey City, Las Vegas, Riverside, Fresno, Reno, Sioux City, and Lima, Ohio. Only Lima's shortfall, however, approaches that for Newark.

Besides the three central cities already discussed, six others in the sample have overlying counties that are also included in the sample. The impact of county shared revenue on these cities is summarized below.

Cincinnati, Ohio (Hamilton County). In our sample, Cincinnati and Hamilton County stand out in that the county's role, typical of the Midwest, is limited. In 1973 per capita general revenue from the county's own sources was only 12 percent of that for the city. The associate reported that the city's fiscal condition is significantly worse than that of the county, and that this situation is compounded by the fact that Cincinnati's population is relatively low income and includes a high proportion of minority residents. He reported further that in 1974 the Hamilton County Commission considered, but rejected, using shared revenue for social services, a county function. County programs in other areas, it was noted, do not affect the disadvantaged. The associate commented on the county's emphasis on providing services in unincorporated areas where it has direct responsibility: "The County does not administer programs besides welfare

18. It is significant that the median city ratios for the four city-size groupings in table 3-8 are very close, although, looking at successively smaller cities, there are wider and more frequent divergences. For the dozen sample cities of 50,000 to 100,000 population, there is an average deviation of 19.5 percent, as against an average difference of only 5.4 percent for the nine cities of over 500,000 for which such a comparison can be made (line 10 of table 3-8).

Table 3-7. City Proportions of County Population and Taxable Property Value, Selected Cities, 1971

City population group (1970)	City's percentage of county		Taxable value percentage divided by population percentage
	Taxable property value	Population	
500,000 or more			
Kansas City, Mo.	73.23	67.34	1.087
San Diego, Calif.	52.92	51.31	1.031
Los Angeles, Calif.	40.19	40.05	1.003
Columbus, Ohio	60.72	64.81	0.937
Chicago, Ill.	56.99	61.30	0.930
Milwaukee, Wis.	63.06	68.04	0.927
Cleveland, Ohio	39.69	43.62	0.910
Pittsburgh, Pa.	28.94	32.41	0.893
Detroit, Mich.	50.65	57.91	0.875
200,000 to 500,000			
Oakland, Calif.ᵃ	35.91	33.69	1.066
Portland, Oreg.	71.71	68.62	1.045
Birmingham, Ala.	48.23	46.65	1.034
Rochester, N.Y.	40.28	41.61	0.968
Wichita, Kans.	74.13	78.86	0.940
Toledo, Ohio	74.30	79.24	0.938
Minneapolis, Minn.	41.31	45.25	0.913
Charlotte, N.C.	61.86	68.00	0.910
San Jose, Calif.	37.56	41.87	0.897
Cincinnati, Ohio	43.87	48.97	0.896
Tampa, Fla.	50.63	56.66	0.894
Jersey City, N.J.	31.11	42.76	0.728
100,000 to 200,000			
Albany, N.Y.	53.19	40.38	1.317
Scranton, Pa.	55.61	44.24	1.257
Colorado Springs, Colo.	67.20	57.24	1.174
Lansing, Mich.	66.83	60.45	1.106
Cedar Rapids, Iowa	71.43	67.79	1.054
Canton, Ohio	28.24	29.57	0.955
Montgomery, Ala.	74.78	79.50	0.941
Evansville, Ind.	76.80	82.22	0.934
Las Vegas, Nev.	39.40	46.03	0.856
Riverside, Calif.	24.77	30.51	0.812
Fresno, Calif.	30.82	40.18	0.767
50,000 to 100,000			
Des Plaines, Ill.ᵃ	1.37	1.04	1.317
Redondo Beach, Calif.ᵃ	1.00	0.80	1.250
Schenectady, N.Y.ᵃ	51.48	48.40	1.064
Fullerton, Calif.ᵃ	6.42	6.04	1.063
Wauwatosa, Wis.ᵃ	5.68	5.57	1.020
Wilkes-Barre, Pa.	17.12	17.19	0.996
Reno, Nev.	54.01	60.18	0.897
Sioux City, Iowa	70.43	83.38	0.845
Alameda, Calif.ᵃ	5.84	6.61	0.732
Roseville, Mich.ᵃ	6.81	9.68	0.704
West Covina, Calif.ᵃ	0.70	1.00	0.700
Lima, Ohio	29.34	48.35	0.607

Source: U.S. Bureau of the Census, *1972 Census of Governments*, vol. 2, pt. 1: *Taxable Property Values and Assessment-Sales Price Ratios: Taxable and Other Property Values*, table 4.
a. Located in a standard metropolitan statistical area with a more populous central city.

Table 3-8. Relation of Per Capita Taxable Property Value of Selected Cities to Per Capita Taxable Property Value of the Counties in Which They Are Located, by Population Group, 1971

Item	All	1970 city population group			
		500,000 or more	*200,000 to 500,000*	*100,000 to 200,000*	*50,000 to 100,000*
Number of cities	44[a]	9	12	11	12
Sampling rate[b]	...	All	1/2	1/5	1/15
Average city percentage of county population	45.4	54.1	54.4	52.6	24.0
City-county ratio of per capita taxable property value					
Percent of cities with a ratio under 1.0	65	67	75	55	58
Median city ratio	0.938	0.930	0.913	0.955	0.947
Highest city ratio	1.317	1.087	1.066	1.317	1.317
Lowest city ratio	0.607	0.875	0.728	0.767	0.607
Intercity range	0.710	0.212	0.338	0.550	0.710
Average deviation	0.104	0.050	0.047	0.115	0.185
Average percentage deviation	11.1	5.4	5.1	12.0	19.5

Source: Same as table 3-7.

a. Except in nine instances, each of these cities is the largest municipality of a standard metropolitan statistical area. The exceptions include one city in the 200,000-to-500,000 group and eight cities of 50,000 to 100,000, each located in an SMSA with a more populous central city.

b. The selection rate applied to those municipalities in each size class that have overlying county governments and for which relevant taxable value data appear in the cited census source.

that can be targeted on the poor and minorities. Moreover, the areas in which the County has service delivery responsibility (i.e., the unincorporated areas) do not contain any significant number of low-income or minority residents."

Two-thirds of the shared revenue allocated by Hamilton County in 1974 was used for new capital purposes; the associate judged the benefit from these facilities, and the benefits from shared revenue generally, to be equally shared by city and county residents. Among the most important new capital projects funded out of shared revenue in 1974 were a downtown addition to the main library, a suburban civic center, and a correctional facility.[19]

Phoenix, Arizona (Maricopa County). Among the larger central cities in the sample, Phoenix stands out as least disadvantaged (in fact, relatively advantaged) compared to its suburbs, with an index number of 85 in table 3-4. Generally typical of the West, Phoenix is a spread-out city,

19. See also appendix A.

accounting for 60.1 percent of the SMSA population in 1970. The associate for the Phoenix area judged the benefits of the county's use of shared revenue in 1974 to accrue to city residents in approximately the same proportion as their share of county population. Half of the county's shared revenue was used for tax stabilization; another 30 percent was used for a new county office building located in the central business district of Phoenix (which proved to be an important boost to the city's downtown redevelopment program). The remaining shared revenue was used, according to the associate, for new capital projects located outside the city.

The associate's report for 1975 stressed social and economic similarities between Phoenix and Maricopa County. He pointed out that as far as the distribution of minority groups and income differences are concerned, Phoenix and Maricopa County are very much alike. "With regard to ethnic distributions, the Mexican-American population in the county is slightly higher than in Phoenix, while the Black population is slightly higher in Phoenix than in outlying county areas. The Indian figures are about the same for the two jurisdictions. Overall, the city-county differences—in terms of income and ethnic balance—are not significant for the question of the relative benefits of the county's shared revenue."[20]

Eugene, Oregon (Lane County). Of all of the central cities and overlying counties in the Brookings sample, relationships between the two types of units with respect to revenue sharing appear to have been the closest in the case of Eugene and Lane County, Oregon. In 1973, the county and the city joined together to set up a new social service program, involving grants to twenty-three private agencies funded with revenue sharing payments. These grants, which were continued in 1974, were an outgrowth of a special city-county planning process for revenue sharing.

Lane County was classified as having used 87 percent of its shared revenue for new spending in 1973 and 88.7 percent in 1974. A major part of these funds in 1973 was devoted to the construction of new public buildings in Eugene. Considerable publicity was given to these uses of revenue sharing funds, so much so that the county commission "was criticized by rural residents for spending too much money for the benefit of urban residents." According to the associate, sensitivity on this point was a major factor in the decision by the county commission in 1974 to use some of its shared revenue for the expansion of office facilities outside of the central city, for housing repairs in unincorporated areas of the county,

20. See also appendix A.

and for the expansion of countywide mass transit service. Efforts were also made to publicize the availability of the social services funded from shared revenue outside the city of Eugene. In overall terms, the associate judged county uses of shared revenue to benefit city and county residents on an equal basis in 1974.

Sioux Falls, South Dakota (Minnehaha County). Most of Minnehaha county's revenue sharing allocated in 1973 ($597,200) was committed to a jointly financed $5 million public safety building (courtrooms and detention facilities) located in Sioux Falls; the city and county will share in the administration of the facilities and the operating costs.[21] The county planned from the outset of revenue sharing to use these funds in future years for the public safety building, and, according to the associate, used 40 percent of the shared revenue allocated in 1974 for this purpose. The associate classified the city of Sioux Falls as benefiting on an equal basis with outlying county area residents from the use of the shared revenue allocated by the county in 1974. Aside from the public safety building, 40 percent of these funds were assigned to tax stabilization, 5 percent to federal aid restoration and 5 percent to borrowing avoidance. In one sense these uses might be expected to benefit county residents outside of Sioux Falls more than those in the central city, since the outlying county area's share of the property tax base is greater than its share of the county's total population (see table 3-6); the difference, however, is not especially large.

Orlando, Florida (Orange County). Although the South tends to have more spread-out cities and consolidated city-counties than other regions, Orlando goes against this pattern. Its 1970 population accounted for only 23.1 percent of that of the metropolitan area. Its tax base is relatively strong, however, and Orlando was classified as facing "relatively little" fiscal pressure in both periods of field research. Orange County allocated a relatively small amount of shared revenue in fiscal 1974 ($1,970,000). But, in the first six months of the program, decisions were made applying to $7 million of shared revenue, equivalent to the first three years of revenue sharing funds anticipated by the county. These funds were assigned to capital purposes, mostly to avoid having to issue previously approved county bonds. According to the associate, these capital facilities can be expected to benefit city and outlying area county residents on an equal basis. Since Orlando's share of the county tax base is 92 percent of its

21. It is a county building in which space has been allocated for the city; the city also benefits from having this public safety building within the city limits.

share of the county population, this avoidance of borrowing effect could be expected to be relatively evenly divided between city and county.

Little Rock, Arkansas (Pulaski County). Like Cincinnati, Little Rock is a case in which the role of the overlying county government is limited. The county's percentage of own-raised revenue per capita compared to that for Little Rock (14 percent) is among the lowest of the central cities with overlying counties in the Brookings sample. According to the associate, "counties in Arkansas have limited governmental functions. They provide for the operation of the county tax collection machinery, maintain land records, administer courts of general jurisdiction, fund the office of the County Sheriff, and provide limited health services. Their most significant function, in terms of expenditures, is the construction and maintenance of county roads."

To date, all of Pulaski County's shared revenue has been used for new spending: roads, cars for the sheriff's department, parks outside of Little Rock, and corrections, as well as one important joint city-county venture—establishment of a combined transit system. The associate reported that county residents benefited disproportionately from these expenditures in 1974, although he noted that one important spending program—new county parks in low-income areas outside of Little Rock—favored low-income residents of the county.

Cities without Overlying Counties

As observed earlier, one of the most important structural differences among central cities is whether or not they have an overlying county. Altogether, there were fifty-four central cities in the nation in 1972 that did not have an overlying county government.[22] Of the five of these combined city-counties included in the Brookings sample, two are poverty-impacted core cities (Baltimore and St. Louis), where the central city accounts for less than half of the SMSA population; two are consolidated city-counties that account for all or most of the population of their metropolitan area (Jacksonville and Baton Rouge); the fifth (New York City)

22. Excluding the District of Columbia and thirty-eight "independent" cities in Virginia, the fifteen other combined city-counties are widely dispersed geographically: Baltimore, Baton Rouge, Boston, Carson City (Nevada), Columbus (Georgia), Denver, Honolulu, Indianapolis, Jacksonville, Nashville-Davidson (Tennessee), New Orleans, New York City, Philadelphia, San Francisco and St. Louis.

Table 3-9. Characteristics of Combined City-County Governments in the Brookings Sample, by Population Size

City	Population (thousands)	City population as percent of SMSA	Percent new uses of shared revenue 1973	Percent new uses of shared revenue 1974
New York	7,894.4	68.2	0	0
St. Louis	622.2	26.3	53	0
Baltimore	621.1	43.7	5.9	0
Jacksonville	528.9	100.0	50	0
Baton Rouge	271.9	95.3	100	34.5

Source: Field research and Census Bureau data.

lies in between in terms of the population share of the central city relative to that of its SMSA as defined in the 1970 census.[23] These five city-counties are shown in table 3-9, along with the percentage of the central city's shared revenue devoted to new uses in 1973 and 1974.

Our main interest in studying these cases is to compare these five cities with each other and also to compare the city and suburban allocations of shared revenue, where we can do so, based on field data. The sections below deal first with the two consolidated city-counties, although these two cases are not as interesting as the three that follow.

Baton Rouge. The Baton Rouge city-parish (in Louisiana counties are called parishes) contains 95.3 percent of the population of its SMSA. According to the associate, Baton Rouge has a "substantial industrial base"; its present consolidated form (established in 1947) "has enabled the city-parish to institute economies of operation." Buttressing this generally healthy financial picture, welfare and public health programs are a state responsibility in Louisiana, in line with common practice in the South. Baton Rouge was classified as being under "relatively little" fiscal pressure in both periods of field research, although increased energy costs were noted as likely to bring about some "belt-tightening."

Baton Rouge stands out in table 3-9 as having financed new spending out of shared revenue in both periods of the field research. Ninety percent of these expenditures in 1973 were classified as having been for new capital projects, and in 1974 most of the new spending was also devoted to capital purposes. Major functional areas of these new capital expenditures were public transportation, public safety, recreation, and environmental protection.

23. Since 1970, two counties on Long Island (Nassau and Suffolk) have been classified as a separate SMSA.

Jacksonville. In 1970 the city of Jacksonville accounted for all of the population of its SMSA, which consists of one county (Duval). A city-county consolidation plan adopted in 1967 made Jacksonville the largest city in population in Florida and the largest in land area in the United States.[24] A major difference between Baton Rouge and Jacksonville (both consolidated city-counties) is that Jacksonville operates its own electric utility system. Although city officials initially decided that shared revenue should be devoted to various new capital projects, this plan was abandoned in 1974 because of the "skyrocketing cost of fuel oil for the Jacksonville Electrical Authority." The authority annually transfers its profits to the general fund of the city; $27.5 million was budgeted for such transfer in fiscal 1974. Rising fuel costs, however, resulted in a change in plans. According to the associate, "in October 1973, the Jacksonville Electrical Authority was paying $2.09 per barrel for fuel oil. In November, the price was $7.00; by January 1974, it had risen to $12.00. The operation of the Authority is entirely oil-based." Electrical charges were increased, but not enough to fill this gap. The upshot was that midway through fiscal 1974, all capital outlays for the city of Jacksonville were frozen, and funds for this purpose, largely derived from revenue sharing, were transferred to the general fund.

Prior to the energy crisis, Jacksonville's overall fiscal condition had been classified as involving "relatively little" fiscal pressure. This rating was said to reflect substantial economic progress for the central city under the 1967 consolidation plan. In 1974, because of the energy crisis, the city was classified as facing "moderate" fiscal pressure.

Baltimore. In contrast to Baton Rouge and Jacksonville, Baltimore, an old city with a combined city-county government, has faced serious social and economic problems for many years. It was recently referred to as "a textbook case of what the term, 'urban crisis,' is all about."[25] The city contains 43.7 percent of the population of its SMSA and is almost completely surrounded by the much wealthier Baltimore County. Although Baltimore County is nearly eight times larger in area than the central city,

---

24. An excellent account of the history of Jacksonville's consolidation plan is by John M. De Grove, "The City of Jacksonville: Consolidation in Action," in *Regional Governance: Promise and Performance*, vol. 2, Case Studies on Substate Regionalism and the Federal System (Advisory Commission on Intergovernmental Relations, May 1973), p. A-41.

25. Quotation is from Baltimore City Council President, Walter S. Orlinsky, "Baltimore: A City in Deep Trouble," *Washington Post*, March 5, 1974.

it contains only two-thirds as much population;[26] the county's per capita income is one-third higher than that of the city. In testimony at the President's 1974 Conference on Inflation, Baltimore Mayor William D. Schaefer emphasized that "within the confines of Baltimore City reside a disproportionately large number of Maryland's poor, elderly, disadvantaged, and handicapped people."[27]

Baltimore and St. Louis rank high on the "hardship index" for central cities shown in table 3-4, Baltimore fourth, St. Louis sixth. In both cases, the central city's population is less than half that of the SMSA as a whole. Both lost population from 1960 to 1970. St. Louis dropped by 17 percent; Baltimore by 3.5 percent.[28] Both have a large minority population: Baltimore's population in 1970 was 47.5 percent black; St. Louis's, 40.8 percent.[29]

The city of Baltimore was classified as being under "extreme" fiscal pressure in both periods of the field research. On the other hand, Baltimore County (also in the sample) was classified as experiencing no fiscal pressure. The associate noted the city is "in deep trouble financially" and that there is a "general hostility by suburbanites toward Baltimore."

Although Baltimore city was found to have used 5.9 percent of its shared revenue in fiscal year 1973 for various new capital projects, in 1974 all the city's allocated shared revenue was classified for substitution purposes, primarily for tax stabilization. Baltimore County also used all of its shared revenue in 1974 for substitution purposes. The associate reported, "the very conservative orientation of the county population and its leaders works against any significant efforts to aid low-income groups and minorities. County officials insist that the county has no need to fund social programs because of the lack of significant poor and minority populations."

Baltimore's situation under revenue sharing is of special interest in another important respect. The city is at a significant disadvantage because of the ceiling contained in the 1972 revenue sharing act limiting cities and townships to 145 percent of the average per capita revenue sharing payment made to local governments in their state. Baltimore would have received 51 percent more shared revenue in 1972 if this ceiling had not

26. The Baltimore SMSA contains four other, much smaller, suburban counties.
27. *Report, The State and Local Governments Conference on Inflation* (Washington, D.C.: 1974), vol. 1, p. 335.
28. U.S. Bureau of Census, *City and County Data Book, 1972*, table 6.
29. Ibid.

applied. The ceiling was strongly criticized by city officials, including Mayor Schaefer. Although revenue sharing was "designed to lessen the fiscal burdens of impoverished cities like Baltimore," the mayor said, "it has, in reality enabled richer counties to benefit to the extent of $8 million at the city's expense."[30] (The $8 million figure is the estimate by city budget officials of the impact of the 145 percent ceiling in 1972.) This upper limit for shared revenue tends to be an especially serious problem for combined city-county governments. Central cities with overlying counties are not affected if their per capita allocations, taken together, are above 145 percent, as long as neither the city or the county alone exceeds this ceiling.[31]

St. Louis. Like Baltimore, the city of St. Louis is significantly affected by the 145 percent ceiling in the revenue sharing formula. St. Louis would have gained even more than Baltimore in 1972 if the 145 percent ceiling had not applied—in its case 78 percent. There was also criticism in St. Louis of another revenue sharing formula issue. Because the so-called Census undercount is said to be greatest for central cities and minorities, it is argued that central cities are treated unfairly under revenue sharing. A study by economist Robert P. Strauss concluded that St. Louis would have received $1.5 million in shared revenue for 1972 were it not for the "Census undercount."[32] If this amount is added to the $9.6 million in additional shared revenue that St. Louis would have received had the 145 percent ceiling not applied, the city's total of shared revenue for 1972 would have nearly doubled—$23.3 million as opposed to $12.2 million.

St. Louis, like Baltimore, is almost completely surrounded by a suburban county (St. Louis County), although in its case the city population is smaller than the county's, whereas in Baltimore the situation is reversed. In both cases, the land area of the county is eight times greater than that of the city and its per capita income is one-third greater. Both cities were classified as facing "extreme" fiscal pressure in all three periods of the Brookings field research.

Again, like Baltimore, St. Louis was found to have used some shared revenue in 1973 for new purposes when the bunching of payments produced a windfall effect, although in 1974 all of the city's shared revenue was classified as have been used for substitution purposes. St. Louis's new

---

30. *Report, State and Local Governments Conference on Inflation*, p. 337.

31. See appendix A for further discussion of Baltimore city-county relations.

32. Robert L. Joiner, "Census Error Said to Have Cost City Aid," *St. Louis Post Dispatch*, July 7, 1974.

spending out of shared revenue in 1973 was mainly for capital projects dispersed for political balance among the various councilmanic election districts. By August 1974, however, the associate reported that "the pressure on the city's finances had become so great that city officials no longer had the privilege of deciding where revenue sharing should be used. It was needed desperately just to balance the budget."

The contrast between St. Louis City and County was highlighted in the associate's report for 1974: "When St. Louis City residents watch as the County spends millions in revenue sharing funds for recreation projects, they hardly feel anything but cheated by the federal government."[33]

New York City. Only New York among the five city-counties in the sample was classified as having undertaken no new spending out of shared revenue in both periods of the field research (table 3-9). Although its relative share of the population and area of its SMSA is larger than that of Baltimore and St. Louis, its fiscal problems are even deeper. The inability of the city in 1975 to continue to obtain bank support for its short-term lending resulted in headline treatment across the nation in 1975 and 1976.

As an earlier section of this chapter points out, New York City's fiscal problems stem in large measure from the fact that the city is responsible for many services—especially social programs—that in other urban areas are the responsibility of overlying governments, either county or state. Despite the fact that its share of the total population of all municipalities in the United States in 1970 was only 5.8 percent, New York City's spending for welfare was 74.1 percent of the total welfare spending of all municipalities in 1973–74.[34] On the same basis, its percentage of hospital spending accounted for 46.2 percent of all municipal government spending for hospitals in fiscal 1973. Higher education is another area where New York stands out. Among the nation's forty-eight largest cities, New York's expenditures for higher education accounted for 74.5 percent of all higher education spending by these governments in 1972–73.[35]

Baltimore is most like New York among cities in the Brookings sample. It has a dependent school district and pays a portion (although lower) of the nonfederal share of welfare benefits. In fact, for three functions—

33. Unlike the Baltimore area, St. Louis County is not included in the sample for this study. Appendix A, however, contains a general discussion of St. Louis city-county relations.

34. U.S. Bureau of the Census, *City Government Finances in 1973–74,* tables 3, 7.

35. Ibid., table 7.

highways, fire protection and parks and recreation—per capita expenditures for Baltimore in fiscal 1973 were higher than for New York City. New York City, however, spent twice as much per capita as Baltimore for welfare, three times as much for health and hospitals, and four times as much for education.[36] And, on an overall basis, New York is at the head of the class: its per capita general revenue in 1973–74 was 31 percent greater than that for Baltimore, and its general expenditures were 35 percent higher.[37] To appreciate the wide variation among cities in these terms, it should be noted that Baltimore's general revenue per capita from own sources was still nearly two times greater than the average for all municipalities in 1973–74 and its general expenditures per capita were nearly three times the average for all municipalities.[38]

Conclusions

Rich and poor, big and little, relatively weak and relatively strong, central cities are by no means homogeneous. Many have a high concentration of social problems within their borders, others do not. Revenue sharing benefits needy central cities somewhat disproportionately; but the 145 percent ceiling reduces even these mild redistributional effects. The fiscal effects of shared revenue as classified by the field associates generally coincide with what would be expected: the more hard pressed the central city, the more likely it is to use shared revenue simply to hold the line fiscally.

Underlying these findings is a fundamental dilemma. To deal with the fiscal problems of the neediest central cities (Newark, Baltimore, St. Louis, New York, and, but to a lesser extent, Rochester and Cincinnati among the sample units) it is surely possible to devise various kinds of indices of financial and social need and channel federal assistance accordingly. Yet this benefits precisely those central cities and metropolitan areas that many would consider least advanced in terms of making structural reforms to ease "urban crisis" conditions. Assuming for the moment that we accept the conventional wisdom that bigger is better—that is, that consolidation and annexation are desired means of urban reform—then the federal government is put in the position of rewarding laggards (including the state

36. Ibid., table 6.
37. Ibid.
38. Ibid., tables 4, 6.

governments involved) if aid is concentrated on those central cities that are most isolated in economic and political terms. Even if it were politically feasible to channel a federal aid program primarily or exclusively to these jurisdictions, it is questionable as to whether this would be appropriate national policy. Could not, for example, Jacksonville decide that it should deconsolidate by separately incorporating the poverty areas of the old city in order to receive its "fair share" under such a federal program?

To summarize, the problems of the most troubled central cities are not in any major way ameliorated by general revenue sharing. Compared to this program, the countercyclical assistance program adopted in 1976 (described in chapter 1) is relatively more beneficial to distressed central cities, though not decidedly so. Even more important for central cities are the formula issues analyzed in the recent report on the Brookings monitoring study of the community development block grant program.

As the analysis in this chapter demonstrates, the distressed conditions of many of the nation's central cities are to a significant degree a function of political structure. Observers will differ as to whether the federal government should adopt national policies designed to bring about structural changes or should concentrate instead on other measures, notably grants-in-aid for distressed urban areas and transfer payments to individuals (both cash and in-kind). This chapter, in looking at the effect of revenue sharing on central city finances, helps to explain the diversity of their conditions and the intractability of the problems of the nation's most distressed central cities.

4 The Role of Revenue Sharing in State and Local Decisionmaking

To some proponents of revenue sharing, its most important—even exclusive—objective is to shift political power. Reacting to the growth of categorical grants during the sixties, these supporters of revenue sharing argued that the system of intergovernmental grants had produced too much centralization of power in Washington, which distorted state and local spending priorities and redistributed power from generalist officials to specialized bureaucracies. The major benefit from the revenue sharing program, in the eyes of these advocates, was to be a redistribution of power from specialized federal bureaucracies and their state and local counterparts to generalist officials such as mayors, councils, governors, and legislatures.

The assumption underlying the expectations of some of these advocates is that by providing greater discretion to generalist officials revenue sharing would stimulate a more competitive environment within which state and local budgets are decided, at least for that portion of the budget affected by intergovernmental grant revenues. Accordingly, a major purpose of this monitoring study is to observe not only what uses are being made of revenue sharing funds by recipient governments, but also how these uses are being decided on. What types of formal budgeting procedures are being adopted by recipient governments with regard to revenue sharing? Are these funds being merged with other sources of revenue in the regular budget, or are they being treated in some special way? In addition, of the various potential actors in the decisionmaking process, which ones are playing significant roles, and does this represent a different pattern of influence among the actors compared to the normal budget process?

In addressing these questions, our approach, as in the preceding chapters on the fiscal effects of revenue sharing, relies on a network of on-the-scene field observers collecting longitudinal data about the kinds of budgetary procedures adopted for handling revenue sharing funds. All the observers have used the same reporting and conceptual framework. Interaction among the field research associates and between the associates and the central staff offer a means to check these data and increase the degree to which there is uniformity in their handling.

In the first part of the chapter we examine the formal budget procedures used by the sample jurisdictions to allocate revenue sharing. In part two, we report the findings of the field associates on the actors who appear to have been influential in deciding the uses of shared revenue and identify the correlates of various patterns of influence.

Before proceeding to the analysis, however, two points should be noted about the question of revenue sharing as an instrument of political decentralization. First, the decentralization objective which some attach to the program may be judged effective if the enactment of this program simply reduces the influence of the national government on domestic programs, irrespective of the policies adopted by state and local governments. If revenue sharing results in a diminution in the rate of growth in categorical programs, or a decline in the issuance of new policies and regulations under existing programs, this too could be considered as having a decentralizing effect—that is, reducing the degree to which the policies of the national government influence state and local units. Our research to date has focused on the state and local effects of revenue sharing, although the third and final volume in this series will also examine the effects of revenue sharing on the executive branch of the federal government.

The second point that needs to be made relates to other purposes of the program. From the point of view of those who in 1972 (as well as in 1976) supported revenue sharing because they viewed it as an instrument for expanding state-local services or providing state-local tax relief, its success or failure as a decentralization device will be of relatively lesser importance.

Budget Process Categories

In the initial phase of the field research (December 1972 through June 30, 1973) the sample jurisdictions were grouped in the following four categories according to the budget procedure used in handling revenue sharing funds: (1) units that used an entirely *separate* budget process to allocate their general revenue sharing funds; (2) units that adopted a *supplemental* appropriation for the allocation of revenue sharing funds; (3) units that allocated shared revenue within their regular and ongoing budget process, but adopted *special procedures* for deciding upon the uses of these funds; and (4) units that fully *merged* shared revenue in their regular and ongoing budgetary process.

The first two categories, separate and supplemental, apply to cases where decisions about uses of shared revenue occurred *outside* the regular budget process, while the second two, special procedures and merged, refer to cases where revenue sharing decisions occurred *within* the normal budget process.

For the second round of field observations (covering the period July 1, 1973 through June 30, 1974) the framework for classifying budgetary procedures was modified in one important respect. Where the uses of shared revenue were decided within the regular budget process, units have been divided into three groups, instead of two. The three categories are:

(1) *Special procedures.* This is the same as the category used in the initial period of the field research. It applies to all units that allocated shared revenue in their regular and ongoing budget process, but where special procedures were adopted for deciding upon the use of these funds.

(2) *Special treatment.* This is a new category for cases in which the use of shared revenue was decided upon in the regular budget process; however, even though no special procedures were adopted, these funds were in some manner treated on a special basis in order to carry out a particular policy as to how revenue sharing funds should be used. The jurisdictions in this category would have been classified as "merged" using the definitions applied to the 1973 data.

(3) *Merged.* This category was reserved in the analysis of the 1974 data for jurisdictions where revenue sharing funds were *fully* merged into the general fund of recipient governments and as a result are indistinguishable from other sources of revenue in the budgetary process.

The new category, special treatment, is best explained by illustrating the kinds of actions that caused units to be classified in this group. A number of jurisdictions in the sample, both in 1973 and 1974, decided to use most or all of their shared revenue for capital projects or to restore anticipated federal aid reductions. Although they did not use a separate budgetary process, it was nevertheless necessary for them to give some measure of special handling in their budget process to shared revenue in order to carry out these policies. Such an approach resulted in their classification

Table 4-1. Sample Jurisdictions According to Type of Budget Process in Fiscal 1973 and 1974

	Number of units	
Type of process	*1974*	*1973*
Outside the regular process	9	20
Separate process	8	7
Revenue sharing supplemental	1	13
Within the regular process	57	43
Special procedure	5	8
Special treatment	25	19
Merged	27	16

Source: Field research data.

as special-treatment jurisdictions. We reclassified the 1973 field reports to separate the merged and special-treatment cases; on this basis, sixteen jurisdictions were classified as merged in 1973, compared to nineteen classified as special treatment.

In table 4-1, the findings relating to budget procedures used in conjunction with revenue sharing funds are summarized for both rounds of field observations.[1] Twenty-seven sample jurisdictions were reported to have completely merged revenue sharing funds into their regular budgets during the second round of field observations. Six of the eight state governments were classified as merged, as were approximately one-half of the city governments in the sample. More than one-half of the local governments with over 100,000 population were classified as merged, compared to approximately one-quarter of those under 100,000. A distinct relationship was also observed between fiscal pressure and the decision to merge shared revenue. Two-thirds of the local governments characterized as under moderate or extreme fiscal pressure during the second round were included in the merged category, compared to only one-fifth of the localities under light or no fiscal pressure.

Given these characteristics, it is not surprising that for the twenty-one

1. For 1974, the units add up to one more than the total of sixty-five sample jurisdictions. One unit made no allocation over the period of observation and two units are counted twice because they acted in two budget cycles during this period and adopted different budgetary procedures for revenue sharing in each cycle. In 1973, sixty-three sample jurisdictions are included in the summary. Three jurisdictions made no revenue sharing allocation in round one of the field observations and one unit acted in two budget cycles, adopting a different budget procedure in each cycle.

local governments that merged shared revenue in 1974, nearly 60 percent of their allocations (on an unweighted mean basis) was accounted for by program maintenance and tax stabilization uses. Correspondingly, only one-quarter of shared revenue allocations by these jurisdictions was accounted for by new spending uses. As noted above, the states in our sample tended as a group to adopt a merged procedure in handling revenue sharing funds, and this precludes any comparisons of net effects data on the basis of alternative budget procedures for these jurisdictions.

Of the thirty-nine jurisdictions that were classified as following a procedure other than merged in 1974, nine adopted procedures that were completely outside of the normal budget process (eight separate process and one supplemental). No pattern was observed for these nine local governments with respect to population size (four were over 100,000 and five under), and in terms of fiscal pressure, six were characterized as under no or little pressure and three under moderate pressure. The one characteristic that these jurisdictions did have in common was a relatively high degree of sensitivity to the five-year life of the program. In seven of the nine jurisdictions, the degree of sensitivity was judged by the associate to be moderate to high, compared to only fourteen of the other forty-six local jurisdictions in the sample.

An examination of the fiscal effects data for the nine jurisdictions that allocated shared revenue completely outside the normal budget process shows that the net effect categories specifically related to capital programs (new capital spending and borrowing avoidance) together accounted for over two-thirds of second-round allocations. The emphasis on capital uses and the complete isolation of shared revenue from the regular budget process is consistent with the relatively greater sensitivity about the five-year limit reported for these jurisdictions.

The remaining nonmerged jurisdictions were reported to have adopted procedures for handling revenue sharing that, while not completely outside the normal budget process, did distinguish revenue sharing funds from other sources of revenue. In five of these cases, a special budgeting procedure was adopted, such as public hearings on the uses of revenue sharing or the creation of an advisory board to review revenue sharing uses. In the other twenty-five cases, revenue sharing funds were afforded some type of special treatment in the sense that the funds were explicitly earmarked for particular uses, in many cases capital projects. Two states, Colorado and Louisiana, are included in this latter group: Louisiana explicitly earmarked all of its shared revenue for highway projects, while

Colorado earmarked its shared revenue for offsetting cutbacks in federal categorical grants.

Of the twenty-eight local governments included in the two special process categories, only seven have populations of over 100,000 and twenty-three were characterized as under relatively little or no fiscal pressure. The net effects data for these jurisdictions show new spending accounting for an average of 57 percent of shared-revenue allocations in round two. Borrowing avoidance uses were not significant for these governments, while program maintenance and tax stabilization uses combined to account for an average of about one-quarter of shared revenue allocations.

CHANGES IN BUDGET PROCEDURES BETWEEN THE
FIRST AND SECOND ROUNDS

Between the first and second rounds of field observations, major changes occurred in two of the budget process categories. First, there was a net decline of twelve units in the supplemental category. Of the thirteen jurisdictions that switched from this category after round one, six were classified as special procedure or special treatment in round two, four as merged, and three as separate process.[2] It is significant that two-thirds of these jurisdictions are on a calendar year budget cycle, compared to less than one-third of the other local governments in the sample. This suggests that the initial use of a supplemental budget was primarily a reflection of the fact that revenue sharing entitlements in round one started after the regular budget was adopted and, therefore, could only be deployed through a supplemental. By round two of the field observations, revenue sharing entitlements could be anticipated with certainty over the coming budget year, and there was no longer the need for a supplemental.

The other major shift was the increase in the number of jurisdictions that fully merged shared revenue into the normal budget in round two. Thirteen jurisdictions switched into and two switched out of the merged category between the first and second rounds, resulting in a net increase of eleven merged jurisdictions. Eight of the thirteen governments that switched to a merged procedure were classified as being under moderate

2. Longmont, Colorado, was the only sample jurisdiction to budget revenue sharing through a supplemental in round two. Prior to this, the city's revenue sharing entitlements had simply been accumulating in the trust fund account. During the second-round observations, the city made a second appropriation, which occurred within the regular budget and was classified as special treatment.

or extreme fiscal pressure, and in five cases fiscal conditions were reported to have deteriorated between the first and second rounds of field observations.

Los Angeles, California, is one of the governments that switched from special procedure to merged between the first and second rounds of field observations. Characterizing the city as under moderate fiscal pressure, the associate described the circumstances surrounding the switch in budget procedures as follows: "The budget was not a controversial item this year (1974) because of the tight fiscal picture. . . . In the past, the Council's Finance Committee and the Los Angeles Human Relations Bureau held hearings on revenue sharing. For the present fiscal year there was virtually no extra input."

The city of Jacksonville, Florida, switched from special treatment in round one to merged in round two. As noted in chapter 2, the city's public electric authority experienced a sixfold increase in the price of oil and reacted to a deteriorating fiscal situation by canceling capital improvements for which revenue sharing had been designated, using the funds instead to support programs in the operating budget. In round two, St. Louis, Missouri also switched to a completely merged budget procedure. The associate noted that extensive plans for the use of revenue sharing for a variety of capital projects, developed in consultation with community groups, were short-circuited by an abrupt worsening in the city's already troubled financial situation. According to the associate, "The city's financial position had slipped so badly that revenue sharing money was just thrown into the pot along with other city revenue as a means of financing a budget to keep the city going . . . the capital improvements proposed from the original revenue sharing appropriations were cancelled."

In general, it is not surprising to learn from these field reports that the probability of revenue sharing playing a prominent role in the budget and being afforded some type of special treatment is significantly reduced as the overall fiscal health of a recipient jurisdiction deteriorates.

SUMMARY OBSERVATIONS ON REVENUE SHARING AND
BUDGET PROCESS

To summarize the field information about the types of budget procedures used in allocating shared revenue, the following generalizations can be made. First, jurisdictions under relatively high fiscal pressure are most likely to integrate revenue sharing into the normal budget. Included in this group is a relatively high proportion of larger city governments in our sample. For these jurisdictions, a high proportion of shared-revenue allocations can be accounted for by tax stabilization and program maintenance uses and, correspondingly, a relatively low percentage by new spending uses.

Second, despite a sharp increase in the number of sample governments that merged shared revenue in round two, over three-fifths of the sample jurisdictions continued to allocate these funds through some type of separate or special procedure. Smaller and less fiscally hard pressed jurisdictions are more likely to be included in this group. Jurisdictions that adopt a procedure entirely outside the normal budget process are most likely to be especially sensitive to the uncertainty associated with the five-year life of the program. For these jurisdictions, uses of shared revenue will tend to be devoted primarily to capital projects, either in the form of direct allocations or borrowing avoidance.

Revenue Sharing and the Politics of the Budget Process

To understand the impact of revenue sharing on the decisionmaking processes of recipient governments, it is necessary not only to examine the formal budgeting procedures adopted for handling these funds, but also to identify those officials who are most instrumental in deciding the uses of these funds. As already noted, some advocates of revenue sharing base their support on the belief that under a general-purpose grant, generalist officials in state and local government are more likely to be the key decisionmakers; under a categorical grant, in contrast, federal agencies and their counterparts in state and local governments would be expected to play important roles in determining the specific uses of grant money, thereby limiting the role of generalist officials.

In reporting the effect of revenue sharing on the budget processes of the sample jurisdictions, the field associates were asked to describe the roles played by various officials. Which ones played significant roles, and did this represent a change in influence vis-à-vis the regular budget process? Using the information provided during the second round of field observations, we have classified the local governments in our sample into three groups, according to who appeared to play dominant roles in deciding the uses of shared revenue.

1. *Executive dominance.* The units in this group are those in which

mayors, managers, finance officers, or other generalist executive officials were judged to have been most influential in decisions on what to do with revenue sharing. Included in this group are units where executive recommendations were accepted without conflict, and those in which interest groups or factions in legislatures tried unsuccessfully to modify executive proposals.

2. *Legislative dominance.* This category includes both those few jurisdictions in our sample that use a legislative budget process and those where state legislatures and city and county councils made significant modifications in executive recommendations, generated independent proposals, or otherwise played a major role in decisions about how to treat shared revenue.

3. *Interest group influence.* This category contains those units in which interest groups were able to divert revenue sharing funds to favored programs. While interest groups do not directly make decisions on how to spend local funds, they do exert more or less influence on the executive and legislative officials who do.

Not included in these three major categories is a limited number of small governments whose process for allocating shared revenue was highly informal and unstructured. Three local governments in the sample fit this description, including Theresa and Lowell Township, Wisconsin. In her discussion of the budget process in these jurisdictions, the associate noted that "although the town chairman is technically the executive, he, the two supervisors, the town clerk, and the town treasurer normally work closely together in all decision-making apart from the annual town meeting. Almost everyone connected with such town government is a generalist . . . In such a situation, it is difficult to see how revenue sharing could have much impact . . . to go on discussing the situation would be gilding the lily."

Executive dominance. For thirty-two of the local jurisdictions included in the analysis, associates reported that during the second round of field observations executive officials were the key actors in deciding how revenue sharing would be used. That three-fifths of the local governments in the sample are included in this category is not surprising. Students of budgeting have long observed that the budget process in most local and state governments is dominated by executive actors, whether city manager, mayor, finance officer, or governor and budget staff. This traditional dominance can be traced to a number of causes—most importantly, a near-monopoly by officials on adequate staff and time to articulate budgetary choices and define available resources. The definition of resources is a particularly critical element of executive power, because it means that department requests and council deliberations are formulated largely within the framework set by the executive.

From our field data, it would appear that the likelihood of this traditional pattern of executive dominance being maintained in relation to revenue sharing is particularly high in jurisdictions facing serious fiscal pressure. Sixteen of the nineteen localities characterized as under moderate or extreme fiscal pressure were included in this group. Moreover, in line with the observations about budget procedures made in the first part of this chapter, sixteen of the eighteen localities that totally merged shared revenue with other funds in the regular budget were identified as cases where the executive dominated the decisionmaking process.

Among especially hard-pressed jurisdictions, the absence of any major change in the traditional pattern of political influence regarding revenue sharing is clearly illustrated by the situation in Newark, New Jersey. According to the Newark associate, "the broad consensus in Newark that the city's revenue sharing funds should be used to stabilize and reduce the property tax rate continues. The destructive impact of Newark's unusually high property tax rate on the city's financial health has been very apparent to city officials from the beginning of revenue sharing, so that the budget office, the mayor, and the council had no real disagreement about how these funds should be used. Agency officials and interest groups have passively accepted the decision and have not attempted to become involved in the decisions over revenue sharing, at least so far."

Legislative dominance. In eleven of the local governments in the sample, the legislative branch was reported to have played a key role in deciding the uses of shared revenue. Of these eleven, eight are county governments and all were reported by the field associates to be under relatively light or no fiscal pressure. Traditionally, a strong council or commission form of government has characterized the politics of eight of these governments. For the other three, the associates reported that in decisions over revenue sharing uses there was a distinct break from a tradition whereby the council members confined themselves to a series of marginal changes in the executive budget, with relatively little opportunity to impose their own priorities. In each of these cases, the councils were reported to have played significant roles in deciding how revenue sharing funds were to be used.

Hamilton and Butler Counties, Ohio, are two of the jurisdictions in which a shift toward greater council participation in the budget process was reported. In his field report, the Ohio associate provided the following assessment of the political impact of revenue sharing in Butler County:

Butler County's method of allocating revenue sharing funds appears to put more control over operating departments in the hands of the county commissioners. By treating revenue sharing money as contingency fund, the county commissioners reserve the right to pass individually on almost all equipment purchases. Department heads come to the commissioners to argue each individual proposal for equipment expenditure. The clerk of the county board (who is essentially a county manager) is unhappy over this method of budgeting. My judgement is that it has increased the degree of influence of the county commissioners over operating departments. This is especially significant in view of the fact that revenue sharing money is the only major part of the county budget over which the commissioners exercise discretionary control.

Similarly, for Hamilton County the associate noted that "the county commissioners have complete control over revenue sharing money, quite unlike their control over any other county funds. This has radically changed the role of the county commissioners. For the first time, they have a significant sum of money over which they can exercise discretion."

Irondequoit Township, New York, was the other local jurisdiction in which the legislative branch was reported to be unusually active in decisions about revenue sharing. In summarizing the political situation during the second round of field observations, the associate said, "revenue sharing funds are designated for general categorical uses, to be spent by department heads only after the town board has approved detailed requests submitted in advance. Revenue sharing funds are, thus, specifically and directly controlled by the town board. Department heads have considerably less autonomy in the spending of these funds, and the town board members have greater continuing influence than in the case of other allocations."

In terms of formal budget procedures used for handling revenue sharing funds, all three of the jurisdictions in which greater legislative participation was observed were reported to have adopted a separate process, entirely outside the normal budget.

Interest group involvement. The remaining nine local governments included in the analysis are those in which interest groups were identified as playing an important role in determining the uses of shared revenue. In each of these jurisdictions, interest groups were reported by the associates to have been successful in having at least a small proportion of shared revenue used for projects they favored, primarily social service programs affecting the poor and otherwise disadvantaged. In six of the cases, groups were reported to have gained influence in decisions about revenue sharing through the legislative branch of the government, compared to two cases in which the groups operated through the chief executive.

Of the five county governments and four city governments included in this group, only three have populations under 100,000. In terms of fiscal pressure conditions, six were characterized as experiencing relatively light or no pressure. One distinguishing characteristic associated with this group was the degree of overall public interest in revenue sharing reported by the associates. In six of the nine localities, the overall level of public interest was described as significant. By comparison, in only two of the other forty-four local governments included in the analysis was significant public interest reported.

In describing public interest about revenue sharing in Los Angeles County, one of the nine localities where interest groups were influential, the associate noted in her second-round report that "from the numbers and variety of groups requesting revenue sharing funds, it is apparent that public awareness and interest in revenue sharing has increased. In addition, the board is playing a more visible role and has used revenue sharing this year (1974) for the kinds of services that stimulate public interest: community agencies, transportation, and the current 'hot' issue—juvenile justice." In discussing media attention given to revenue sharing, she noted that special revenue sharing hearings appeared to increase the extent of coverage in 1974.

The observation by the Los Angeles associate that public interest had increased between the first and second rounds of field observations is suggestive of a more general trend. Between the two periods of field observations, the number of localities in which interest groups were judged to have gained influence in deciding the uses of shared revenue increased from two to nine.[3] There are two likely explanations for why groups become more involved in revenue sharing decisions only after one full budget cycle had been completed under the new program. First, as the real or potential effects of the Nixon administration's fiscal 1974 budget became more apparent to community groups affected by federal aid programs, they became more active in seeking revenue sharing funds to replace anticipated federal aid cutbacks. In this connection, the associate for Monroe County, New York, noted in her second-round report that "in response to complaints

3. Correspondingly, the number of localities in the sample in which executive officials dominated revenue sharing decisions declined from thirty-eight to thirty-two, and legislatively dominated jurisdictions declined from twelve to eleven.

by two citizen coalitions, the county manager suggested that the legislature hold separate hearings on revenue sharing allocations. Three hearings were held in May and June 1974, at which representatives of groups in danger of losing federal funds made requests for revenue sharing funds."

The second explanation for the delayed response by interest groups is that some potential participants were not aware of the revenue sharing program until 1974. In describing the heightened debate over revenue sharing uses during the second round of field observations, the associate for Pulaski County, Arkansas, noted that "much of this increased activity is undoubtedly due to increased pressure by interest groups, as well as a general awareness of the major contribution to the county budget which the revenue sharing funds have made."

With respect to budgeting procedures adopted by the nine jurisdictions in which groups played important roles in deciding the uses of revenue sharing funds, all were reported to have adopted a procedure other than merged. Moreover, all five jurisdictions that adopted some form of special procedure—involving special revenue sharing hearings or the formation of a revenue sharing advisory board—were included in this group.

The Politics of Revenue Sharing in State Government

An examination of the information on political impact provided by the field associates monitoring the eight state governments in the sample suggests that the role of revenue sharing in state budget decisions varied both in the dominance of particular actors and the overall level of interest in and visibility of these funds. Of the four states in which associates identified a dominant actor, the governor prevailed in North Carolina, Louisiana, and Massachusetts. In his second-round report, the North Carolina associate noted that the governor and his Advisory Budget Commission "took their normal key roles," while for the most part the General Assembly was "quite oblivious to the presence and effects of general revenue sharing." The associate for Louisiana observed that "the Governor is the dominant figure in determining the use of revenue sharing. He stated publicly in advance of the legislative session that the money would be used for highway construction and this decision was never challenged by the legislature, other public officials, or the public." It should be noted that a substantial increase in other revenue due to an increase in state taxes tended to overshadow revenue sharing during the second round of field observations, according to the associate. In Massachusetts, general revenue sharing may have strengthened the position of the governor. The associate noted that "shared revenue enabled him to avoid a tax increase—an election promise —and to enlarge and maintain spending in a few areas."

In Colorado, a state where traditionally neither the executive nor legislative branch has dominated the budget, the Joint Budget Committee of the General Assembly was the key in deciding the uses of revenue sharing. According to our associate, the governor favored using these funds for education, but the legislature passed a law specifically designating revenue sharing for federal aid restoration. As a consequence, state agencies facing federal aid cutbacks and related interest groups were active in decisions about the allocation of revenue sharing.

Associates in the other four states reported that decisions about revenue sharing were not dominated by either branch of government, either because there was general agreement about how the funds should be used or because relatively little explicit attention was given to these funds in designing the budget. In California and Maine, there was general support for the decision to use revenue sharing to support local schools, though the Maine associate did report more involvement by outside interests, particularly education groups, than was normally the case. In New York, general revenue sharing funds had been budgeted even before the program had been enacted. As a result, a former state official acknowledged to the New York associate that responses to agencies and groups requesting particular uses of these funds effectively amounted to "you've already had it." Finally, the Illinois associate reported that "no branch of government, or for that matter any interest group, pays particular attention to the state's share of general revenue sharing. Moreover, because revenue sharing is allocated directly to the Common School Fund, most officials probably believe that revenue sharing funds are 'already' being used, the fungibility issue notwithstanding."

Descriptions of Six Sample Jurisdictions

Capsule descriptions of six sample jurisdictions follow. Drawing on information from both rounds of field observations, these capsules are intended to provide the reader with a closer look at the political impact issues discussed earlier. Looking across both rounds of observations, it is also possible to gain from the descriptions some sense of the dynamics associated with the politics of revenue sharing at the state and local levels.

LOS ANGELES COUNTY (pop. 6,923,813)

According to the Los Angeles County associate, shared revenue has been "treated as a separate program, distinct from the rest of the budget." This was a "conscious policy adopted partly as a political gesture to encourage continued funding by Congress, and partly to preclude dependence on funds that may be terminated." Public hearings were held on the uses of revenue sharing in both periods of the field research and separate budget documents were issued for these funds. Another and related reason given for this policy was to have specific programs and projects funded out of shared revenue in order to demonstrate to the public generally, and particularly to the county's nineteen-member delegation in the U.S. House of Representatives, that the program had produced tangible benefits to the community.

Public hearings were held on the uses of revenue sharing in both periods of the field research; separate budget documents were issued for these funds. Of particular interest is the county's program to use a portion of its shared revenue to aid community social service groups. In June 1974, the Board of Supervisors earmarked $22.5 million in shared revenue for fiscal year 1975 to be made available to community groups. More than 480 proposals were received from nonprofit community groups during the fiscal year, requesting $102,800,000. Of this amount, $9,336,891 eventually was funded. The Greater Los Angeles Community Action Agency also received $1,320,000. The County Department of Urban Affairs retained responsibility for making final recommendations to the supervisors.

In October 1974, the supervisors created a special advisory committee on general revenue sharing for community groups to recommend priority categories to the board. The chairman of the advisory committee was an official of the United Way; two other members were from the county Community Action Agency. Each of the members of the county Board of Supervisors appointed one other member. Jockeying among advisory committee members and interested community groups was said to be intense. Major factions involved were the United Way, the Community Action Agency, the Chicano Coalition, and a fourth group consisting of more than one hundred community organizations organized as the Coalition for the Equitable Distribution of Revenue Sharing. The ensuing political controversies, plus three other factors —a division on the Board of Supervisors as to this use of shared revenue, continued federal funding for community action agencies, and increased fiscal pressure on the county government—resulted in significant reductions over time in the amount of shared revenue allocated to the community groups. At one point, county officials described this situation as "a major firestorm," and said their original plan for community involvement "appeared to be back-firing."

Political activity involving the use of shared revenue for community groups was intense. Coalition members and spokesmen for various community organizations attended board meetings and mobilized their congressmen to assist them. Two congressmen wrote letters on behalf of community groups, and the chief assistant of one congressman testified before the board in support of particular social service uses of shared revenue.

The field research report for fiscal 1974 concludes: "The most significant impact of revenue sharing in Los Angeles is the increased involvement of citizens groups of all kinds in the budget process of county government."

The role of the members of county Board of Supervisors was also portrayed as having been increased primarily because of the revenue sharing funds used for new capital purposes, "always an important political tool in a politician's district." Besides revenue sharing, another important factor in the changed role of the five-person county board in this period was the election of three new members making the board more "liberal and activist."

WINNSBORO, SOUTH CAROLINA (pop. 3,411)

When its first revenue sharing check was received, the manager of the city of Winnsboro, South Carolina, contacted each department head to make certain that their priority capital items were on his most recent list of "needed projects." Citizen groups and city council members were then asked for their opinion as to how these funds should be used. In the final analysis, the manager's choices were said to have dominated. "He used an artist's pad on an easel, wrote down the possible projects in pencil, and when they were approved traced them over in ink."

The five-man council was described as playing an active role in this process. They generally agreed with the manager, but did withhold funds from some of his "pet projects." The most active interest group was said to be the Winnsboro Merchants' Association, which pressed for funds for downtown development to ward off competition from a planned shopping center outside of the city. Several requests were made to have driveways paved with these funds, but were rejected.

Blacks account for half the population of Winnsboro, but no black organizations took an interest in these decisions, although the local newspaper urged editorially that some revenue sharing funds be allocated for human resource purposes. More interest groups participated in decisions about the use of shared revenue for the overlying Fairfield County, also in the sample. These groups requested shared revenue funds for libraries, the voluntary fire company, recreation, and child care, all of which received some funds from the county out of their initial allocations of shared revenue. The associate described the interest of these groups as declining in fiscal 1974.

WORCESTER, MASSACHUSETTS (pop. 170,730)

The use of shared revenue for social services was the most prominent public issue in the impact of revenue sharing in Worcester, Massachusetts. In 1973 an ad hoc committee was formed by the city manager of Worcester to advise him on which social programs that had suffered cutbacks in federal aid should be aided by the city out of its revenue sharing funds. Although there was some discussion of converting this committee into an office of human services, this had not been done as of the field report for 1974.

The dominant individual in framing the city's budget, as well as deciding on the uses of revenue sharing funds, has been the city manager. "As a generalist official, revenue sharing seems to have increased his budget powers, since he was provided with 'free' money to which no significant strings were attached. This was a windfall to which no groups inside or outside city hall had special claim, and the manager, until the furor arose over federal aid cuts, acted as if all revenue sharing funds were in addition to the city's general revenue."

Interest groups were relatively inactive in attempting to influence the city council on the use of revenue sharing funds in the early days of revenue sharing. The principal exception was the Worcester Taxpayers Association, which requested that the funds be used "to stabilize the tax rate." They received a "sympathetic" review from both the city manager and the city council.

In the spring of 1973, when social welfare groups were faced with the possibility of federal program cuts, "the manager made them part of the budget process", establishing the ad hoc committee described above. A year later, during the presentation of his 1974 budget, the manager claimed that Worcester "was the first municipality in New England to set aside revenue sharing money for social services, including funds for the retention of neighborhood centers." At this time he stated his intention of recommending that a special fund be established in which 10 percent of the city's revenue sharing money— approximately $470,000—would be earmarked for "essential activities, particularly [those] of a social nature."

BANGOR, MAINE (pop. 33,168)

The budget process for revenue sharing in Bangor, Maine, was basically a closed one. The timing of revenue sharing payments was responsible for the special budget handling of these funds by the city government. Because the initial checks arrived late in the budget process, city agencies were not consulted about their use; the decision was made by the city manager and the city council, primarily its finance committee. The council caused the manager to make several changes in his plans for the use of these funds. "There was a bit more centralization in the executive branch, and a bit more bucking by the council against the executive." Both of these changes, however, were described as minimal.

"Interest group involvement was limited to social-service agencies, such as senior citizens and United Way groups." The associate added that "among smaller localities in the state, especially those using the town meeting, revenue sharing had more impact. The revenue sharing program was extensively discussed by citizens in some town meetings." Illustrative of a lack of public interest in revenue sharing and budget issues generally in this period, the associate noted that the night the budget was passed, there was a large crowd in the council chamber, but it was there mainly because of a zoning issue.

The initial decision in Bangor was to use a significant portion of the city's shared revenue to ease its cash-flow problem. Prior to revenue sharing, officials were concerned about the emergence of what was described as a "cash flow crisis."

Social service groups were seen in Bangor as having moderately increased their influence, although the main reason here was a change in state law, which the associate notes encouraged such groups to seek revenue sharing funds at the local level.

STATE GOVERNMENT OF COLORADO (pop. 2,534,000)

At the outset of the revenue sharing program, Governor John Love sought to have these funds used as a part of his proposed program of state aid for education then being developed. He did not consult with other agencies of the state's executive branch, a decision that later contributed to the budget policy problems experienced by the governor. In Colorado, budgeting is typically carried out under a joint arrangement between the executive and the legislature, in which for a long while the legislature has been "very powerful and has taken the lead."

Leaders of the legislature in 1973 wanted to use shared revenue to replace funds that it was anticipated would not be forthcoming because of proposed or actual reductions in grants-in-aid from the federal government. The legislature won out, passing a statute which said: "Revenue sharing funds are used in those state programs which have been or are expected to be reduced or terminated for the fiscal year of this act. In the event that additional federal funds are available, the general fund amount noted as '(RS)' or as otherwise noted shall be reduced by the amount of federal funds received in excess of the figure shown in the 'federal funds' column for that program." The associate ascribed three important changes to revenue sharing: "(1) the Joint Budget Committee and its staff as well as other people and institutions in the state government are developing a heightened interest in the relationship of state programs to federally funded operations. There is an attempt to look at overall program priorities and trends based on better information and more adequate communication. This involves state officials communicating more frequently with each other as well as with federal officials. (2) State agencies have pressed the legislature more strongly than in past years. Since decisions about the uses of general revenue sharing funds are made by the legislature, the legislature is the obvious place to seek favorable decisions on these matters. (3) Interest groups have also lobbied the General Assembly more vigorously; this has particularly been true of associations of local governments."

GREECE (TOWN), NEW YORK (pop. 75,136)

For the town of Greece, New York, the budget is adopted in November for the next calendar year. Because the first revenue sharing check was received in December of 1972 and the second shortly thereafter, a supplemental budget process was adopted early in 1973 to handle these funds. This was not necessary in 1974, and as a result shared revenue was merged with the normal budget process.

"The residents of Greece are mainly conservative, middle-class, white homeowners who are employed in semiskilled and skilled positions in large industry." Over half of the allocations of revenue sharing funds for 1973 and 1974 were assigned by the associate to stabilizing property taxes, so the "impact was on the general population of the town."

It was noted in the first field report that there seemed to be little public interest in the determination of the use of revenue sharing funds. At that time only two groups—the library and neighborhood sidewalk committees—attempted to influence the decisionmaking process. As of the last report the library board was the sole body which "thought of revenue sharing as extra money." The library director and board of trustees requested $50,000 in revenue sharing money to help finance an addition to the town library. Although the library board argued that "other town libraries received revenue sharing" and that Greece's library "was entitled to it, too," their request was turned down by the town board.

National Interest Groups and Revenue Sharing

We turn now to the effect of the general revenue sharing program on interest groups at the national level. With the advent of revenue sharing and other changes in federal grants policy, particularly the increasing importance of block grants, it might be expected that some national organizations would step up their efforts, or make new efforts, to encourage state and local affiliates to obtain their "fair share" of these funds. To get at this subject, the field research associates were asked in 1974 whether interest groups active with respect to the uses of revenue sharing funds had been urged to do so by their parent national organizations. Out of thirty-nine local jurisdictions where some interest group activities were reported, the influence of one or more national groups was noted by the associates in six cases, while local groups were said to have been influenced by state-level interest groups in four cases. The national and state organizations cited by field associates were those for libraries, police and fire employees, mental health, senior citizens, the League of Women Voters, and a state historical society.

On the whole, the influence of these state and national organizations does not appear to have been strong. Library groups were mentioned several times, and the American Library Association was active nationally, pointing out to its affiliates that the inclusion of libraries as one of the priority-expenditure categories in the act offered a basis on which they should petition for revenue sharing funds. Employee organizations for policemen and firemen were cited in three cases, although as a significant actor in only one (Hamilton County, Ohio). The League of Women Voters was mentioned in two cases as pressing for the use of shared revenue for housing and other social programs. But despite active efforts, the effect of national interest groups on the decisionmaking process was not judged to be great by the associates.

To supplement these data, fifty national organizations were polled in the spring of 1975. This sample, which did not include national associations of state and local governments, was designed to provide a reasonably balanced cross-section. Thirty-six groups, representing 72 percent of the total, responded. Twenty-one (58 percent of the respondents) said that their organization had attempted to influence state and local governments to spend revenue sharing funds for purposes which they favored. For more than half of these respondents, their efforts were said to represent "an important activity"; for two of them it was said to be of "the highest priority," and for ten groups, it was said to be one of several major activities.

Respondents fell basically into three categories. One type of organization concentrated on the fiscal impact of revenue sharing. The National Taxpayers Union, for example, urged its members to oppose the use of shared revenue to "increase the scope of local government"; their preference was for substitution uses, such as tax reduction and tax stabilization. The Union said it strongly opposed the basic idea of revenue sharing, calling it "a signpost on the road to bankruptcy." A second group of organizations urged the use of shared revenue to finance particular functions of government. The International Conference of Police Associations, for example, urged that these funds be used to "prevent layoffs of police officers." The American Association for Retired Persons said that their organization "utilized the revenue sharing program in a catalytic effort to involve local units and chapters in local budget considerations." A third group of responding organizations, which clearly were the most active with regard to revenue sharing, both nationally and locally, included social action groups favoring increased citizen participation in revenue sharing decisions, stricter enforcement of the civil rights provisions of the act, and more spending for the poor and minorities. The National Urban League, the United Way of America, and the National Association of Social Workers fall into this category. Several of these organizations have joined in coalitions at the national and local levels to oppose, or at least basically change, the revenue sharing program.[4] Typical of responses from organizations in this third group was that from the Center for Community Change: "Our affiliates and the other groups with which we work are continuing to try to enforce civil rights regulations, secure greater citizen participation in general revenue sharing decisions, as well as to influence total budget decision-making."

As might be expected, a number of the national organizations polled are involved in similar efforts with regard to block grant programs. One-third of the respondents reported activities having to do with the Comprehensive Employment and Training Act of 1973 (CETA) or with the Community Development Block Grant program under Title I of the Housing and Community Development Act of 1974. The National Council of Senior Citizens, for instance, mailed a brochure to prime sponsors under the CETA program offering its assistance in developing manpower programs for the elderly.

The conclusion to be drawn from these data is that while some national organizations indicated that they have devoted new lobbying efforts to localities that receive revenue sharing, these efforts do not appear to have had a widespread effect, as of June 1974, on the sixty-five units in the Brookings sample.

Effect of Revenue Sharing on Budgetary Processes and Systems

The revenue sharing law includes several requirements relating to the budgetary processes of recipient governments. Recipients must submit annual planned- and actual-use reports to the U.S. Treasury Department;

4. Respondents were asked to provide information as to whether they favored the renewal of revenue sharing. Of the twenty-one groups that reported local efforts to obtain shared revenue, only one supported renewal of the act in "about its present form"; eight favored renewal, but with substantial modifications; five were opposed; six had no position; and one organization did not answer this question.

these reports must be published in a general-circulation newspaper and background information on them must be available for public inspection. Each recipient government is required to set up a trust fund for shared revenue, which must be expended according to the laws applicable to that government's own revenues. Accounts must be kept in order to document compliance with the nonmatching provision and to permit audits showing that revenue sharing expenditures in all other respects are in compliance with the act.

To summarize the Brookings field data, there were few significant changes observed in the areas affected by these provisions. For the first round of the field research, effects were reported for only four jurisdictions. In two cases the associates identified what would have to be considered minor accounting or budget policy changes said to have been brought about by the revenue sharing program. For the two South Carolina counties in the sample, however, the effect was said to be significant. Fairfield County officials reported that they had revised their entire bookkeeping system to ensure compliance with the requirements of the revenue sharing program. Similarly, for Kershaw County the associate said that revenue sharing provided "an impetus for making needed changes in financial operations to improve their coordination and increase their efficiency." In both cases, the associate noted that these relatively small governments, which had previously not received federal aid, were stimulated by the revenue sharing program to develop more systematic financial systems and procedures.

For the second period of the field research, effects of revenue sharing on financial systems and procedures were identified for six jurisdictions.[5] In two of these cases—the town of Greece, New York, and Hamilton County, Ohio—revenue sharing was said to have encouraged the development of a new capital budgeting system. In two other cases, the impact of revenue sharing was found again to have been a result of accounting requirements contained in the law. North Little Rock now issues monthly financial reports on its revenue sharing fund and also on its total cash balances. Seminole County, Florida, established a special budget category for its shared revenue "in order to avoid a two-step appropriations process." Fairfield County, South Carolina, is the only government mentioned in this

5. Data were also collected on the political effects of revenue sharing for the city of Troy, New York, which, although not in the sample, was monitored in 1974 by the New York State associate. In Troy, the city comptroller said that the city's five-year capital budget adopted in 1973 was a "direct result of the advent of revenue sharing." Through July 1974, the city had allocated three-quarters of its shared revenue to new capital uses.

connection in both periods of the field research, although the impact in the second is much less significant than what was reported for the first period. To facilitate the reporting of revenue sharing expenditures, the county in 1974 hired a special consultant to prepare the required Treasury Department reports. Los Angeles County in 1974 allocated $69,000 for a revenue sharing audit "to determine whether private agency requests for shared revenue meet federal guidelines."

Revenue Sharing and Civil Rights

The report form for our field research both in 1973 and 1974 asked associates about civil rights provisions and enforcement in the revenue sharing program.[6] This was also discussed as a major topic at the conference of associates in April 1976. In their field reports, associates were asked to rank the effect of the antidiscrimination provision of the act for each sample unit on a five-point scale—from 0-none to 4-significant. This provision was found to have had a significant effect in only one case (the city of Los Angeles); it was indicated as having had no effect in all but six other jurisdictions, for which it was ranked as 1 ("little" effect).

In the case of Los Angeles, a lawsuit was filed by the U.S. Department of Justice under Title VII of the Civil Rights Act of 1974, charging discriminatory recruitment by the fire department. After a consent decree was entered in June 1974, in which the city agreed to an affirmative action program, a letter was obtained from the director of the Office of Revenue Sharing to the effect that the decree put the city in compliance with the revenue sharing act, and that payments would be continued under this act. (They were never suspended because the city did not contest the suit.) Nevertheless, the city decided in its second budget not to allocate any of these funds to either the police or fire departments. The city administrator stated, "This will provide no hardship whatever to the Fire and Police Departments inasmuch as they will receive exactly the same number of dollars from the General Fund that they otherwise would have received from general revenue sharing funds."

6. See chapter 1 for a discussion of the national debate over revenue sharing and civil rights.

Summary

Few questions are as difficult to answer with any degree of certainty as those dealing with the distribution of power and influence in state and local government and the impact of federal policy on that distribution. The preceding analysis of our field data does not purport to provide a precise accounting of the political net effects of revenue sharing, but it does provide a perspective on this aspect of the program. For approximately one-fifth of the local governments in the sample, there is evidence that revenue sharing has been associated with either a shift in political influence among generalist officials (particularly an increase in the role of local legislatures) or with a relatively competitive decisionmaking process in allocating these funds (especially where interest groups were successful in gaining access to the decisionmaking process).

In the other jurisdictions the political impact of revenue sharing appears to have been less pronounced. For a few of them, particularly at the state level, revenue sharing was reported to have had practically no effect. Among many local governments, traditional patterns of influence, particularly one of executive dominance, characterized decisions about revenue sharing. Yet it would not be correct to conclude that revenue sharing has been politically neutral. In some cases, associates noted that while traditional patterns of influence were maintained, revenue sharing served to further strengthen key actors in the budget process. Moreover, in other jurisdictions, interest groups, while not notably successful in having their demands met, were nevertheless active.

It would seem reasonable to conclude that the expectations of some that there would be a dramatic change in the politics of state and local governments as a result of revenue sharing have not been borne out. At the same time, however, the evidence from our field associates does not support those who expected no political effect, that state and local decisions about revenue sharing would merely be business as usual. There has been some shifting and broadening of political influence, as well as a strengthening in the traditional roles of generalist officials.

What are likely to be the long-term consequences of the political effects described in this chapter? To the extent that fiscal conditions are a determinant of whether and how revenue sharing affects the budgetary process, the effects reported here are most likely to be sustained if the fiscal condition of the jurisdictions involved does not deteriorate. This possibility is clearly illustrated in the case of St. Louis, Missouri. In his first-round report, the associate observed that the roles of generalist officials and interest groups were strengthened by revenue sharing; the funds were allocated in 1973 in a log-rolling fashion after extensive consultations with neighborhood groups, and a variety of capital improvement projects around the city were funded. By round two, however, an already troubled fiscal situation for the city worsened because of inflation and recession, and, according to the associate, "the actors were without a stage; revenue sharing funds simply went into the operating budget to maintain existing programs." However, it is also possible that where outside interest groups have seen their influence increased in the budget process, a worsening fiscal situation may not eliminate all of their gains. Where revenue sharing, perhaps along with one or another of the block grants, has caused interest groups to take a greater interest in the budget process, basic changes in political roles and relationships may be lasting regardless of what happens in the future to revenue sharing funds.

On the other hand, there are also cases in the sample where, as revenue sharing funds become an established source of revenue and are claimed for particular purposes, they lose some of their political impact. In the second period of the field research, the number of units that merged shared revenue into their regular and ongoing budget process rose appreciably. Yet the number of sample units with increases in activity by interest groups in the budget process also rose in the second period.

In the final period of the field research for this study (July 1, 1974 to December 31, 1976), further attention will be given to the determination of the most important and lasting political effects of the revenue sharing program, both for this eighteen-month period and over the duration of this monitoring project.

5 *Structural Effects*

It has become an article of faith among experts on intergovernmental relations that the revenue sharing program, despite its "no strings" rhetoric, is not neutral with respect to the structure of American state and local government. General-purpose units of local government are eligible; special districts are not. All local units of general-purpose government, no matter how small, that are eligible for more than $200 per year can receive payments. Tax receipts are included in the allocation formula in a way that benefits recipient units; user fees are excluded. Early predictions (including some of our own) were that these and similar features of the revenue sharing program would cause it to have a significant impact on the structure of state and local government: that, for example, it would perpetuate the existence of small and limited-function units; that it would discourage the establishment, and perhaps promote the dissolution, of special districts; that it would discourage annexations and mergers; that it would cause user taxes paid to special districts to be reassigned, sometimes along with the pertinent functions, to general-purpose units; that it would discourage intergovernmental cooperation among local units; and that it would cause state governments to reduce the level of their financial support to local units.[1]

Despite the strength of these and other incentives to structural change, the principal conclusion of our investigation is that they have not been strong enough or clear enough to affect appreciably the behavior of the recipient governments. Although there are several areas in which policy changes were observed that appeared to be at least partly attributable to the revenue sharing program, the structural effects were not strong or widespread. The major areas in which a structural impact of revenue sharing appears involve: a tendency for the program to reinforce and maintain the position of small and limited-function governmental units in rural

1. For a comprehensive discussion of the program's potential effects, see Robert Reischauer "General Revenue Sharing: The Program's Incentives" (Brookings General Series Reprint no. 313, 1976).

(though not urban) areas; a similarly positive, but very modest, effect on decisions on the part of some local units to take on new programs and new functions; and a tendency in some states for revenue sharing to stimulate increased levels of state aid to local governments.

The first and perhaps the most controversial question addressed in this chapter is the extent to which the revenue sharing program has propped up small and limited-function units of local government by encouraging them to expand their operations and functions, or by enabling them to withstand pressures that might otherwise have eliminated or downgraded these units. Second, the broader effect of revenue sharing on the role and relationships of local units is analyzed, particularly in terms of its impact on special districts (their establishment or dissolution), its effect on other proposals for structural modifications (such as annexation and intergovernmental agreements), and its impact on decisions on the adoption of new functions. Third, the chapter examines the impact of revenue sharing on financial relationships between state and local governments.

Has Revenue Sharing Propped Up Small Governments?

The first report on this study of the general revenue sharing program, in discussing the impact of the formula on Midwestern townships and New England counties, concluded that "the revenue sharing law is likely to have a material influence on governmental structure over the course of time."[2] The fact that small and limited-function governments are eligible to receive revenue sharing inevitably constitutes an incentive for their continued existence. Literally thousands of governments that had previously received no federal funds are now eligible to receive revenue sharing, which may amount to a substantial portion of their total budgets. To the extent that the continued existence of these governments is affected by their financial viability, this provision of new money increases their ability to resist abolition. These units receive further preferental treatment from the guarantee to each recipient government of 20 percent of the average statewide per capita grant. While this amount cannot exceed one-half of a unit's total taxes and intergovernmental receipts, any locality that receives only minimal support from other levels of government can count on receiving 50 cents of additional revenue for every dollar it collects in taxes. This

2. Richard P. Nathan, Allen D. Manvel, and Susannah E. Calkins, *Monitoring Revenue Sharing* (Brookings Institution, 1975), p . 308.

incentive is strengthened by two policies of the Office of Revenue Sharing. First, new units do not have to collect taxes in order to receive revenue sharing funds, but instead receive allocations during their first year of operation on the basis of "estimated revenues" derived from the collections of other governments of similar size. Second, there is no incentive for neighboring governments to oppose incorporation, since the funds necessary to bring a unit up to the 20 percent floor do not come from the county area entitlement, but rather from the statewide pool. This means, in effect, that county areas with few governments subsidize those with large numbers of subordinate jurisdictions.[3] Together with the 20 percent floor, these policies create a strong incentive for the retention and even the creation of small governments.

Two points should be made before reviewing the data. One involves the policy issue raised here. Although governmental units below 5,000 population accounted for 80 percent of all recipient units in 1975, they accounted for only 5.03 percent of all revenue sharing payments. In the debate over renewal, the argument was often made that the funds involved are not worth raising an issue on which it was clear that the outcry from local officials would cause formidable problems for proponents of change in this area. The second point is that where this "propping-up" effect occurs, it works against the traditional "good government" or "reform" model which places emphasis on economies of scale and intra-jurisdictional burden-sharing. This model, strongly reflected in the work of the Committee for Economic Development in the 1950s and 1960s and currently urged by many governmental "reform" groups, advocates the reduction of the number of small units and the absorption of their functions by regional governments, both in metropolitan and rural areas. This report does not take a position on this issue. There are, in fact, strong arguments to be made on the other side. The so-called public choice theory of governmental structure is often used to support the retention of small units, and, as discussed in the next section, the retention or establishment of special districts.

REVENUE SHARING AND INCORPORATION ACTIONS

As table 5-1 demonstrates, the number of cities has increased at a slightly higher rate since the advent of revenue sharing, but a previously existing downtrend in the number of townships has accelerated since

3. Reischauer, "General Revenue Sharing," p. 76.

Table 5-1. Number of Units of General-Purpose Local Government, 1962–74

Type of government	Number of governments, 1962	Number of governments, 1967	Average annual change, 1962–67	Number of governments, 1972	Average annual change, 1967–72	Number of governments, 1974	Average annual change, 1972–74
Counties	3,043	3,049	1	3,044	−1	3,043	0
Municipalities	18,000	18,048	10	18,517	94	18,776	130
Townships	17,142	17,105	−7	16,991	−3	16,940	−26

Source: U.S. Bureau of the Census, *1972 Census of Governments*, vol. 1: *Governmental Organization* (GPO, 1973), p. 1, and unpublished information from the Bureau of the Census.

1972.[4] Overall, there has been a slight increase in the number of new governmental units since the adoption of revenue sharing, but almost half of these new units were incorporated in a few states, making it difficult to attribute this increase to the onset of revenue sharing.

These data are not conclusive. It is entirely possible that the rate of incorporation would have been lower and the rate of disincorporation higher in the absence of revenue sharing, but data from our sample cannot be used here, since it is impossible to sample units that did not exist when revenue sharing was enacted. Consequently, we address this question with data from three mail surveys which we conducted in the spring of 1975. Surveys were conducted of state departments of local government and local boundary commissions to ascertain, among other things, the influence of revenue sharing on incorporation rates within their jurisdictions. A separate survey was conducted of forty local governments that incorporated between July 1973 and December 1974.[5] The results of these surveys are reported in tables 5-2 and 5-3. While a majority of incorporation advocates and officials of new governments were described as being aware of the program's existence, few respondents indicated that it had strongly encouraged the formation of new governments.

4. Preliminary census figures suggest that the rate of incorporation for cities slowed appreciably in 1974 and 1975. See Richard Forstall, "Annexations and Corporate Changes 1970–1974," *Municipal Yearbook 1976* (Washington: International City Management Association, 1976), p. 60, and idem, "Annexation and Corporate Changes, 1970–1975," *Municipal Yearbook 1977* (forthcoming).

5. Local boundary agencies are quasi-judicial bodies, concentrated in western states, that are charged with responsibility for reviewing and approving annexations, incorporations, or other changes in local boundaries. For details, see Advisory Commission on Intergovernmental Relations, *The Challenge of Local Governmental Reorganization* (1974), pp. 86–91. The local government survey was sent to all new units with a population greater than 1,000 and to a 10 percent sample of smaller governments. Twenty-eight responses were received; nonrespondents were concentrated in the smaller size category.

Table 5-2. Effect of Revenue Sharing on Incorporation, by Type of Respondent

Respondent	Revenue sharing strongly encourages incorporation	Revenue sharing encourages but is not major factor	No effect
State agencies (*n* = 43)	2	11	31
Boundary agencies (*n* = 12)	1	4	7
Local governments (*n* = 28)	7	8	13

Source: Survey data.

Table 5-3. Awareness of Revenue Sharing among Officials of New Governments, by Type of Respondent

Respondent	Local officials very much aware of revenue sharing	Somewhat aware	Not aware
State agencies (*n* = 41)	9	12	19
Boundary agencies (*n* = 11)	6	1	4
Local officials[a] (*n* = 28)	17	. . .	11

Source: Survey data.
a. Questionnaire administered to local officials provided only "aware" and "not aware" categories.

Several reasons were cited for the limited impact of revenue sharing. A number of respondents indicated that the formation of new governments was generally motivated by factors other than financial feasibility, such as local desires to avoid annexation, prevent encroachment on tax bases by other governments, or improve the level of services. Financing arrangements in general and revenue sharing in particular appear to have been considered only after the decision to incorporate had been made. The executive officer of a California boundary commission illustrates this sequence of events: "Those . . . who advocate incorporation generally do so for more emotional reasons . . . They would be more likely to advocate incorporation for land use and zoning considerations . . . We require proponents of each incorporation to give us a two year proposed budget. This happens last in the procedures . . . and is generally done to substantiate conclusions rather than to be the leading argument for the change. . . ."

Local respondents generally isolated one of the above factors as the primary reason for incorporation. The mayor of one Oregon city, for example, indicated that inadequate services were the primary motivation for incorporation: "A high ground water table was causing much septic system failure, which created health hazards and the possible degradation of our lakes. Rapid growth compounded our problems. Our law enforcement came from 50 miles away. Streets were maintained only at the whim of the individual property owner and were often near impassable for emergency services. Other needed community services were lacking. The creation of another special service district would not aid in a total solution."

Revenue sharing appears to have been explicitly considered in a limited number of incorporations, and then only after the basic decision to incorporate had already been made. Several respondents indicated that its influence was further diluted by the fact that new governments became eligible, upon incorporation, to receive funds from a number of state programs. All but ten states operate some form of revenue or tax sharing program with local governments. A smaller number of states also provide property tax reimbursement to individuals living in incorporated areas, so that new governments can levy taxes up to the amount of the reimbursement without increasing the net local tax burden. These payments, both direct and indirect, provide more resources nationally than revenue sharing. State general support payments to local governments amounted to $4.6 billion during 1974–75, compared to $4.2 billion in general revenue sharing payments from the federal government to local units in the same period. The resources available to a new government from the state can amount to several times that available from revenue sharing. As an extreme example, a new municipal government in Wisconsin that received the mean per capita payment of both general revenue sharing and state programs would receive $14.25 per capita in shared revenue and $78.75—over five times as much—from the state.[6] Revenue sharing thus does not constitute the only, or even the most significant, source of outside funding for newly incorporated governments.

The extent to which revenue sharing has perpetuated the existence of small and limited-function governments, either by removing incentives to disincorporate or by providing substantial amounts of new money and hence an incentive to engage in new functions, is more difficult to assess since it is impossible to identify units that were considering dissolution but had not initiated formal disincorporation procedures. To the extent, however, that communities wish to maintain the protection of land use and local autonomy, generally identified in our survey as the major reasons for incorporation, their financial viability will be more or less irrelevant to disincorporation decisions. This should be particularly true for small sub-

6. U.S. Bureau of the Census, *Taxes and Intergovernmental Revenue of Counties, Municipalities, and Townships: 1974–75* (1976), tables 3, 4.

urban governments, which wish to avoid annexation by cities. While it is possible that the availability of revenue sharing postponed the dissolution of some governments, its impact has probably been limited.

SMALL-GOVERNMENT EXPENDITURES AND FUNCTIONS

The impact of revenue sharing on the range of activities supported by smaller governments is potentially more significant, as the program provides a strong incentive for these governments to expand their levels both of taxation and expenditures.[7] This is because the formula provisions and differences in the financial conditions of recipients mean that revenue sharing represents a greater increase in discretionary resources for smaller governments than for larger units. Shared revenue generally provides a larger fraction of total revenue to small governments than to large ones, and can generally be shown to produce an even larger disparity in revenue growth and "untied" revenue. The magnitude of this disparity is shown for the units in our sample in table 5-4. In sum, the combination of this bias in distribution and the general tendency for the budgets of larger governments to be under greater financial and political pressure than those of smaller units indicates that revenue sharing represents a more significant resource, both in absolute and marginal terms, for officials of smaller governments than it does for those of larger units.

Another difference between small and large governments is that many smaller governments typically provide only a limited range of services. As many observers have noted, townships, especially in the Midwest, often provide only road maintenance and, in some cases, general (welfare) assistance; counties in many states do no more than operate local courts and employ a sheriff.[8] Even small municipal governments, which provide a broader range of services, tend to spend less money per capita and have fewer employees relative to population than larger city governments.[9]

This combination of increased resources and a limited functional base

7. The following is drawn from Reischauer, "General Revenue Sharing," pp. 82–86.

8. See Comptroller General of the United States, *Revenue Sharing Fund Impact on Midwestern Townships and New England Counties* (General Accounting Office, 1976), for a detailed discussion of functional responsibilities of these units. See also Nathan, Manvel, and Calkins, *Monitoring Revenue Sharing*, chapter 11.

9. For expenditure data, see Bureau of the Census, *1972 Census of Governments*, vol. 4: *Finances of Municipalities and Township Governments*, table 16, p. 35. For employment data, see ibid., vol. 3: *Compendium of Public Employment*, table 20, p. 342.

Table 5-4. Shared Revenue (Fiscal 1975) as a Percent of Own-Source General Revenue (Fiscal 1973), for Sample Local Governments, by Population Group

Population group	Shared revenue as percent of own-source general revenue	Number
Under 50,000	17.4	19
50,000–100,000	11.1	15
100,000–500,000	11.8	11
500,000–1,000,000	8.3	9
Over 1,000,000	6.4	3
All	12.7	57

Source: Shared revenue, estimates of entitlement period 5 entitlements in Office of Revenue Sharing, *Payment Summary, Entitlement Periods 1-4, with Period 5 Estimate* (ORS, 1974). Own-source general revenue, U.S. Bureau of the Census, *City Government Finances in 1972–73*, (GPO, 1974) table 5; idem, *Governmental Finances in 1972–73* (GPO, 1974), table 17; and unpublished data from the Census Bureau.

would appear to create a strong incentive for smaller governments to expand their activities into new functional areas. Likewise, the displacement of existing expenditures in order to provide tax relief or divert dollars to other uses would be expected to be more difficult for small units, since few accounts are large enough to absorb an increase of the size of the revenue sharing payments received without an expansion in real terms in these functional areas. Use of shared revenue to provide tax relief is discouraged for these units if they are affected by the 50 percent ceiling in the formula, since they can receive an additional fifty cents in shared revenue for each additional dollar they raise in taxes. These practical considerations suggest that the most likely response to revenue sharing would be an expansion either in the number of activities supported or in the level of support provided to functions that previously received relatively little attention and money.

The data from our sample units indicates that the response of small units to this incentive to spend in new areas, while not negligible, has been limited. The two Wisconsin townships (both under 2,000 population) were described by the field associate as "road maintenance districts"; both spent all of their shared revenue on this function. One purchased a higher quality of resurfacing mix; the other bought a dump truck with its first two years of shared revenue. More generally, the evidence developed in the fiscal effects analysis in chapter 2 suggests that smaller governments were unwilling to allocate shared revenue to operating programs or to allocate funds to new programs. Smaller units were found to be especially sensitive to the revenue sharing program's limited life span and to be more likely to adopt special procedures for allocating shared revenue to ensure its use for nonrecurring expenditures. This concern with the possibility of expiration appears to have reinforced a general propensity to spend shared revenue on capital intensive functions, such as transportation and sewage, which have historically composed the dominant share of the budgets of small governments. While some smaller governments did allocate shared revenue to program areas that had traditionally received little support, most limited their support to capital projects. Pulaski County, Arkansas, for example, allocated 15 percent of its shared revenue for recreation facilities, which the associate described as "one of the few efforts in recent years by the county to provide social services except at the welfare level." The associate also noted that the county was careful to avoid committing its own funds to the facilities: "the recreational facilities have been built for the most part in those communities where there is an assurance of a local citizen group which would maintain the facilities. The recreational facilities have been in the nature of parks, picnic tables, basketball courts, and similar low maintenance items. No substantial structures of any nature have been built."

Actions on the part of smaller governments to expand their activities was noted by the associates in two states. The most widely publicized case was that of townships in Illinois. Before revenue sharing, Illinois townships were responsible only for road maintenance and the provision of general welfare assistance. When these functions proved incapable of absorbing the large increase represented by revenue sharing, the Illinois Legislature enacted a statute allowing townships to spend both local and shared revenue for service contracts in any of the priority areas specified in the 1972 revenue sharing act. The associate noted that most townships have been unwilling to spend their own funds on new services: "One [major use] has been for townships to enter into contracts with private providers. These contracts, for example, are for items such as ambulance services and transportation for the rural aged. These are annual contracts or two year contracts and expire close to the anticipated termination of the present revenue sharing act. A second move for townships . . . has been to enter into cooperative agreements with municipalities, again with a specific and limited time period. In many cooperative agreements, projects are identified as having been funded with revenue sharing funds." Increased activity by limited-function governments was also noted by the Maine associate, who indicated that some county governments had used shared revenue to establish grant-in-aid programs or cooperative agreements with municipalities.

To summarize, the strong incentive provided by revenue sharing for small governments to expand the scope and level of their activities seems to have been largely neutralized by uncertainty about the program's continued existence. This uncertainty apparently reinforced a general unwillingness on the part of local officials to move into new program areas, and thus to have caused smaller governments to allocate shared revenue to capital expenditures for traditional functions, such as roads and sewage. Now that the revenue sharing program has been extended to 1980, however, the incentive to expand may be felt more strongly, as smaller governments become less uncertain about the program's future and come to regard it as part of their normal operating budgets.

IMPACT ON GOVERNMENTAL "MODERNIZATION"

The most controversial issue of revenue sharing for small governments has been its effects on the "modernization" of local government. Advocates of governmental and functional consolidation have argued that revenue sharing has served to shore up small and allegedly inefficient governments in instances where consolidation or the transfer of functions to higher levels of government was becoming more attractive. To the extent that the attractiveness was the result of increasing financial pressure, revenue sharing can be held to have undercut or delayed consolidation efforts and perpetuated the fragmentation of local government.

The strength of this disincentive to governmental streamlining is difficult to assess. If the results of the incorporation survey can be generalized, its impact appears to be limited, since local attitudes toward consolidation appear to be quite independent of financial considerations. On the other hand, the reformers' argument could hold in a sizable number of places, where smaller units have withdrawn from cooperative agreements or deferred functional consolidation and financed programs independently as a result of revenue sharing. Further, the availability of revenue sharing may have strengthened the arguments of smaller governments against consolidation attempts at the state level.

The reports of our field associates tend to support the first interpretation. Although active reform movements at the state and local level were noted by a number of associates, revenue sharing was felt to have had a deleterious effect on these efforts in only two places—Illinois and South Dakota, where the associates indicated that revenue sharing had impeded efforts to reduce the number of townships, particularly in rural areas. The

Illinois associate pointed to the expanded expenditure authority assigned to townships as a direct consequence of revenue sharing. The South Dakota associate maintained that revenue sharing caused many rural townships in that state to pull back from entering into joint activities with county governments, particularly in the cooperative use of road maintenance equipment.[10] The South Dakota associate also cited a retreat from what had been an emerging trend prior to revenue sharing for the state to establish multipurpose regional districts to provide services to rural areas. In conclusion he stated that "the recognition of townships by the present revenue sharing program and its effect in alleviating any financial crunch they face, and that might have compelled change, results in revenue sharing serving as an impediment to the restructuring of these governments."

This adverse impact of revenue sharing on governmental modernization appears to be limited to rural areas. None of the associates for urban areas identified ongoing or nascent modernization efforts that were frustrated even marginally by the availability of revenue sharing funds.

In the debate over the extension of the general revenue sharing program, this issue of governmental modernization, especially as it applies to small and limited-function units, was raised at a number of points. The House Subcommittee on Intergovernmental Relations attempted to limit revenue sharing payments to governments with more than one function, using complex procedures for classifying local expenditures according to fourteen functional categories. But this provision was not adopted by the Senate, and the House language was deleted in conference, essentially on the grounds that it was unworkable. More specifically, an amendment requiring state and local governments to have modernization plans as a condition of receiving shared revenue was added by the full House Committee on Government Operations, but deleted on the House floor.[11]

Structural Impact on Urban Units

Although the structural impact of revenue sharing has been felt principally by small governments in rural areas, we are interested also in its effect on urban areas. The incentives provided by revenue sharing to an individual government are examined here in relation to four possible kinds of structural modifications: the use of special districts, annexation, the

10. See appendix A for additional information on this point.
11. See chapter 1, pp. 18–19.

provision of new services, and cooperative agreements with other units. The analysis is based on data from the associates' reports and from the surveys of state and boundary officials.

THE USE OF SPECIAL DISTRICTS

Revenue sharing provides a disincentive to the use of special districts to perform functions that could be provided by a general-purpose government. Since special districts are not eligible to receive shared revenue, a government that establishes one forgoes receiving credit for any taxes assessed by the district and, if it is constrained by the 50 percent ceiling, credit for any intergovernmental grants the district receives. On the other hand, a government can gain credit for special-district taxes or grants by exercising sufficient supervision of special districts within its borders to meet the census definition of a "dependent" district; and local governments can claim credit for the taxes levied by such districts for the purpose of computing their shared-revenue allocation. There is a moderately strong incentive, therefore, for local governments to create fewer special districts and to absorb, or at least to expand their control over, existing special districts. While the potential gain from such action may vary widely, some governments can increase their tax revenue substantially thereby.

The evidence to date suggests that the impact of revenue sharing on the use of special districts has been limited. None of the field associates reported any change in the rate of formation of special districts or any tendency for these districts to be absorbed. The assessments of state and boundary agency officials are presented in tables 5-5 and 5-6; both sets of officials report overwhelmingly that revenue sharing had little impact on either the creation or abolition of special districts. Awareness of the relevance of revenue sharing to this issue, while lower than that for incorporation, appears to be moderate, particularly with regard to the formation of new districts. A small number of respondents reported that the potential loss of revenue sharing was being regularly considered by governments contemplating the formation of new districts. Awareness of the potential gains from abolishing existing districts was more limited. Two respondents reported that revenue sharing had actually discouraged the abolition of special districts, since revenue sharing funds can be used to purchase services from such districts. There were scattered reports that individual governments had filed appeals with the Census Bureau to clarify the dependent

Table 5-5. Effect of Revenue Sharing on Creation and Abolition of Special Districts

Respondent	Revenue sharing strongly encourages	Revenue sharing encourages	Revenue sharing discourages	Revenue sharing has no impact
	Creation of special districts			
State officials (*n* = 40)	0	1	6	33
Boundary agency (*n* = 12)	0	1	0	11
	Abolition of special districts			
State officials (*n* = 41)	2	3	2	34
Boundary agency (*n* = 12)	0	1	0	11

Source: Survey data.

Table 5-6. Awareness among Local Officials of Relevance of Revenue Sharing for Creation and Abolition of Special Districts

Respondent	Very much aware	Somewhat aware	Not aware
	Creation of special districts		
State officials (*n* = 35)	6	6	23
Boundary agency (*n* = 12)	4	3	5
	Abolition of special districts		
State officials (*n* = 35)	4	4	27
Boundary agency (*n* = 12)	3	6	3

Source: Survey data.

status of particular districts within their borders, but exploitation of the potential gain from absorbing or supervising existing districts appears to have been minimal. The respondent from Florida, for example, said that the state had passed legislation allowing counties to review and approve the budgets of special districts within their borders, but noted that no counties had taken advantage of this legislation as of mid-1974.

There are a number of explanations for this limited effect. One would appear to be a low level of awareness among local officials, at least initially, of the impact of special districts on local revenue sharing allocations. Perhaps more important is the limited amount of revenue that most jurisdictions would realize from absorbing coterminous or underlying districts. While particular jurisdictions may be able to increase their tax effort substantially, the potential gains to the average jurisdiction are relatively modest, since a considerable majority of special districts finance the bulk of their operations through a combination of user charges and grants and rely on property taxes very little, if at all. According to census figures, property tax collections by special districts amounted to $919 million in 1971–72, which represents less than 15 percent of all special-district revenues and less than 5 percent of property tax collections by general-purpose local governments. Over half of this revenue was collected by districts in three states—California, Texas, and Illinois.[12]

A number of potential political and legal problems may have reduced the willingness of local officials to attempt to realize even this modest gain. Many special districts have been created either to evade state limits on the debts and taxes of local governments or to avoid the use of local tax revenue to guarantee bonds. Absorption would cause local governments to forfeit the advantages gained from special-district financing. Furthermore, many special districts have been created as the result of other federal programs, such as soil and water conservation, mass transit, public housing and urban renewal, and health. Attempts to absorb these districts may have been perceived as impractical because of potential problems with federal officials. In addition, the governing bodies of many districts are elected, which may have made local officials unwilling to risk the controversy that could arise from an attempt to exert public control over special-district operations.[13] While we have no evidence to indicate the extent of these problems, they provide plausible explanations for the limited response to what would appear to be a relatively strong incentive effect of the revenue sharing program.

IMPACT ON ANNEXATION

The incentives offered by revenue sharing for local governments to annex additional territory can be characterized as less strong and more uncertain than those against the use of special districts.[14] If a unit is not affected by either of the floor or ceiling limitations, the impact of annexation on its allocations will be dependent on the size of the population in the annexed area and the increase in taxes realized from the annexation.[15]

The incentive to annex is weakened by Treasury Department regulations that prevent any government from increasing its allocation through

12. U.S. Bureau of the Census, *1972 Census of Governments*, vol. 4: *Finances of Special Districts*, table 4, p. 12.

13. For a discussion of these factors, see Advisory Commission on Intergovernmental Relations, *Regional Decision Making: New Strat gies for Substate Districts* (1973), chapter 2.

14. Reischauer, "General Revenue Sharing," p. 78.

15. It is possible for the effect of increased population to be offset by an increase in the per capita income level of an annexing jurisdiction or a decrease in its tax effort. However, if it is affected by the 20 percent floor or 145 percent ceiling, it will be assured an increase from annexation.

Table 5-7. Characteristics of Annexations in Cities over 2,500 Population, 1970–75

Characteristic of annexation	1970	1971	1972	1973	1974	1975
Estimated area (square miles)	663.5	924.9	965.5	930.0	800.0	550.0
Estimated population (thousands)	256	359	539	300	300	220

Source: 1970–73, U.S. Bureau of the Census, *Boundary and Annexation Survey* 1970–1973 (GPO, 1975), table 3, pp. 10-13; 1974–75, Richard Forstall "Annexation and Corporate Changes, 1970–1975," 1977 *Municipal Yearbook* (Washington: International City Management Association, forthcoming).

annexation until the population in annexed areas amounts to 5 percent of the population of the annexing unit. While not conclusive, census figures suggest that the majority of individual annexations fail to produce population changes of this magnitude. The average area annexed in 1973, for example, contained only forty-six residents.[16]

Perhaps more important, any gain in revenue sharing allocations may be offset, either wholly or in part, by the cost of extending services to the annexed area. If the area requires such capital-intensive services as water and sewage connections, the net cost of the annexation may exceed the increase in revenue sharing by a large amount.

Available evidence on the effect of revenue sharing on annexation is mixed. Nationally, the amount of annexation activity declined over the life of the program, as shown in table 5-7. Both the total area and population annexed declined substantially between 1972, when the program was adopted, and 1975. The importance of revenue sharing to the annexations that did take place is more difficult to assess.

Tables 5-8 and 5-9 present survey data gathered from state and boundary agency officials, supplemented by a survey of local governments that added large amounts of territory through annexation between 1970 and 1973.[17] The assessments of the two groups are quite different. State and boundary agency officials report high levels of both awareness and activity, while local officials report much less awareness and no annexation activity at all as a result of revenue sharing. Large annexers generally cited

16. This is the average population gain for individual annexations for cities of over 2,500 population. See U.S. Bureau of the Census, *Boundary and Annexation Survey*, series GE 30-1 (GPO, 1975), p. 10.

17. The local government survey was sent to the fifty municipalities that added the largest amount of territory through annexation between 1970 and 1973. Thirty-six questionnaires were returned; the twenty-five cases reported in tables 5-8 and 5-9 are those reporting annexations in 1973 or 1974.

Table 5-8. Effect of Revenue Sharing on Annexation, by Type of Respondent

Respondent	Revenue sharing strongly encourages annexation	Revenue sharing encourages, but is not major factor	Revenue sharing discourages	No effect
State officials	2	12	2	25
Boundary agencies	0	4	0	8
Local officials	0	0	0	25

Source: Survey data.

Table 5-9. Awareness of Local Officials of Revenue Sharing Impact on Annexation, by Type of Respondent

Respondent	Very much aware	Somewhat aware	Not aware
State officials ($n = 40$)	15	13	12
Boundary agencies ($n = 13$)	7	4	2
Local officials[a] ($n = 25$)	6	...	19

Source: Survey data.
a. Questionnaire administered to local officials provided only "aware" and "not aware" categories.

liberal state laws and increased service needs as the major reasons for annexation. The response from Austin, Texas, provides an illustration of the way in which other cost considerations can offset the impact of the federal revenue sharing program on annexation decisions. "Areas which are annexed are usually developed only sparsely. While revenue sharing is an important source of funds, the costs of providing principal services together with an effective decrease in the water and wastewater rate more than offset the small increase in revenue sharing receipts. Therefore the effect of revenue sharing has not been considered a factor one way or the other in the decision to annex."

It is difficult to explain the relatively higher levels of awareness and effect reported by state and boundary agency (both state and local) officials as compared to that reported by local officials with significant annexation actions. One possible explanation is that state and boundary agency officials may be reacting to annexation activity on the part of units not eligible for our sample because they were not among the fifty municipalities that added the largest amount of territory through annexation between 1970 and 1973. A second explanation is that in some cases revenue sharing may have encouraged annexation not by raising the possibility of additional revenue but rather by providing resources to finance services to newly annexed areas. This use of shared revenue was reported in Little

Rock, Arkansas, the only unit in the sample to undertake a major annexation during the monitoring period. The associate observed: "Two million dollars in revenue sharing was set aside to be used for capital improvements in the annexation area, particularly for fire stations and also for other purposes, such as a police substation and some road improvements. That $2 million was the carrot they put out in front of the citizens to get them to go along with the annexation. The city clearly could not have committed to those service and capital improvements if it had not been for revenue sharing."[18]

This speculation is supported by the widespread use of annexation by suburban governments to provide basic services such as water and sewage to newly developed areas, whose demands for these services exceed the capacity of existing special districts. Residents of these areas frequently petition adjacent municipalities to annex them in order to receive services. By providing these governments with additional resources, revenue sharing may have made them more receptive to such petitions.[19]

In sum, we did not observe an appreciable increase in annexation actions attributable to an incentive effect created by the general revenue sharing program. Annexation decisions tend to be influenced by noneconomic factors in many cases, but at the same time the additional resources provided by the revenue sharing program may in some cases (as in Little Rock) facilitate annexation actions.

EFFECT ON THE ADOPTION OF NEW FUNCTIONS

The incidence of spending for new functions, and particularly "innovative" spending, has been the target of considerable criticism by opponents of revenue sharing. Conservatives have charged that the program encourages recipient jurisdictions to undertake new activities that may be marginal or unnecessary; liberals, on the other hand, have argued that shared revenue has not been devoted in sufficient measure to new functions and innovative uses. In this section, we examine the new functions and programs that have been funded with shared revenue and the reasons and motivation for the decisions behind them.

For the two years covered by the field research, thirteen jurisdictions were found to have used shared revenue either to begin new functions or

18. For a complete description of the Little Rock annexation, see appendix A, pp. 203–06.

19. ACIR, *The Challenge of Local Government Reorganization*, pp. 84ff.

Table 5-10. Shared Revenue Used to Fund New Programs, 1973 and 1974

Jurisdiction	Program area(s) funded	Cumulative percentage of allocations for new programs	Financial pressure[a]
Counties			
Kershaw, S.C.	Recreation	30.9	Light
Orange, N.C.	Environmental protection	28.6	Moderate
Fairfield, S.C.	Public safety	14.7	Moderate
Harford, Md.	Public safety	2.3	Light
Seminole, Fla.	Public safety	4.2	Light
Pulaski, Ark.	Recreation	10.1	Light
Hamilton, Ohio	Street beautification, restoration	3.8	None
Los Angeles, Calif.	Transit subsidy	16.9	Moderate
Monroe, N.Y.	Transportation	3.9	Light
Cities			
Phoenix, Ariz.	Recreation, social services	6.2	Light
Eugene, Oreg.	Housing	4.3	Moderate
Little Rock, Ark.	Art center, health	3.8	Moderate
Bangor, Maine	Social services, public safety	6.1	Moderate

Source: Field research data.

a. Cumulative financial pressure ratings are for the two periods of field observations; in cases where the average fell between two levels, the higher of the two levels was used.

to finance discrete new programs in existing functional areas. These jurisdictions are listed in table 5-10, together with the appropriate functional area, the cumulative allocations of shared revenue for new programs, and the jurisdiction's financial pressure rating. The amounts of shared revenue allocated for new functions and new programs, as coded for this analysis, are relatively small in comparison to the total amount of revenue sharing allocated by the thirteen sample units: on an unweighted mean basis, these allocations account for 11 percent of total shared-revenue allocations.

Revenue sharing, as already suggested, has not caused large numbers of small governments to appreciably expand the scope of their activities. Only two jurisdictions that used shared revenue to finance new functions and programs have fewer than 50,000 residents (Kershaw and Fairfield Counties, South Carolina), and only one of these governments (Kershaw) used revenue sharing funds for a completely new functional area.

Our findings suggest that spending for new functions and programs is a product of both the financial condition of the recipient unit and the political orientation of its leaders. The analysis of fiscal effects in chapter 2 indicates that jurisdictions under serious fiscal pressure used their shared revenue more heavily for substitution, as opposed to new, purposes. Even in cases where fiscal conditions were not judged to be adverse, local officials in many cases adopted a conservative attitude toward the use of shared revenue, reflected in the allocation of these funds to tax stabilization or capital projects in established functional areas.

The jurisdictions in our sample that allocated shared revenue for new functions or programs were units in which there was both a lack of fiscal pressure and the presence of political leadership interested in initiating new programs. In four of the thirteen cases shown in table 5-10, the dominant actors in revenue sharing decisions appear to have been local officials interested in the idea of using shared revenue to engage in new activities. This was most clearly noted in Eugene, Oregon. The associate indicated that several members of the city council were interested in seeing the city provide additional social services for the poor and disadvantaged and took the opportunity presented by revenue sharing to fund programs in this area. A similar situation was reported in Los Angeles County, where the associate noted that "revenue sharing provided an activist county board of supervisors with the means to exercise more visible power." In this case, too, social services were a major new use of shared revenue, involving grants by the county to various social agencies and also to the rapid transit district to subsidize bus fares. This interest on the part of local officials in the use of shared revenue to expand the scope of local governmental services was also noted, but to a lesser extent, in Little Rock, Arkansas and Hamilton County, Ohio.

In three other governments, the development of new programs was associated with high levels of interest group activity. In Bangor, Maine, and Phoenix, Arizona, this activity was directed toward securing the use of shared revenue to replace cutbacks in federal social service programs, previously not a city function. The Bangor associate noted that social service groups were motivated to seek shared revenue by a state law encouraging social agencies that had lost federal funds to seek replacement funds from local governments and providing state funds to match local funds.

The remaining six cases are more complex. All are southern counties, and all but one (Fairfield, South Carolina) encompass suburban areas. These counties have traditionally provided a fairly limited range of services, largely public safety and a number of state-financed social service programs. Two of the southern associates noted that increased suburbanization had produced pressure on these units to expand their services to include such "urban" services as environmental protection and garbage collection. The South Carolina associate reported that county government had been restructured to allow it to provide a large number of urban services. He also noted that "county councils in South Carolina are beginning to take themselves more seriously. The word 'policy' is not alien anymore. There has been a fairly dramatic growth in the number of professional administrators and managers hired by county governments." In Orange County, North Carolina, the associate reported that it was the requirements of the state that led the county to establish a new sanitary landfill.

The southern associates also reported long-term political changes in several counties. The Arkansas and Florida associates noted that established county political coalitions were beginning to be challenged by civil rights groups and other social action groups, even before revenue sharing came on the scene, leading to increased competitiveness in the political process.

This combination of structural and political change suggests that the role of revenue sharing is somewhat less significant in these places than in the other seven cases where funds were allocated in a relatively stable institutional and political environment. While the availability of shared revenue may have made it easier for these governments to respond to new demands for an increased range and level of services, it is quite likely that they would have been provided even without revenue sharing. Revenue sharing thus appears to have accelerated the rate at which these demands were fulfilled, rather than being instrumental in their creation, as in the other jurisdictions.

Aside from the six southern counties, there are seven jurisdictions where revenue sharing is related to the adoption of new functions. The mean percentage of shared revenue so allocated is, again, relatively low—6.4 percent for these seven units. Furthermore, in at least two of these cases, a major determinant of the decision to undertake new functions and fund new programs was the reduction in previous federal grants, which encouraged municipal governments in particular to enter the social service field, previously an exclusive state and county function. All of this suggests that we have not had, at least in our sample, a blossoming of new governmental activity caused by revenue sharing. Perhaps this reflects a generally conservative orientation on the part of state and local governments in this period as well as conditions of fiscal stringency, which if not actually present for a particular unit, were nevertheless widely publicized and perceived in the period in which the revenue sharing program was getting underway.

REVENUE SHARING AND INTERGOVERNMENTAL COOPERATION

There is no direct incentive to the revenue sharing program for local governments to use shared funds to participate in cooperative arrangements with neighboring governments. In fact, there has been considerable speculation by proponents of municipal reform that revenue sharing would reduce the willingness of many governments in urban areas to participate in cooperative activity and lessen the power of metropolitan governmental institutions, such as councils of governments and federal planning and review systems. By making local governments better able to go it alone, these critics say, revenue sharing delays the formation of more comprehensive regional institutions.

Generally speaking, our findings do not support this prediction. Revenue sharing was found in a number of cases to stimulate intergovernmental cooperation, although these ventures for the most part have been in program areas where cooperation was already widely practiced. Altogether, fourteen jurisdictions, or about one-quarter of the local units in our sample, allocated shared revenue for cooperative programs with other governments or to make payments to other governments for the provision of services. These cases reflect considerable variation, in both the functions and the structural arrangements involved. Lane County and the city of Eugene, Oregon, used shared revenue to establish a joint social services program involving private agencies; they also set up a special budget process to plan on a combined basis for the allocation of revenue sharing funds. Minnehaha County and the city of Sioux Falls, South Dakota, used shared revenue for the construction of a public safety building. Although the building is a county facility, the city has been allocated space and is committed to pay a corresponding portion of the construction and related operating costs.

Orange County and Chapel Hill, North Carolina, used shared revenue to jointly build and operate a sanitary landfill. Kershaw County and Camden, South Carolina, established a cooperative recreation program with revenue sharing funds. Pulaski County, Little Rock, and North Little Rock, Arkansas, used shared revenue to establish a regional public transportation authority. In fact, transportation emerged in the 1974 data as the main functional area for intergovernmental cooperation out of revenue sharing funds. The use of county shared revenue for new spending for intergovernmental transportation purposes in 1974 was also reported for Monroe County, New York, Los Angeles County, California, and Lane County, Oregon.

The associate for Monroe County and Rochester, New York, reported that the county allocated revenue sharing funds to the regional transportation system for the Rochester area, "marking the first time that the county has participated directly in joint financing with the Transit Authority of current operations." Monroe County also allocated shared revenue in 1974 to the Rochester school district for health units in inner-city schools.

The associate for Los Angeles County reported in 1974 that revenue sharing funds have been used for several joint ventures. Los Angeles County appropriated revenue sharing funds to the Rapid Transit District (a multicounty special district) to subsidize transit fares; "in effect, this program is a voluntary payment made to another level of government. The county has no jurisdiction over transportation." As in the case of Monroe County, Los Angeles County also appropriated revenue sharing funds in 1974 to the Los Angeles City school district to fund a drop-out prevention program and a special project to enable the schools to use the county's swimming pools. Historically, Los Angeles County has been a leader in promoting joint agreements and programs. The associate reports that revenue sharing has aided and abetted this process: "Joint powers agreements in the past have provided several examples of inter-governmental cooperation; the County and City of Los Angeles have consolidated some functions already, notably health care. But functional consolidation discussion has picked up in the past year in the areas of beach operations, consumer affairs, and airports. Revenue sharing funds make it easier for the county to accept the fiscal responsibility for these kinds of activities."

If cooperation is a prerequisite to more comprehensive regional approaches to urban problems, then revenue sharing has made a contribution to urban reform by stimulating local governments to participate in joint ventures and to coordinate their efforts more closely. Some observers of the urban scene, however, have argued that cooperation on relatively routine and noncontroversial matters does not represent a willingness to cooperate on more controversial issues, and in fact, may impede it by reducing the strength of arguments for more comprehensive kinds of cooperative arrangements.[20] What are the respective merits of these two points of view?

20. The argument that cooperation in noncontroversial areas may produce cooperation on controversial areas is made in a number of sources. See Matthew Holden "The Governance of the Metropolitan Area as a Problem in Diplomacy,"

An examination of the cooperative arrangements in our sample metropolitan areas indicates a wide level and variety of intergovernmental activity. This is not surprising; a recent ACIR survey indicates that over 60 percent of all cities are party to at least one agreement to receive or provide services to another unit of government. Smaller, but still significant, numbers of governments are parties to agreements for the joint provision of services or other cooperative activities, such as joint construction and leasing agreements or arrangements for the loan of personnel or equipment.[21] Participation in multigovernmental arrangements such as regional special districts is also widespread.

The popularity of these arrangements has a number of sources. They are relatively easy to implement, as they usually do not require voter approval and can be arranged by the governing bodies of the participating jurisdictions. Further, they allow participating governments to take advantage of economies of scale or technological improvements without a large investment of their own funds. A suburban police department, for example, may not have sufficiently large demands for the training of new officers to justify setting up its own training program; contracting with the state police academy provides a good solution.

The functional areas in which these agreements are concentrated are generally noncontroversial program areas perceived as lending themselves readily to "technical and nonpolitical" arrangements. The ACIR survey indicates that most agreements are for the provision of such support services as police and fire training, street lighting, and sewage disposal. Most multijurisdictional special districts provide such basic services as mass transportation, water and sewage.

The absence of cooperative activity in such potentially controversial activities as zoning and education suggests that cooperation may not be a prelude to more comprehensive reform. This conclusion is bolstered by findings from the ACIR survey that few agreements cover the provision of a package of services and that the major obstacle to further cooperation is fear of the loss of local autonomy. The weight of the evidence from our sample suggests that local governments are much less willing to engage in permanent arrangements in politically sensitive areas, which create the potential for controversy and may limit their freedom of action in the

---

Journal of Politics, vol. 26 (August 1964), pp. 627–47; and ACIR *Regional Decision Making*, pp. 34–36. The opposing argument is stated in Oliver Williams, *Metropolitan Political Analysis* (New York: Free Press, 1971), chapter 6.

21. ACIR, *The Challenge of Local Governmental Reorganization*, chapter 3.

future. All of the agreements but one are in relatively noncontroversial areas, such as transportation and sanitation.

To summarize, our data indicate that, contrary to what might have been anticipated, revenue sharing does not seem to have impeded intergovernmental cooperation in urban areas. But, at the same time, it has been in the customary mold of most such arrangements, and has not involved either an observed inducement or impediment to more basic and far-reaching kinds of regional cooperation for multiple or more controversial functions. Nor did our associates find much to suggest that the availability of revenue sharing had handicapped existing regional institutions. The only exception was in South Dakota, where the associate reported that a state attempt to establish a system of substate planning districts had been handicapped because these districts were not eligible to receive shared revenue. Otherwise, there is little evidence to suggest that either new programs or cooperative arrangements would have required the involvement of regional bodies in the absence of revenue sharing.

Revenue Sharing and State Aid

The data on the effect of revenue sharing on state aid to localities reported in the first volume of this study were inconclusive, but the 1974 results give a sharper picture. On balance, revenue sharing appears to have stimulated increased state aid. This is not necessarily the outcome that might have been anticipated. In many cases, the state government's share of total state-local revenues and expenditures is much larger than its one-third share of revenue sharing funds. In states where this disparity is particularly pronounced, state officials might be expected to view revenue sharing as a substitute for growth in their own local aid programs and thus exhibit a marked lack of sympathy to local requests for increased assistance.[22] This attitude was reported to have been prevalent among state officials in New York, Massachusetts, and California. In North Carolina, where the state accounted for nearly three-quarters of total state-local revenue in fiscal 1974 but received only one-third of the shared revenue

22. Actual cuts in state aid presumably were prevented by a maintenance of effort provision in the revenue sharing legislation. Under this provision, states would have their own revenue sharing allocations reduced if they reduce their actual dollar level of support payments to local governments below that of fiscal year 1972.

allocated for the entire state, the associate reported that the revenue sharing formula was regarded as especially unfavorable by state officials. He observed that this situation has "probably made North Carolina officials even less inclined to increase state support for local units."

There are also grounds for expecting that the advent of revenue sharing would cause some state governments to expand major programs, among the largest being their financial aid to localities. Revenue sharing was directly related by the Maine associate to a significant increase in state financial aid for local school districts. Similar observations were made for other states in 1974, both in terms of actions taken and plans considered. The associate for Colorado noted an increase in state grants to local units for such purposes as water and sewer construction and education, which he attributed to revenue sharing. In Arizona our associate reported significantly increased financial assistance to city governments, though it was not directly tied to revenue sharing. Florida, too, is reported to have adopted new grant programs for local units in this period.

Associates also provided less systematic data for four state governments not in our sample (Missouri, South Dakota, New Jersey, and Wisconsin), although local units for these states are included. For Missouri, the St. Louis associate observed increased state aid, primarily to replace federal aid cuts for such purposes as water and sewer systems and housing; these increased payments were directly linked to revenue sharing by the associate. The South Dakota associate reported in 1974 that the entire state allocation of revenue sharing funds had been used for school aid, significantly increasing the level of this assistance. The New Jersey associate also reported increased school aid as a result of revenue sharing. For Wisconsin, it was reported that revenue sharing had resulted in significantly increased state aid to localities and that in 1975 the state was considering picking up most county welfare costs. In two other states (Illinois and Oregon) important changes in state aid programs were said to be under consideration in 1974, in part because of the availability of revenue sharing funds.

Comparing the information provided by the associates in 1973 and 1974, we observe a stronger tendency in the 1974 data for states to increase their financial aid to localities, either directly or indirectly, in response to the adoption of the general revenue sharing program. The largest increase reported was in school aid. A number of associates observed that recent, or anticipated, federal and state court decisions regarding educational equalization were at the root of these decisions.

Revenue Sharing and Governmental "Reform"

The enactment of revenue sharing legislation in 1972 was accompanied by considerable speculation, including our own, to the effect that it would appreciably influence governmental structure. Most of the concern was expressed by proponents of the consolidation model of "good government," apprehensive that revenue sharing would impede regional solutions to public problems and efforts to establish governmental structures on a broader geographical basis. One observer at the time predicted that the availability of shared revenue to small and limited-function units would cause them to spring up "like mushrooms after a rain."[23]

Our investigation has disclosed that the structural impact of revenue sharing has been much more modest than was originally anticipated. While the program provides incentives for local governments to modify the way in which they organize and finance their activities, these incentives have not been substantial enough to induce significant changes in local governmental structure. With the exception of small governments in rural areas, revenue sharing does not appear to have unduly hampered efforts toward governmental "modernization" or to have hindered the activities of regional institutions.

There is some evidence to suggest that the long-term effects of the program may be somewhat more pronounced. Much of the unwillingness of smaller and limited-function governments to use revenue sharing to finance new activities was found to be the result of uncertainty about the program's future. The program's extension until 1980 may remove some of this uncertainty and make officials of smaller governments more willing to use shared revenue to provide new services.

The most significant finding from this research, however, is that revenue sharing does not appear to provide incentives of significant strength to make a substantial impact on the structure of state and local government. The roles and functions of various levels of government appear to be determined by political and economic forces that may be reinforced by revenue sharing, but are not significantly altered.

23. Testimony of Robert Strauss, in *General Revenue Sharing*, Hearings before the Subcommittee on Fiscal Policy of the Joint Economic Committee, 94:1 (GPO, 1975), p. 105.

6 *Issues and Prospects*

This second report on the Brookings monitoring study updates both the history of the general revenue sharing program and the presentation of the field data; it is an *interim* report. The third and final volume in this series will contain a cumulative analysis of all three rounds of field data (covering the period December 1972 through December 1975), as well as an analysis of the overall impact of the "revenue sharing idea," defined as encompassing all "grant-broadening" devices of national policy, including both general revenue sharing and block grants. Under a contract with the Department of Housing and Urban Development, the Brookings Institution is monitoring the first two years of the block grant program for community development (replacing urban renewal, model cities, and five other urban grant programs); this is the largest ($3 billion per year) and, in our view, most important of existing block grant programs. The final volume in the series will interrelate data from the two studies. It will also contain: an overview of the impact of the revenue sharing idea on American federalism; an analysis of its effects on the federal bureaucracy; an assessment of the impact of the revenue sharing idea on the role of lobbying organizations in Washington that represent general-purpose governments, both state and local; and a report on linkages in planning for the uses of shared revenue and block grant funds on the part of local units.

In this concluding chapter, we summarize our findings to date in relation to the central policy issues raised by the general revenue sharing program. First we consider the record of the program since 1972; second, the issues surrounding its extension; and third, the possible agenda for the Ninety-sixth Congress (1979–80), which will have to tackle again the question of a legislative extension.

159

The Record of Revenue Sharing

As we have stressed in our work on both revenue sharing and block grants, judgments about a program's effectiveness depend on one's point of view. Program evaluation requires a set of criteria against which performance can be measured; but, like many government programs, revenue sharing encompasses a number of diverse and sometimes contradictory objectives. The goals most frequently cited for the program can be characterized as follows: (1) to reduce fiscal disparities between states and among local governments; (2) to stabilize state and local taxes and thereby help produce a more progressive national tax structure; (3) to assist in the financing of needed state and local services; and (4) to move in the direction of governmental decentralization by increasing the discretion of state and local governments in determining the uses of federal grants. The extent to which each of these objectives has been achieved is briefly discussed below.

REDUCING FISCAL DISPARITIES

Because the formula established in 1972 for distributing general revenue sharing funds was not basically changed by the new law, we will not repeat here the discussion of the formula already presented in *Monitoring Revenue Sharing*. There, particular attention was given to the distributional impact of the revenue sharing allocation system on large central cities and poor states. The general policy issue raised was whether these and other "needy" jurisdictions received "appropriate" treatment under the formula contained in the original law. Taking into account the way in which most of the framers of the original program described their aims, we concluded that some provisions of the law appeared to work in ways that were not anticipated and that these features should be changed. Our analysis also indicated the need for better measures of certain variables included in the original allocation system.

Specifically, it was suggested that the floor and ceiling provisions of the law—requiring county areas, cities, and townships to receive at least 20 percent of the statewide average of shared-revenue payments to local units in their state and no more than 145 percent of this amount—be eliminated. If these floor and ceiling provisions had been removed, it would also have been necessary to take other steps. Among the other steps urged for consideration in *Monitoring Revenue Sharing* were: (1) replacing per capita income as the measure of relative fiscal capacity and as a factor in determining relative fiscal effort with new indicators that relate more closely to a jurisdiction's actual tax base and therefore more accurately reflect the comparative financing capability of areas and jurisdictions; (2) ending the uniform two-to-one local preference feature of the formula (two-thirds of each state's shared revenue must go to local units) and instead varying the portions of shared revenue that go to state and local governments according to their respective fiscal roles; and (3) modifying the provision that limits the shared-revenue entitlements of each local government to half the sum of its tax revenue and intergovernmental receipts, so that only tax revenue would be taken into account.[1]

Subsequent research on the distributional effects of the current formula revealed significant differences in the revenue sharing entitlements received by local governments having identical allocation factors as determined by relative tax effort and relative income. Based on this finding, a fourth modification can be added to the above list—namely, the elimination of the county-area allocation currently used in determining entitlements to individual local governments within a state.[2] All these changes, while important, are essentially modifications of current law. Other researchers have studied the effects of more basic formula changes in the form of alternative allocation systems. One such alternative recommends adding to the revenue sharing formula a new factor for "service requirements," separately computed for states, counties, and municipalities, and involving for each type of government approximately twenty statistical measures of service requirements by major functional area.[3]

These and other formula modifications were discussed in the renewal hearings and in the press. Some of them were encompassed in proposed changes in the law—in one case as advanced by the Ford administration, which proposed raising the 145 percent ceiling by six percentage points per year over five years. However, even limited modifications to the exist-

1. See Richard P. Nathan, Allen D. Manvel, and Susannah E. Calkins, *Monitoring Revenue Sharing* (Brookings Institution, 1975), chap. 6.

2. See Allen D. Manvel, Jacob M. Jaffe, and Richard P. Nathan, "Revenue Sharing Alternatives: Final Report to the National Science Foundation" (Brookings Institution, March 1976; processed).

3. Gregory Schmid, Hubert Lipinski, and Michael Palmer, *An Alternative Approach to General Revenue Sharing: A Needs-Based Allocation Formula* (Institute for the Future, June 1975).

ing law did not find their way into the versions reported in either the House or the Senate.

Although the law was not changed, the issue of the degree of equalization to be achieved under revenue sharing has been widely debated. The formula as it currently operates is most strongly influenced by population. As pointed out in *Monitoring Revenue Sharing*, state-area allocations (including both the state and local shares) under the original act ranged from $20.08 per capita in Ohio to $39.90 per capita in Mississippi, with a U.S. average for state areas of $26.08 per capita in 1972. Somewhat more variation was found for the largest cities compared to the balance of their SMSAs.[4] In 1972, the per capita amounts of shared revenue received by the twenty-three largest cities, where the city is part of a larger SMSA, in every case exceeded that for the balance of the SMSA, and in nine cases was over twice as much. However, as pointed out in chapter 3, these variations in per capita revenue sharing entitlements do not in any major way ameliorate the problems of distressed central cities.

The overall distributive pattern of the general revenue sharing program is a function of the "something for everyone" philosophy of the program. In other federal countries—notably West Germany, Canada, and Australia—the equalization effects of general grant programs tend to be much more pronounced because the allocation systems used involve a redistribution from wealthier (donor) jurisdictions to a limited number of recipient jurisdictions, defined as having special and acute problems and fiscal deficiencies.[5]

This is not to say that revenue sharing fails to reduce disparities, only that its equalizing impact is relatively limited. Many proponents of the existing formula, although it is not often expressed in these terms, regard other federal programs as more appropriate equalization devices, particularly income-transfer programs and social service grants. In debates on revenue sharing, spokesmen for local governments that would be considered fiscally healthy, particularly suburban jurisdictions, have argued

4. In these calculations, the amounts of shared revenue received by overlying governments are prorated to central cities on a per capita basis.

5. Considerable research on comparative fiscal federalism has been conducted recently by the Directorate-General for Economic and Financial Affairs of the Commission of the European Communities. This work is under the supervision of its Study Group on the Role of Public Finance in European Economic Integration. See especially "Budget Equalization and Other Unconditional Redistribution between Federal and State Governments" (Brussels, June 13, 1975; processed). The authors are indebted to Klaus Schneider of the EEC for his assistance in obtaining and working with these materials.

that their units also have needs and that inflation has reduced their ability to respond to these needs; thus, while other federal programs should focus on poverty needs, revenue sharing should give recognition to the financial problems of *all* governmental units.

The distributional effects of revenue sharing are closely related to the next objective to be discussed.

IMPACT ON THE TAX SYSTEM

One of the ideas important to backers of the original revenue sharing program was that it would have a desirable effect on the national tax structure by causing a heavier reliance on more progressive and efficient federal tax sources and, in turn, less reliance on state and local sales and property taxes. The research to date shows significant indications that this has occurred. Revenue sharing has been an important factor in allowing some governments to stabilize or limit tax increases; as seen in chapter 2, this effect has been particularly pronounced among hard-pressed municipal governments. At the same time, however, sample jurisdictions characterized as being under no fiscal pressure are also reported to have used a relatively high proportion of their shared revenue to cut or stabilize taxes.

Some regard this tax stabilization effect as generally desirable; others criticize the revenue sharing program because in some instances it may increase rather than reduce fiscal disparities among recipient governments. For example, the efforts of hard-pressed central cities to improve their fiscal position by using shared revenue to stabilize taxes may be significantly or fully offset as more fiscally healthy suburban jurisdictions take similar measures. The competitive position of the central cities could as a result be relatively unchanged or even worsened. This issue of the extent to which revenue sharing should be oriented to urban or poverty needs has been extensively debated. The point of view that appears to have prevailed, or at least been dominant, is that revenue sharing is a *general-purpose* program.

EXPANDING PUBLIC SERVICES

Another purpose of revenue sharing advertised by its supporters in 1972 was that it would expand the capability of state and local governments to meet public needs. This objective, of course, conflicts with the idea that revenue sharing should cause a heavier reliance on federal taxes and provide tax relief at the state and local levels. It implies a pro-spending orientation and emphasizes the impact of revenue sharing at the local level on the public, as opposed to the private, sector.

Persons with this pro-spending orientation may be encouraged by the significant amounts of new spending uses reported for the sample jurisdictions. For the vast majority of jurisdictions, at least some portion of revenue sharing has been used for new spending. Smaller local governments experiencing relatively little or moderate fiscal pressure were observed in chapter 2 to be the most likely to use a significant portion of their shared revenue in this way. For these governments, capital projects accounted for the bulk of their new spending uses. This bricks-and-mortar emphasis has also generated controversy. Critics of capital-intensive patterns in the use of shared revenue have urged instead that the funds be channeled into operating programs to improve and increase basic services. Among local jurisdictions, only county governments have evidenced any significant tendency to use shared revenue for new or expanded operating programs.

DECENTRALIZATION

Although it is discussed last in this section, the decentralizing objective of revenue sharing was the most prominent reason for its enactment in 1972. As in the case of other purposes of the program, however, decentralization has different meanings for different observers. Generalist officials (governors, mayors, managers, legislators) regard the basically "no-strings" character of these grants as an important means of allowing them greater discretion. Above and beyond the dollars and cents, these officials and supporters of decentralization generally see revenue sharing as a symbol of a new willingness on the part of the federal government to reduce the level and specificity of the controls placed on federal subventions in order to give greater emphasis to the role and significance of subnational governmental units in contemporary federalism. The fact that the program allows a high degree of discretion to generalist officials in determining the uses of these funds is reason enough for some observers to judge the program a success.

However, the experience to date suggests that the program has not decidedly changed the nature and type of participation in the political processes of recipient governments. In only about one-fifth of the local jurisdictions in the sample has there been either a broadening of the decisionmaking process, with new groups gaining access, or some shifting in relative influence among generalist officials.

Under the decentralization heading, one body of opinion measures the success of revenue sharing in terms of its ability to increase the role and leverage at the state and local level of citizens' groups with a decidedly social-service orientation and purpose. Of the twelve cases where there was a broadening of the decisionmaking process, nine involved social action organizations. There is also evidence that other grant-broadening programs of recent vintage, especially the block grant for community development, have had a greater effect in these terms.[6] In the third volume on this study, we will especially focus on the way in which various grant-broadening programs have interacted at the local level in a manner that has increased the level or changed the character of citizen participation.

CHANGES IN THE PROGRAM'S IMPACT

The design of this monitoring project provides a means for considering not only differences in fiscal and political impacts across recipient governments, but also changes in these effects over time. For example, between the first and second rounds of field observations a significant decline in new capital spending out of revenue sharing was reported by the associates, particularly for municipal governments. The number of jurisdictions that fully merged shared revenue into their regular budgets was also observed to have increased between the first and second rounds. Somewhat contrary to this last point, the number of jurisdictions where interest groups were reported to have gained influence in decisions about revenue sharing also increased.

In part, these changes in response patterns may simply reflect a normal process of adjustment to a new grant program by recipient governments. The initial bunching of revenue sharing entitlements in round one, for example, did not recur in round two. Hence, for many governments a more orderly deployment of these funds may have occurred in round two, reflected in the reduction in the number of cases in which shared revenue was treated separately in the budget process. Also, interest group awareness of revenue sharing may have increased over this period, prompting them to seek a greater role in deciding on the uses of these funds.

In some cases, however, changes in fiscal conditions prompted changes

6. See Richard P. Nathan and others, "Block Grants for Community Development" (Department of Housing and Urban Development, 1977).

in the uses of revenue sharing funds and the manner in which decisions were made. As seen in chapter 2, for several of the cities in the sample the shift away from capital uses and into program maintenance and tax stabilization uses was clearly related to deteriorating fiscal conditions.

In sum, any evaluation of the program's impact on local politics and budget decisions must be considered not only with regard to how recipient governments differ from one another in terms of various social, economic, and structural characteristics, but also with regard to how these characteristics change over time within individual jurisdictions.

The analyses of the third-round field data, covering allocations made from July 1, 1974 through December 31, 1975, will be of interest in this context because of the deterioration in the national economy and in the fiscal conditions of many state and local governments during this period. The analyses of the first two rounds of data already suggest that there may be a move away from new spending uses and, possibly, tax cuts, borrowing avoidance, and increased fund balances, and a move toward greater emphasis on program maintenance and tax stabilization. However, it is also possible that where new programs were initiated with shared revenue, local preferences for these programs may have become sufficiently well established so that even under greater fiscal pressure they will be maintained. Likewise, increases in political influence for some groups gained through revenue sharing may endure even under conditions of significant fiscal constraint. The analysis of the third-round field data and comparisons with earlier periods will provide important insights on the permanence of the initial political and fiscal effects of the general revenue sharing program.

The 1976 Amendments

Turning next to the 1976 renewal legislation, we must ask what inferences can be drawn from the field data about the likely repercussions of various changes made in the original program. As discussed in chapter 1, the formula provisions of the 1972 act are basically unchanged. Congressional critics of the program, mainly liberals in the House, concentrated their attention instead on process issues, such as civil rights enforcement, public participation, and auditing and accounting—the so-called accountability provisions.

CIVIL RIGHTS

The most prominent issue in revenue sharing in the Ninety-fourth Congress involved civil rights. The nondiscrimination provisions in the original act were significantly expanded by the 1976 amendments. Age, handicapped status, and religion were added to race, color, national origin, and sex as forms of discrimination specifically prohibited. Extensive hearing and compliance procedures are now spelled out to deal with discrimination, and private civil suits are explicitly authorized after administrative remedies have been exhausted. In order to demonstrate compliance with the nondiscrimination provisions of the act, a recipient government must demonstrate by "clear and convincing" evidence that the program or activity over which an allegation of discrimination has been made is not funded in whole or in part with revenue sharing funds.

The House wanted to go further than the Senate in this connection. The language in the original House bill required that recipient governments provide "clear and convincing" evidence that any alleged discriminatory activities were not funded "directly or indirectly" with revenue sharing. The keyword is "indirectly," which was eliminated in conference. Had it been retained, complaints of discrimination could have been lodged not only against activities funded under the accounts to which revenue sharing funds were transferred, but also in other areas in which revenue sharing may have affected the finances of recipient governments. At issue here is the familiar concept of fungibility discussed in chapter 2: if shared revenue simply substitutes for funds that otherwise would have been used to finance a particular program or project, then the real impact of revenue sharing must occur elsewhere in the budget.

In the process of renewing the program, attention was given to the fungibility problem and its implications for recipient governments having to account for the uses of shared funds. Evidence of this is provided by the decision to eliminate the priority-expenditure categories previously imposed on operating uses of shared revenue by local governments. Designations showing how revenue sharing funds were allocated among these categories often bear little or no relationship to the real impact of these funds in the budget. But Congress did not deal with the problem of fungibility in the 1976 amendments in the case of the nondiscrimination provisions; it limited the extent to which recipient governments could be held accountable to "direct" uses of revenue sharing funds. Not to underestimate the ambiguity of the House usage of "indirect," it is clear that, by dropping it, compliance efforts, especially those by private groups, will be more difficult to press. Governments that choose to do so can practice "careful" bookkeeping and directly transfer shared revenue to accounts clearly in compliance with the nondiscrimination provisions of the law, fungibility notwithstanding.

PUBLIC PARTICIPATION

The provisions relating to public participation in decisions about the uses of shared revenue were also expanded by the 1976 amendments. In the original act, recipient governments were simply required to inform citizens about uses of shared revenue by publishing actual- and planned-use reports in a local newspaper. Now, recipient governments must hold public hearings on revenue sharing unless explicitly waived by the secretary of the treasury. In fact, they must hold two public hearings, one on the proposed use of revenue sharing before the budget is presented to the legislature and a budget hearing which, according to the conference report, is to give citizens an opportunity to comment on the proposed uses of revenue sharing "in relation to the government's entire budget."

As discussed in chapter 4, twenty-seven of the sample units fully merged shared revenue into their budget in fiscal year 1974 without any special attention—either within the government or in relation to outside groups—to policy questions involving the use of these funds. Only eight of the sample units held special hearings on the uses of shared revenue in the first period of the field research, and an even smaller number, five units, in the second. In this context, the hearing requirements could have an important effect on state and local political processes.

Even before the new law went into effect, controversy arose about the implementation of these hearing provisions. According to the *Revenue Sharing Bulletin,* Treasury officials took steps shortly after enactment to establish a policy that would involve granting extensive waivers of the hearing requirements. Under the proposed regulations, as many as 75 percent of local governments below the county level may be eligible for exemption from the first required hearing on the proposed uses of revenue sharing funds.[7] With respect to the second hearing, to be held prior to adoption of the final budget, the law allows a waiver if existing state or

7. *Revenue Sharing Bulletin* (November 1976), p. 6.

local law mandates a budget process that "assures" an opportunity for public participation and "a portion of such process includes a hearing on proposed uses of (revenue sharing) funds in relation to the entire budget." The proposed regulations in this case appear to provide a tighter standard, in accordance with the intent of the act, regarding the waiver of this second hearing.

On balance, those who support greater public participation in decisions about revenue sharing uses may be encouraged by the actions taken by Congress in the renewal legislation. However, there remains the question of the extent to which the implementation of these provisions by the Office of Revenue Sharing will reflect the intent of Congress to strengthen the public participation provisions of the program. A closely related issue, discussed below, is the way in which the Treasury Department implements the reporting system on the basis of which the public discussion of the uses of shared revenue is carried out.

"STRINGS" REMOVED

There were two changes made in the 1976 amendments aimed at removing "strings" in the original revenue sharing act. First, the provision against using revenue sharing funds to match categorical grants was eliminated. As discussed in chapter 2, the sample jurisdictions gave evidence of some sensitivity to this provision. Associates for eleven sample jurisdictions noted that concern about violating this provision may have deterred government officials from using shared revenue in program areas affected by matching grants. Many state and local human resource programs are aided under matching grants from the federal government; hence, to the extent that a bias existed against using shared revenue in certain areas because of the nonmatching requirement, human resource programs were most likely to have been affected. Because of this, social action groups were the most frequent critics of the nonmatching requirement. Its elimination may have some impact on the distribution of shared revenue allocations to human resource and social programs generally.

The other change, already noted, eliminated the restriction on local governments whereby revenue sharing funds for operating expenses were limited to specified priority-expenditure categories. In chapter 2, however, we noted that there is little reason to believe that this provision has seriously restricted local governments from using shared revenue in areas outside of the priority categories. For example, in the case of public safety, one of the priority categories, we found a significantly smaller real impact from revenue sharing than that suggested by the actual-use information reported by the Office of Revenue Sharing. A special report on this subject concluded that, "[O]fficially reported expenditures of shared revenue compiled by the Treasury Department's Office of Revenue Sharing were six times greater than new spending for law enforcement out of revenue sharing in the Brookings field research in 1973 and four times greater in 1974."[8] In general, the restriction imposed by the priority-expenditure categories appear to have been satisfied through accounting adjustments rather than through real adjustments in spending patterns.

REPORTING ON REVENUE SHARING USES

Although the priority-expenditure categories have been eliminated, recipient governments will still be required to report to the Secretary of the Treasury about how revenue sharing funds have been spent. Specifically, the 1976 amendments require governments to submit at the end of each fiscal year a report, "setting forth the amounts and purposes for which funds . . . have been appropriated, spent, or obligated . . . and showing the relationship of those funds to the relevant functional items in the government's budget. Such report shall identify differences between the actual use of funds received and the proposed use of such funds."[9]

By removing the priority-expenditure categories and requiring a reconciliation between planned and actual uses and the reporting of these uses in the context of the entire budget, official reports could actually provide a more accurate accounting of the real fiscal impacts of revenue sharing. It is also possible that even within this revised format, reports submitted by recipient governments will continue to reflect what are essentially accounting transactions, bearing little or no relationship to the real uses of revenue sharing funds. Careful attention will still have to be given to the fungibility issue when using data based on officially reported uses of shared revenue.

In addition to reporting to the Treasury on proposed uses of shared revenue, recipient governments are required under the 1976 amendments, as in the original law, to "publish in at least one newspaper of general

8. See chapter 2 for a more detailed discussion of the findings of this special study.

9. The State and Local Fiscal Assistance Amendments of 1976, sec. 121 para. (a). See appendix C for the text of the amendments.

circulation, the proposed uses of (revenue sharing) funds together with a summary of its proposed budget . . ."[10] This report is to be published at least ten days before the required public hearing on the adoption of the budget. Recipient governments must also make a summary of their budget and proposed uses of revenue sharing available for public inspection thirty days after the budget is adopted. Governments only have to notify citizens that this latter type of information is available; they are not required to publish it.

Under the original act, governments were required to publish the planned- and actual-use reports submitted to the Office of Revenue Sharing. For the reasons discussed earlier, these reports in many cases gave little insight into the real impact of revenue sharing on state and local budgets. By requiring a summary of the entire budget to be made public, along with information about the proposed uses of revenue sharing, the revised publication provision could provide a framework that puts revenue sharing into a more comprehensible perspective—depending, as indicated, upon the regulations adopted to implement this portion of the law.

ISSUES NOT ADDRESSED

It is important to consider the relationship of our research findings not only to issues that were addressed by the 1976 amendments, but also those issues that were raised but were not dealt with, at least not in any significant way, by the new law. Especially notable in this area are issues affecting the level and distribution of shared revenue.

Funding level. The renewed program provides spending authority at an annual rate of $6.85 billion over three and three-quarters years; this is an increase of $350 million over the 1976 calendar year amount. However, in real terms the level of funding will continue to decline. Using the GNP deflator based on 1972 price levels, funding under the original act declined from $5.31 billion in 1972 to about $4.89 billion in 1976, or by about 8 percent in real terms. Assuming the deflator increases by 5.5 percent annually through 1979, the level of funding in calendar year 1979 will be approximately $4.40 billion in real terms. This means that the program will have declined by 17 percent from 1972 to 1980.

An obvious implication of this declining real level of funding is that whatever the initial fiscal impact of revenue sharing on recipient govern-

10. The State and Local Fiscal Assistance Amendments of 1976, sec. 121 para. (c).

ments, that impact will diminish over time. Hard-pressed cities that have been using revenue sharing to hold down tax increases or maintain programs will find it increasingly difficult to sustain whatever benefits were initially derived from the program. Similarly, governments that expanded or created new operating programs will find it increasingly difficult to sustain these programs without raising taxes or reducing spending on other programs. A number of proposals were made in the renewal process to tie the annual level of revenue sharing to the U.S. individual income tax base. Such an approach was proposed in the original Heller-Pechman revenue sharing plan as a way to make the state-local revenue base more responsive to growth in national income.[11]

A small but unintentional step was made in this direction in the final stages of congressional debate on renewal legislation in 1976. In considering the conference bill, a point of order was raised in the House concerning a possible conflict between the funding arrangement included in the conference bill and the requirements of the Congressional Budget and Impoundment Control Act of 1974. This conflict was resolved (actually side-stepped) by indexing annual revenue sharing entitlements to federal individual income tax receipts. Specifically, the annual entitlement is now determined by multiplying $6.65 billion (the annual entitlement included in the House bill) by the ratio of personal income tax collections in the last calendar year before the end of the current entitlement period to tax collections in 1975. In the absence of a major recession or discretionary reduction in tax liabilities, the ratio used in the calculations should be higher than 1, so as to yield an annual entitlement greater than $6.65 billion.[12] However, the actual entitlement cannot exceed $6.85 billion (the amount agreed to in conference). Based on projected increases in individual income tax receipts, annual entitlements will in all likelihood be equal to the maximum of $6.85 billion.

While an indexing procedure has been added by the 1976 amendments, it is constrained so as to yield a fixed annual entitlement. But, the very fact that this concept has been incorporated into the program, albeit for

11. The Heller-Pechman plan, proposed in 1967, would have funded revenue sharing at an annual amount equal to 2 percent of taxable personal income. For 1972 this would have provided funding at about $10 billion, increasing to an estimated $13.6 billion in 1976. Adjusted for inflation, funding under this arrangement would have increased by about 2 percent in real terms over this period.

12. Since 1949, calendar year personal income tax receipts have on six occasions dropped from one year to the next as the result of some combination of recession and legislated reductions in tax liabilities.

technical rather than substantive reasons, may prove to be a first step toward a full indexation of the revenue sharing program, as originally envisioned in the Heller-Pechman plan.

Distributional issues. Easily the most important area in which changes were *not* made involves the distribution system, including both the formula and the criteria governing eligibility for entitlements.[13] Despite voluminous reports, computer printouts, and recommendations, the original distribution formula survived the renewal process intact. Indeed, changes —at least those not accompanied by additional funds—would have been politically difficult to make since they would necessarily cause some jurisdictions to lose. The most important formula revision recommended by the Ford administration (although not with any special vigor) was that the ceiling on per capita entitlements to local governments be raised from 145 percent of the statewide average for localities to 175 percent over a period of five years. An analysis of this proposal showed that (subject to the retention of the 145 percent ceiling for municipalities and townships with under 5,000 inhabitants and county areas with under 10,000) the amount of redistribution would have been relatively minor, though some large central cities under significant fiscal stress, such as Baltimore, Cleveland, and St. Louis, would have been aided appreciably.[14]

Although the Senate Finance Committee was emphatic in opposing major formula changes, the House Government Operations Committee was willing to act in this area. Several members of the committee introduced bills involving changes in the basic distribution system. One proposal adopted by the full committee, but rejected on the House floor, would have added what was felt to be a stronger needs factor (reflecting poverty conditions), although applying only to funds added under the new law.[15]

Another proposal, this one adopted by the House, would have significantly altered the criteria used in determining the units that will receive shared revenue by making single-purpose local governments ineligible. While the number of governments affected by this provision would have been very large, the amount of money involved was very small, a consideration which no doubt influenced the outcome. The customary re-

13. Several relatively minor changes in the distribution system were made by the 1976 amendments, such as adding county (parish) sheriffs in Louisiana as eligible recipients and modifying the special formula provisions for Alaska and Hawaii.
14. See Manvel, Jaffe, and Nathan, "Revenue Sharing Alternatives."
15. This proposal by Congressman Dante Fascell is discussed in chapter 1.

sponse to proposals along these lines was that since the amount of money to be recouped for other units is so small, it is not worth the political outcry that would result from eliminating so large a number of governmental units (perhaps as many as 17,000)[16] from eligibility.

But the real question in this case, even more than resources, involves political structure. A major criticism of the revenue sharing program from its inception was that it would prop up small and limited-function governments, especially townships in the Midwest, which account for approximately one-third of all local units eligible for assistance. Despite the prevalence of this argument, we found little evidence to support the charge that the revenue sharing program significantly reinforces the role of marginal and limited-function government units.

Related to the issue of small and limited-function governments, was one other important structural issue considered by the Congress but not included in the renewal legislation. As discussed in chapter 1, revenue sharing was seen by some of its earliest proponents as a means of promoting broad structural reforms of state and local government; in fact, a proposal was included in the House committee bill in 1976 requiring state governments to report annually on steps taken to develop a master plan for "modernizing" state and local government. Such proposals for tying revenue sharing payments to basic structural reforms have been widely discussed. Beginning in the late sixties, Representative Henry S. Reuss and others urged that such procedures be included under revenue sharing for both state and local units. In any event, even the more limited version of the Reuss plan, offered in 1976 by Representative Benjamin Rosenthal of New York, was rejected on the House floor.

Issues for the Future

The Ninety-sixth Congress, which will convene in 1979, will be faced again with the question of whether and how to renew the general revenue sharing program. It is not too early to consider the way in which policy research can contribute to the examination of the questions that will come to the fore in this debate. Several such issues are briefly discussed here under three headings involving the distributional, structural, and procedural aspects of revenue sharing.

16. Unofficial estimate of the upper limit of the effect of such a change provided by the staff of the House Committee on Government Operations.

DISTRIBUTIONAL

A new element on the revenue sharing scene is the inauguration in 1977 of a president who has on numerous occasions recommended that state governments be eliminated as recipient units of revenue sharing. Although others took this position in the renewal debates in 1976, it never surfaced as an important issue; now it could.

Economic conditions are also bound to have an important effect on distributional issues in 1979–80. The hold-harmless principle has had a strong influence in Washington in the consideration of formula changes in grant-in-aid programs. If, however, there was an opportunity and disposition to add funds to the revenue sharing pot, such a decision would open the way to formula changes, while at the same time adhering to the hold-harmless principle. Under these conditions, various proposals made by practitioners of and researchers on state and local government could be considered. By adding such formula factors as population density, dependency, and age of housing to the allocation system, greater recognition could be given to urban hardship conditions. On the other hand, new or strengthened poverty- and income-related factors tend to be more beneficial to rural areas and smaller communities. The former kinds of formula changes would aid the Northeast and Midwest; the latter, the "sunbelt" region. Of course, if state governments were removed from the revenue sharing picture, this too would open up possibilities for formula changes without increasing the overall size of the general revenue sharing program.

Another issue that could be added to this agenda involves the eligibility criteria applied to local governments. In *Monitoring Revenue Sharing,* it was suggested that one technique for eliminating limited-function governments from the revenue sharing program would be to tie eligibility to some percentage of the national average of local nonschool employees in relation to population. Even a low threshold, such as 10 percent of the national average, would disqualify the overwhelming majority of Midwestern townships, as well as some New England counties and numerous minimally active municipalities.

Another approach to reduce the number of small units would be to raise the current $200 minimum annual payment to local units. Still another would be to insert a population cut-off. The vast majority of recipient jurisdictions are small; four-fifths are under 5,000 population, although they receive only 5 percent of all shared revenue distributed to local governments. If a population cut-off of 2,500 were adopted, it would eliminate 70 percent of the cities eligible for shared revenue; a 1,000 minimum would halve the total number.

In the first Brookings volume on revenue sharing, suggestions were also made that would alter the definition of fiscal capacity and effort, the state-local split, the floor and ceiling provisions, and other formula provisions of the current law. We believe greater attention should be given to these and related formula issues in the Ninety-sixth Congress.

STRUCTURAL

Structural and formula issues are closely related, especially with respect to eligibility. Should limited-function governments classified as general-purpose units be restricted from eligibility under revenue sharing? Should small municipalities be excluded? What about the eligibility of state governments; what should be the division between states and localities?

Under the 1976 amendments, the Advisory Commission on Intergovernmental Relations is given responsibility to "study and evaluate the American Federal fiscal system." Such a study should provide valuable information about the effects of revenue sharing and other new forms of grants on American federalism. At the same time, however, we believe that questions about intergovernmental relations must be addressed locally as well as in Washington.

While recognizing that proposals for attaching strings to the revenue sharing program have been resisted, we nevertheless offer one possibility for consideration next time around. As a condition of keeping state governments in the program (which President Jimmy Carter has previously opposed), consideration should be given to adopting a requirement for the establishment, if one does not already exist, of some form of independent or quasi-independent state advisory commission on intergovernmental relations or commission on local government. Such agencies can stimulate attention to intergovernmental issues, including the way in which revenue sharing has affected state-local fiscal relationships, as well as serve as vehicles to propose new measures that could be adopted to alter state-local fiscal relations and the role and structure of local governments in this context.

Our research on the problems and conditions of central cities demonstrates that the role of state governments in dealing with what can be considered the "urban crisis conditions" of some (though not all) central cities is a critical ingredient to progress in dealing with these conditions.

One could argue therefore that the role of states as the middleman in American federalism should be highlighted in the current period, and that both the substance and politics of the revenue sharing debate in 1979–80 offer an opportunity to move in this direction.

PROCEDURAL

Under the heading of procedural changes can be grouped all three of the major areas in which revisions were made in the general revenue sharing program in 1976—nondiscrimination, public participation, and auditing and accounting.

A key question concerning the efficacy of these revisions is whether the issue of fungibility has been adequately dealt with. In the case of the nondiscrimination provisions, the Ninety-fourth Congress in effect sidestepped the issue. Charges of discrimination and subsequent administrative and court decisions will have to be watched to see whether, in fact, this becomes a pivotal factor in determining the outcome of such cases.

Fungibility is also a critical point in relation to the significance of the new reporting requirements. In implementing the reporting requirements, every effort should be made by Treasury to insure that the data which are generated by official reports relate to the real choices of state and local decision makers as to the uses of shared revenue. National policymakers should be alert to developments in this area in order to determine whether further legislative action is required. Attention should also be given to the implementation and effects of the nondiscrimination, public participation, and independent audit requirements of the 1976 amendments. The revenue sharing agenda of the Ninety-sixth Congress, should include both accountability and formula issues. There is no necessary trade-off between the two, except insofar as the time and energy of participants limits their ability to cope with modifications of the program.

Appendixes

A Excerpts from the Transcript of the Concluding Conference of Field Research Associates, April 8–9, 1976

The participation of the field associates in this study was completed April 8–9, 1976, when the third research conference, chaired by Richard P. Nathan, for the general revenue sharing study was held in Washington at the Brookings Institution. Associates had submitted their last field reports two months prior to the conference. For the conference, associates were requested to prepare in advance to speak on selected topics relating to findings of special importance for their sample jurisdictions. The discussion at the conference was divided into panels. The first was a general panel to indicate the range and variations in responses to the revenue sharing program; the second focused on central cities; and the third considered the structural impact of general revenue sharing funds.

Panel 1: Patterns of Response

CHAIR: In dealing with what happens under any national program such as revenue sharing, an important point to make is that the patterns of response will be different. We have picked a cross-section of sample units for this first discussion topic to indicate the variety of ways in which revenue sharing has affected individual recipient governments. We start with Los Angeles County.

RUTH ROSS: During the first two rounds of our study, shared revenue in Los Angeles County was used largely for new capital spending, especially parks, improving health service facilities, and juvenile justice facilities. Although a large proportion of the funds was not involved, the county has done some rather innovative things with shared revenue. It has sub-

181

sidized the local bus fare to create a cheaper rate throughout the county and to give the supervisors greater decision power over bus routes. The county also bought a commuter train to augment the Amtrak service between San Diego and Los Angeles Counties.

Another innovative use was funding nonprofit community groups with general revenue sharing funds. Although this funding has been reduced from the originally planned level, the county has so far allocated over $16 million for this purpose, largely for social services to low-income or handicapped people, health services, and delinquency prevention. As of this fiscal year, 766 nonprofit groups had applied for this funding; last year alone 480 applied. These are sizable numbers. Right now, though, there is only $3.4 million left for this purpose, so there will not be many groups funded this year.

By the third round of our field research, the fiscal situation was such that the county simply merged its shared revenue into the general fund. This was partly a political decision, in my view reflecting the ideas of a new county administrative officer who is strongly budget-oriented. His view is that the county should not put revenue sharing funds into new capital projects; the county is now funding mostly the capital projects for which they already had legal commitments.

CHAIR: The point that seems to me to be important is the visibility of revenue sharing in Los Angeles County, particularly during the early stages of the program.

ROSS: Yes, extremely visible.

CHAIR: The state government of Colorado is next.

ROYAL D. SLOAN, JR.: When general revenue sharing funds were made available to Colorado, the state was under practically no fiscal pressure. There was initially a delay in deciding how shared revenue ought to be used. Then, as the Nixon administration began to impound various categorical grant funds, and also as appropriations from Congress in some cases were reduced, the state adopted a basic strategy to put general revenue sharing funds into areas where these categorical-grant programs were being cut back. That is still, to a large extent, what the state is doing.

Recently the list of uses of general revenue sharing funds has changed; it is now difficult to identify reasons for the way in which Colorado is allocating its shared revenue. Earlier, a substantial proportion of these funds went for capital construction, especially for water treatment projects that had been cut out or cut back by the federal government. Gradually, more and more of these general revenue sharing monies have been used for operating programs unrelated to federal aid cutbacks.

The decision process in Colorado involves a legislative budget. The governor and his executive budget director have relatively little to say in preparing the budget; it is the Joint Budget Committee of the State Legislature, a group of six people with a small professional staff (the only committee in the legislature with its own staff), which basically makes the decisions. Pressure groups have not been particularly influential in guiding or even trying to influence the budget process. This was particularly true when the Republican Party was in control of the state. Now we have a Democratic governor and the legislature is split (a Democratic House and a Republican Senate). As a result, the system has opened up somewhat, although the basic decisions are still made by the Joint Budget Committee and its staff.

CHAIR: We have heard about a county and a state. The next government on this panel is a municipal government, Bangor, Maine.

KENNETH T. PALMER: When revenue sharing began, Bangor regarded itself as being under moderate to heavy fiscal pressure, primarily because of a fund-balance problem that had existed since about 1970. The city wound up its fiscal year 1972 with virtually no cash balance. Its assets tended to be nonliquid—uncollected taxes, deferred assessments, and so forth.

In its use of revenue sharing, Bangor became a very heavy substitution user. Almost all of its revenue sharing money for the first three years went into either improving its fund balance, which I roughly calculated at 40 percent, or tax stabilization, which I also calculated at about 40 percent. Bangor has had the highest tax rate of any major community in Maine. Only about 10 percent of its shared revenue went to new programs and an additional 10 percent to program maintenance.

One lesson from the Bangor experience is that the required actual- and planned-use reporting forms are not necessarily accurate concerning what a jurisdiction does. The manager and council, in filling out the report forms, allocated somewhere between $100,000 and $200,000 to each of the several "priority-expenditure" categories such as environment, public safety, public transportation, and recreation. But this did not mean there was any real increase in these areas. What was really happening was that revenue sharing money was going into these accounts, and funds that would otherwise have been spent from the city's tax revenue for these programs went into a new surplus account. Bangor started a new surplus fund at a level of about $500,000 in 1973 and kept adding to that up to the present time. So what really occurred in Bangor was that from a point of practically a zero surplus early in 1973, the city now has over $2 million in surplus funds in 1976.

The five-year duration of the revenue sharing program was very important in Bangor because the city fathers wanted to know where they were going to be in 1976. They made their decisions in the fall and early winter of 1972–73, and they kept to that plan.

As far as political impact is concerned, the revenue sharing program, unlike the situation in Los Angeles, had very low visibility. There was relatively little public participation in the allocation of these funds; it was very much an in-house operation conducted by the council and the manager.

The city council did help the various social service agencies in Bangor with some revenue sharing dollars; this was the only major area of new programming. Private nonprofit organizations were able to secure some additional funds, but a very limited amount, from the revenue sharing program.

CHAIR: Thank you. So revenue sharing had fairly high visibility in Los Angeles County, generated controversy in Colorado, and had no visibility or very low visibility in Bangor. Eugene and Lane County, Oregon, are next on this panel.

HERMAN KEHRLI: Eugene is a rapidly growing city, especially since World War II, and now has a population of nearly 100,000. In the post-war period, the city government has been quite progressive in developing services. This is reflected in the way they have planned for the use of revenue sharing funds. In its 1972–73 budget, the city included a special program for shared revenue. Even though the voters turned down this budget, city officials kept right on going and committed about one-third of their first allocation of shared revenue to this special program months before Congress acted. This was not a legal commitment, but since they expanded certain activities in anticipation of receiving these funds, it had that effect. About a third of this special fund went at the beginning for facilities and services. The services involved practically every department—a new major-crimes team for the police force, bicycle paths, social services.

Eugene's budget committee consists of eight city council members and eight citizens. They work on the budget prepared by the city manager. They have been frustrated over the years. The manager prepares the budget and about all they can do is rubber-stamp it. Under revenue sharing, however, the members of the budget committee felt that they did have some choices to make. While there was public exposure, there wasn't much public input other than by the public members of the budget committee. So the committee did a couple of things. First, as in Los Angeles, the committee appropriated $200,000 in the 1972–73 budget to subsidize private agencies providing social and health services. This became a joint program also involving Lane County and, initially, the city of Springfield. [Lane County overlies the city of Eugene.] The other new program was to provide housing for the low-income elderly.

The point I would stress about these two programs is that they were not in the manager's budget. They came right out of the budget meeting. There was no staff work done on them, no justification, and so forth. One of the councilwomen, who used to be a social worker, simply made a motion to set aside the $200,000, about 10 percent of the initial revenue sharing allocations being considered, for social services. The committee agreed, though they did not quite know how they were going to do this. Then someone else proposed $150,000 for low-income housing. They worked out the details later, and Lane County joined in these programs. I asked the councilwoman who made the motion how she arrived at that figure. She said, "I don't know. If I had it to do over again, I would have said a half a million and it would have carried."

This reflects the strength of the budget committee. There was a split in the council on this issue. But the liberal majority of the budget committee prevailed; they also allocated revenue sharing funds for recreation facilities for the elderly, the physically handicapped, and children and youth.

After the first round, the city also purchased new equipment for the fire department, police department, computer time—everybody got something. From then on, they just supported these various new programs and activities; the status quo was maintained.

As for Lane County, the original plan was to use revenue sharing money for one-time projects; county officials intended to put most of it into a new office building and a social-service center. They also joined in a social-service program with Eugene, as I mentioned earlier, and said that revenue sharing gave them the resources to do that. The county also appropriated shared revenue to buy buses for the rapid transit system so they could provide new routes into suburban areas and rural areas surrounding Eugene; they were not going to use shared revenue for operating expenses. However, local governments in Oregon are very dependent on what the voters in referendum are willing to levy in property taxes, and the voters have not been good to Lane County. This year, Lane County officials as a result say they have been forced to use most of their shared revenue for county operating expenses.

CHAIR: We have a township in our group of six cases, Greece, New York.

SARAH LIEBSCHUTZ: In my judgment, the overriding effect of revenue sharing on the town of Greece, which is Rochester's largest suburb, has been to strengthen its determination of its own destiny—to minimize the pain of growth to its taxpayers and to minimize political risks for its incumbent officeholders. To be more specific, general revenue sharing has facilitated continuing development. The town's population is currently estimated at 86,000, an increase of 15 percent since 1970.

From the outset of general revenue sharing, the town supervisor understood the fungible nature of revenue sharing funds. Decisions with regard to revenue sharing and the entire budgetary process were carefully managed and directed by the supervisor. Citizens who inquired were told to get involved, not just with revenue sharing allocations, but with the whole budgetary process. As a consequence, they got involved with neither.

The planned- and actual-use reports showed the allocation of revenue sharing to public safety, transportation, and environmental protection, all considered to be essential services. The net effect of the funds, however, is substitution. These revenues would have been raised by increasing property taxes or borrowing to enable the town government to provide services to residents and to plan for the future.

CHAIR: We have one more case to consider, New York City.

HENRY COHEN: I should mention that our participation in this project has been through groups of students over the past three years. They are doing the work under my supervision.

In the 1973 report on fiscal year 1971–72, the students rated New York as under "extreme" fiscal pressure. In the 1974 report on the 1972–73 fiscal year, they reported "extreme pressure with some improvement." This was three months or so after the end of the Lindsay administration and four months after Moody's had upgraded New York bonds to "A." The current team reported last month for the last year and a half and rated the city as facing "extreme pressure with significant deterioration."

The recent deputy mayor, who was the key person for the budget, told the students that municipal financing takes place in one of three atmospheres. One is "relaxed scarcity," a period of relative plenty in a city in which revenue sources such as general revenue sharing are used to initiate new programs. New York has never had relaxed scarcity. The second category is "acute scarcity," which describes fiscal 1974–75, during which sources such as general revenue sharing are used to keep existing programs and services funded without tax increases. Third, he said, you have "scarce-scarcity," which describes 1975–76, during which funds such as general revenue sharing can only be used to minimize cuts in programs and services but cannot prevent tax increases.

For New York, the $250 million it gets out of revenue sharing is a drop in the bucket. What has been going on in terms of the budget process is that New York is a big blotter. You throw in $250 million, it's absorbed; you throw in a billion, it would be absorbed. No one really knows what the deficit is. It started at $724 million in November, which everyone agreed to. Now it is approaching one and a half billion.

The students made a gallant effort in this last review to try to determine what would have been the nature and degree of budget cuts if you had not had revenue sharing. In effect, what they reduced it to was not revenue sharing money as a percentage of the total budget, but revenue sharing as a percentage of the total general fund budget, and then applied it to the parts that were more or less controllable—not the debt services, not pensions. They came up with a figure of something like an 8 percent budget cut across-the-board on this basis, although they applied their cuts differently to different functional areas.

So in effect, even while you are cutting, if you did not have revenue sharing funds, you would have had to cut another 8 percent, which is a lot of cutting.

Panel 2: Central Cities

CHAIR: We have five central cities on this second panel. Again we have diversity—for example, as between Newark and Phoenix. We will start with Newark and its overlying county, Essex County, New Jersey.

ROBERT CURVIN: In the Brookings city-suburb hardship index, Newark is right at the top. For many years the city has been under extreme fiscal pressure; conditions have become worse over the last couple of years with increasing economic duress at both the local and state levels. The city's tax base continues to decline by about 5 percent each year. Tax collections have decreased over the last two years, after a few years of increasing rather significantly just after Mayor Kenneth Gibson took office. For 1976, the city's tax rate has been set at $10 per $100 of assessed valuation; that is at a 100 percent valuation, so one literally purchases his house in taxes every ten years in the city of Newark.

This high tax rate, particularly as it affects business and industry in the city, has been the most significant factor in determining the uses of revenue sharing funds in Newark. It is not surprising that all of the city's revenue sharing funds have gone for tax reduction and tax stabilization.

I want to stress that even though the amount of revenue sharing which comes to approximately 8 percent of the city's budget is not enough to have what I would call a fundamental impact on the city's fiscal condition, it has been extremely important for several financial and political reasons. On the financial side, revenue sharing funds allowed the city to reduce the tax rate for two consecutive years, in 1973 and 1974. This was completely unanticipated, given the history of fiscal crisis in the city. It resulted in a new sense of optimism in Newark. The tax cut made in 1974, an election year, was on the order of 78 points. The size of this reduction is, to my knowledge, unparalleled in the city's recent economic history. This has also had important political implications, giving the mayor an enormous amount of support.

One of the striking features of the impact of revenue sharing in Newark is the almost total absence of citizen participation. It is difficult, if not impossible, to identify the reasons why this is so, given that Newark is generally a very highly politicized city. But as a guess I would say one of the reasons is that the high level of political activity that was characteristic of the period before Mayor Gibson's election subsided quite a bit when Gibson became mayor and recruited some of the more vocal activists into the city government. In addition to that, Gibson himself has been one of the more prominent advocates of federal revenue sharing. He is a vice president of the U.S. Conference of Mayors and has not only testified frequently before Congress on revenue sharing legislation, but has made many speeches around the country about the program and its importance to cities like Newark. Having this kind of exposure and identification with the revenue sharing program, I think, has given him an edge and flexibility in determining the uses of these funds. Indeed, one local official told me that he had nothing to say about the use of general revenue sharing funds because the community development block grant program is his thing and general revenue sharing is the mayor's thing.

The overlying county of Essex is quite a contrast to Newark. The county is in relatively good fiscal health for several reasons. It still has within its boundaries some of the more affluent communities in New Jersey; indeed, communities like South Orange and Livingston rank among the more affluent in the nation. In addition, Essex County has not depended upon the state and the federal governments, particularly the state government, in funding the services it provides. The county initially started out using its shared revenue in a mixed way, some for capital expenditures, some for service expenditures. It was also able at the outset to set aside some of this money for tax reduction on a basis that would level out the impact of revenue sharing funds over a period of years. In the last two years, the county has moved more toward using revenue sharing funds for operating expenditures because of adverse economic developments.

CHAIR: An interesting point here is that when Essex County cuts taxes, it discriminates against Newark because the per capita tax base of the county is much higher in the outlying areas than it is in the city. Next is Cincinnati and Hamilton County.

FREDERICK D. STOCKER: I would like to use my few minutes to make some observations on fiscal interactions between the county and the city. We have talked a lot in this monitoring project about fungibility. I don't think that before revenue sharing came along I knew what the word fungibility meant, and I am still not sure that I know what the process involves, although I now know what the word means. Our discussion of fungibility has focused primarily on substitution effects among functions and uses. Presumably, the same phenomena would work among overlapping levels of government. I thought perhaps we could observe in the Cincinnati–Hamilton County area a picking up of some responsibilities for city governmental services by the county with revenue sharing funds.

Cincinnati has been under considerable financial pressure, and when revenue sharing came along, the city merged revenue sharing in its regular budget and used it for the most part to maintain and marginally expand services across-the-board. The county, on the other hand, being under relatively little fiscal pressure, held onto its money. They did nothing with it for over a year, and then they allocated most of it to capital improvements.

One might have expected that the further reduction in fiscal pressure that revenue sharing provided for the county would have resulted in some increase in capital expenditures in the city or the greater participation by the county in functions for which there is a joint or perhaps overlapping responsibility by city and county. One visible way in which the easier situation for the county has helped the city is that the county allocated $650,000 for expansion of the public library. While the public library is fiscally independent of the county, the additional county funds in this case clearly took a burden off the city. In Ohio, libraries are financed by a system in which libraries get first crack at the revenue from an earmarked tax, and the cities get what is left. The allocation by the county of revenue sharing funds to the library thus allowed more of this earmarked revenue to revert to the city of Cincinnati. In that sense, more obviously perhaps than in any other, the easier financial situation of the county has helped the city under revenue sharing.

I might note parenthetically that in the other two jurisdictions I have looked at, Butler County (the county adjacent to Hamilton) and its central city of Hamilton, I have been able to observe nothing like this. To generalize, I would have expected more visible evidence that the easier fiscal situation created for the county by revenue sharing somehow would have redounded, either directly or indirectly, to the benefit of the city, but it didn't.

CHAIR: What is the attitude of Hamilton County officials toward the central city?

STOCKER: There is little interaction; they operate in two separate worlds. They have separate political bases. Republicans dominate the county, whereas the city is primarily Democratic.

CHAIR: Is the county government sympathetic to city needs or unsympathetic?

STOCKER: I would say indifferent bordering on unsympathetic.

CHAIR: Now we will hear about Baltimore and after that Phoenix and St. Louis.

CLIFTON VINCENT: The city of Baltimore is under extreme fiscal pressure caused by the loss of the middle class, both black and white, over the last twenty-five years. Baltimore has a high poverty rate, a high percentage of the aged and unemployed, and cannot expand its boundaries.

The first round of revenue sharing had considerable exposure in the press. When Congress enacted the bill, the budget chief and the mayor immediately decided how the money would be spent, even before they had received their first check. The budget chief and the mayor were the most influential figures in deciding on the use of these funds. In the first round of our field research, most of it was spent to restore cuts in the 1972 budget, in such areas as police, parks, fire, and public works. Also, for the first time in five years, in 1973 Baltimore did not increase its tax rate, which was and continues to be the highest in the state. In sum, Baltimore used most of its shared revenue for tax stabilization and program maintenance.

If you look across the line at Baltimore County, which rings the city. like a horseshoe and is the second wealthiest county in Maryland, you find an expanding tax base, a relatively affluent white middle class, and 5 percent black population. There was very little public exposure for revenue sharing funds in Baltimore County. The county has an executive committee on the budget. An announcement was made that federal revenue sharing funds would be used to reduce the tax rate, and this was done. The county has about $40 million in reserves and they are quite proud of that fact. As far as city and county cooperation is concerned, people in the county have the attitude that they don't want to have anything to do with Baltimore's problems. The tax rate in Baltimore County is almost one-half that of the city. Also, the birth rate has gone down in the county. It's cutting down on expenditures for education; just this year, they closed four public schools.

CHAIR: We turn now to Phoenix, Arizona, and Maricopa County, which overlies Phoenix.

WILLARD PRICE: Maricopa County contains the city of Phoenix and several other significant cities—Glendale, Scottsdale, Tempe, and Mesa. It also has a lot of good Arizona farmland. At the same time, Maricopa County is a metropolitan county in the sense that county facilities are next to the city hall, and to a great extent it seems like one big happy family. Approximately 50 percent of the people who live in Maricopa County live in the city of Phoenix.

Phoenix is a dominating feature of Maricopa County. What I want to do is not go into much detail about Phoenix's use of revenue sharing monies but to spend a little time talking about what Maricopa County has done to see if that tells us anything about the county's ability to effect the central city.

First, Phoenix somewhat shocked me when I found out that it is not really as fiscally secure as I might have anticipated. My view, though, is not as longitudinal as it ought to be.[1] Phoenix, probably earlier than some of the other wealthier communities in Maricopa County, merged its revenue sharing funds into its overall budget. With regard to the round of field observations that I participated in (round three), the net effect has been

1. Price was named an associate in June 1975, after the death of David Shirley.

a distribution, as many of you I am sure have found, between program maintenance, tax stabilization, and some fund balance increases.

At the same time, Phoenix has had a fairly low property tax for quite some time. As in the case of many Arizona cities, it is living mainly off of its sales tax. We do not have any local income taxes; that was voted out as an option of local government. Phoenix is faced right now with a fairly significant revenue-expenditure gap for the next year. To a great extent, revenue sharing funds helped to close this gap.

Maricopa County, on the other hand, is in fairly good financial shape. This is because of its broad and stable property tax base, its sales tax (although a low one), and because of the growth that has occurred in the metropolitan area. When you combine rounds one and two for Maricopa County, there was the much more typical initial impact on the capital side, using revenue sharing to build some new buildings, acquire land, and buy equipment, although a good chunk of what Maricopa County did was to reduce its existing budget gap, essentially a tax stabilization effect.

The question then is whether these capital items had an impact on what maybe some of you may not realize has been a declining central city in Phoenix. In my view, general revenue sharing has added substantially to the vitality of the central business district in Phoenix, because Maricopa County decided to build new buildings in the downtown area out of shared revenue. Who benefits from that? The county clearly did not decide to provide special programs particularly for outlying areas, though it could have. A lot of people told me during the field research for the third round that county officials could have built out in the rural areas and provided other things for people in the county who have been good supporters of the Maricopa County government. They didn't; they chose capital development downtown.

The population is about the same between the city and county, so you might say they benefit equally. But I think the city of Phoenix has benefited somewhat more than the outlying county residents because of the county's help in the revitalization of the downtown area, which in Phoenix is now getting underway with new hotels and new convention facilities.

CHAIR: Robert Christman will tell us about the city of St. Louis. Even though he is not monitoring St. Louis County for general revenue sharing, he has agreed to consider what revenue sharing means when you compare the city and the county.

ROBERT CHRISTMAN: The city of St. Louis has been on the slide since 1950, when the population peaked at 850,000. The population today is estimated at about 515,000 and is continuing to decline. Demographers say that the exodus from the city will continue until it levels off at about 400,000, and that could come before the year 2000. But many of the experts are not unhappy about that; they say it could be a nice city at 400,000. They say crowding people together isn't necessarily good. It is better to spread out and thus also have room for industrial development.

The city's budget sessions generally revolve around what to cut. The severity of its fiscal problems can be seen by looking at the coming fiscal year, which begins May 1. The initial proposed budget was a few hundred thousand more than the $180 million budget of the current fiscal year and yet provided for a 7 percent pay increase for city employees that will cost between $5 and $6 million. It was estimated that nearly 650 employees would lose their jobs so that the rest of the city's employees could get this pay increase. That would have left the city with about 6,600 employees, down from 9,000 employees in 1969. Although these cuts may seem severe, in many cases the employees dropped have been picked up under other federal programs. Up until this year, the city has operated four hospitals, including two acute-care hospitals. In the coming fiscal year, it was proposed to close one hospital and turn one hospital into a domiciliary-care facility. Also, the budget director initially proposed no street cleaning for residential, streets, a reduction in fire department personnel, and cuts in health services. All of this was said to be necessary to bridge a $10 million gap. The picture has changed, however, in the past few weeks.

The budget currently before the Board of Aldermen totals $189 million, using estimated carry-over funds and relying on a heavy dose of prayer and optimism. The latest proposal represents weeks of revisions of the original budget proposals. The city will continue to operate four hospitals until advised by an outside consultant on which of the two general hospitals to eliminate. The 7 percent pay increase has been approved, but it now appears that approximately seventy persons will lose their jobs, at least until the hospital decision is made. A total of 287 unfilled job slots are eliminated in this latest proposal, leaving the city with a total of 7,100 employees. The latest recommended budget contains no cuts in fire department personnel or residential street cleaning.

When revenue sharing first came to St. Louis in 1972, it was not anticipated in the budget, so the money was available for projects the city had been putting off. City fathers were intent on spending revenue sharing for nonrecurring programs if possible; but, as in many other cities with the same intention, it did not work out that way. Among the capital uses proposed for the first $12 million in revenue sharing funds were $300,000 for a new firehouse, $486,000 for a new city jail, $408,000 for new refuse equipment, $560,000 for new street cleaning equipment, $1 million to air-condition the city's two acute-care hospitals, $1.2 million for three ice- and roller-skating rinks, and $1.6 million for recreation and senior citizen's centers. City officials brought all of the department directors together and called on city residents to express their opinions as much as possible, contacting about 130 neighborhood groups in making the allocations. In St. Louis, budget proposals come from the Board of Estimate and Apportionment, which is made up of the president of the Board of Aldermen, the mayor, and the comptroller. In 1972, all three were candidates for mayor, so all three were trying their best to please.

In the end, a substantial amount of this $12 million went for building demolition and street repairs and reconstruction. There was about $2 million left from 1972 funds that were carried over to the 1973–74 budget, providing a total of about $16 million in revenue sharing in that year.

However, by 1973–74, the city's fiscal state had worsened so much that $13 million of the $16 million went for city employees' salaries—that is, program maintenance. This helped to provide $5 million for a 5 percent pay increase for city employees. There was a great pressure on the city for pay increases because none had been granted in the previous year and there had been a refuse strike in the meantime. Two weeks of a refuse strike can put any mayor right up against the wall. Out of the $16 million of available revenue sharing funds, only $2.3 million went for new equipment and capital improvements. By the end of the 1973–74 fiscal year, the city faced a $20 million gap for the coming budget estimated at $170 million. The Board of Aldermen figured there was nothing to do but cash in capital improvement ordinances that had been approved in 1973 for the use of 1972 revenue sharing funds. The ordinance approving the recreation and senior citizens centers, the hospital air-conditioning, and the ice- and roller-skating rinks were all repealed. Some amounts—for example, $500,000 to buy land—were already spent; but the total amount unspent came to $3.3 million. That amount, plus revenue sharing money anticipated in the 1975–76 budget and the little bit that was not spent the previous budget year (1972–73), added up to $21 million that went entirely for program maintenance purposes. In the 1975–76 fiscal year, the city included five quarters of revenue sharing payments in the budget to help the city over a rough spot. Thus, there was only about $10.2 million in revenue sharing money to be appropriated for the coming fiscal year, again all going to program maintenance.

So, out of a total of about $70 million in revenue sharing money that the city will receive, or has received, $62.7 million has been used for salaries (program maintenance)—almost 90 percent.

Turning to St. Louis County, the county's fiscal year is the calendar year, so the first revenue sharing payments were appropriated in the regular budget process. By the way, in the city the revenue sharing money just came into the regular budget process as well; it was not considered separately. In St. Louis County, the first year's appropriation of $8.2 million in revenue sharing funds went mostly for parks and recreation, including $750,000 for a golf course. About $1.8 million went for recurring programs, mostly police services. In the following budget year, 60 percent of the $6.2 million in revenue sharing money allocated went for parks and recreation, highway work, health facilities, and code enforcement; the remainder went toward the recurring costs of police services.

In 1975, the county's operating budget was $65 million. Some 70 percent of the $6.7 million in revenue sharing allocated was used for recurring costs such as police services, and 30 percent for new programs, mainly code enforcement and recreation. The 1976 budget in the county uses $6 million of shared revenue, three-quarters for recurring costs and the remainder for capital improvements and code enforcement.

It is interesting to note that in 1974, revenue sharing money provided 5 percent of the county's operating (as opposed to capital) budget. The next year, revenue sharing money made up 15 percent, and in the current budget year, revenue sharing money accounts for about 9 percent of the operating budget.

It is also interesting to note that in the past two budget years, county officials have referred to their budgets as "austere." In the early seventies, growth in St. Louis County provided an automatic increase in revenue annually that county officials could bank on. In the past two years, however, the growth rate has been reduced by half; budget belt tightening has been the result in a county that is just now beginning to feel the effects of urbanization, the problems resulting from an influx of poor persons needing costly services, and a housing stock that has reached an age where code enforcement is necessary to prevent blight.

But the county has not done so badly on revenue sharing overall. Out of about $34 million in revenue sharing, including interest, I estimate that about $13.5 million has been used for new purposes—nearly 40 percent of the total.

CHAIR: I remember a comment from one of the St. Louis reports to the effect that within the St. Louis area there has been considerable discussion in the press about the fact that the county has been able to do new things with its revenue sharing—the golf course is a symbol of that—while the city has not been able to use its shared revenue for new purposes. I wonder if you might say a word or two about attitudes toward revenue sharing in relation to the contrasting conditions of the city and the county.

CHRISTMAN: As I said, in St. Louis County revenue sharing is considered free money, new money that can be used for such purposes as recreation and parks.

ARTHUR R. THIEL: Can't people in the city use the facilities? If you live in the city, can't you play on the county golf course?

CHRISTMAN: There's not that much interaction between St. Louis and St. Louis County.

THIEL: I'm talking about the people.

CHRISTMAN: I'm talking about the people.

THIEL: They don't go outside of the city?

CHRISTMAN: No. We had a serious problem of county people using St. Louis city park facilities, especially baseball diamonds. There was a proposal, and it went into effect, to charge $10 a year for a permit for a county person to use city tennis courts. But there's no way to enforce it so it went out the window.

PAUL R. DOMMEL: With regard to the idea of burden sharing between the central city and its suburbs, from these five cases it is clear that burden sharing has many dimensions and manifestations. One example is the case of the public library in Cincinnati; another is Phoenix, with downtown capital development being undertaken by the overlying county government. In Newark, it is the tax side that is important; county tax relief out of shared revenue benefits outlying county residents more than those living in the center city.

COHEN: Why are some of these counties in such good shape? Is it a population mix for them, higher income? Is it that despite their developmental costs somehow they don't have the burden of the full infrastructure that the central cities have?

CHAIR: Two of the five counties on this panel are not overlying counties. St Louis and Baltimore Counties are completely outside of the central city. They are suburban governments, whereas Hamilton, Maricopa and Essex are overlying counties.

ROSS: I would like to comment on the Los Angeles situation, which is an overlay. Most of Los Angeles County's shared revenue went into capital expenditures. The County Board of Supervisors functions according to what is called the "rule of five," that is, splitting up capital items among the five supervisorial districts. The five districts are relatively equal in population, so Los Angeles City gets as much as the outlying areas. That is the way the board operates, whether it is courts or parks or health facilities.

Major county responsibilities are, for example, health and welfare. The city has no responsibility for these functions, so there is a great deal of burden sharing because of the assignment of duties of local government in California.

CHARLES R. HOLCOMB: It is not only a matter of whether or not counties overlie the central city or just surround it as in Baltimore County; it is partly a matter of not having to provide the infrastructure. County governments often don't have to have areawide water systems and sewerage systems because people in outlying areas have septic tanks. Also, when you are putting in a sewer line, it goes into essentially virgin territory; you don't have to tear up streets as in a central city.

Also, as to the matter of function, I think it is interesting that in New York State in the last decade, welfare expenditures, including Medicaid, have mushroomed. Welfare is a county function throughout New York State. It is interesting to hear wealthy counties like Westchester, Nassau, and Monroe howling with pain because of mushrooming welfare expenditures. They are used to having expenditures reflecting the needs of the poor loaded on the central cities; that is not so much the case anymore.

CLARA PENNIMAN: Some of these structures and governmental organizations flow from old state legislation dealing with shared taxes or grant formulas. In many cases you will find that these old patterns of taxing and functional relationships produce new kinds of problems.

STOCKER: In relation to the different fiscal situation of cities and their overlying counties, I want to comment on one other factor evident in Cincinnati and Hamilton County and in the city of Hamilton and Butler County. The two central cities face strong, aggressive unions, whereas in the counties, at least in Ohio, there is practically no union organization. The county sheriff does not have a unionized police force as you have in the case of city police departments.

VINCENT: The same thing is true for Baltimore city and county. With the exception of the teachers' union, there is practically no union organization in the county. The city, on the other hand, is highly organized.

LIEBSCHUTZ: I want to pick up on the point Charles Holcomb made with respect to Rochester and Monroe County, New York. It is true that state mandates and program growth have put the county in a different position vis-à-vis the city in terms of welfare services. But I think that the net effect of revenue sharing for county government has been to accelerate service consolidation in non–state-mandated areas, including parks, purchasing, and, most recently, the assumption by Monroe County of the cost of the disposal of solid waste for the city. Interlocal cooperation has been accelerated by revenue sharing.

JOHN DE GROVE: We certainly do have an interesting contrast in city-county combinations. Let me add to this. In Orange County and Orlando, Florida, you have a situation where neither the county nor the city is under any particularly severe fiscal pressure. Both have operated in a pretty relaxed atmosphere in their use of revenue sharing funds. This is just to make the point that this is quite a different picture here than you have in some of the old northeastern and midwestern metropolitan areas.

CHRISTMAN: There is almost an arrogance in St. Louis County toward people in the city. The attitude is, "well, it was your idea that took you out of St. Louis County. It was not our doing at all, so you live with it." About half of the people living outside of the city in St. Louis County have moved there from the city of St. Louis; they automatically take on the county attitude.

Panel 3: Structural Effects

CHAIR: First we will hear about the state of Illinois, especially the impact of revenue sharing on township governments.

ROBERT SCHOEPLEIN: Illinois maintains its dubious distinction as having the most units of local government of any state, including a proliferation of 1,432 townships. I would group the townships into three categories: (1) rural townships; (2) coterminous townships, that is, townships with political boundaries that virtually match and overlap those of municipalities; and (3) townships adjacent to municipalities. The latter two categories are the most controversial in Illinois. (Seventeen of Illinois' 102 counties have no township governments.)

Prior to the adoption of revenue sharing in 1972, the prescribed functions that townships could perform were restricted by the new state constitution adopted in 1970. Two functions were specified, road maintenance and cash-grant poor relief or general assistance, although the latter is rarely very important for townships in Illinois because of their conservative political orientation and the fact that poor relief tends to have been displaced by state and federal funds. Moreover, townships could not transfer monies to municipalities or counties.

The effect of revenue sharing on townships depends in part on cash-flow and spending decisions, as we have come to appreciate in our study. In Illinois, township lobbyists and certain special interest groups lobbied with the state legislature to expand the allowable functions that townships could perform. Many townships withheld decisions on spending revenue sharing funds until their allowable functions were expanded by statute in June 1973 to include all the priority-expenditure categories in the federal revenue sharing act of 1972. The enabling legislation permitted townships to expend revenue sharing monies only on programs in these functional areas and only in cooperation with another governmental unit or community organization.

But in February 1974, an Illinois attorney general's opinion held the statute to be ineffective because the federal revenue sharing act expressly states that revenue sharing monies may be spent only on programs that local governments can provide out of their own revenues. Thus eighteen months after adoption of the federal revenue sharing act, Illinois townships found themselves either in legal jeopardy from financing new programs without state sanction or with extraordinary accumulated cash reserves. Not until the legislature passed a second statute in September 1974, did Illinois townships have the authority legitimately to expend monies on programs other than road maintenance.

Townships now have moved forward to commit revenue sharing receipts in two general ways. One has been for townships to enter into contracts for services with private providers for such items as ambulance service and transportation for the rural aged. These are annual or two-year contracts and expire close to the anticipated termination of the present revenue sharing act. A second move by townships that are coterminous with or adjacent to municipalities has been to enter into cooperation agreements with a municipality for the provision of a particular service, again for a specific time period.

These various programs and projects are clearly identifiable. In many cooperation agreements, they are specifically identified as having been funded by revenue sharing funds. One finds in some municipal areas signs posted with a credit line that some particular project or service was funded by federal revenue sharing money under agreement between the city and a particular township.

We have no hard data at this time about any changes in interest levels in township politics. Therefore, I would have to fall back on casual observation. It is my assessment that the revenue sharing act has increased the interest in township government at the rural level. In the urban counties, however, where the bulk of the population resides and where there are coterminous townships and townships adjacent to municipalities, I would say there is no perceptible change so far in the interest in town government. Local political parties that were in the minority in the last elections seemed to have had the same degree of difficulty in fielding a complete slate of candidates for township boards. Perhaps this November we will be able to perceive, if there is any, a change in the interest level in these township governments. As it stands now, the visibility of township government is very low. Revenue sharing funds have provided an extension of the life of a form of government that in the nonrural areas was on the decline.

CHAIR: William Farber will speak next about Midwestern townships and related structural issues.

WILLIAM O. FARBER: In South Dakota, most shared revenue paid to township governments has been used for road maintenance and construction. The value of federal revenue sharing funds for townships can best be determined on a state-by-state basis, but the case for its continuance, at least in my area, is vulnerable on at least two counts.

First, township governments lack viability because of the arbitrary character of their boundaries and their smallness. Second, for the most part, either legally or in practice, township government is limited-purpose government. Both of these counts make township government ripe for reform efforts.

But the recognition of townships by the present revenue sharing program and its help in alleviating any financial crunch they face, which might have compelled change, means that revenue sharing serves as an impediment to the restructuring of these governments. Attempts to recast the revenue sharing formula to make sure that only general-purpose or multipurpose townships receive funds should, in my opinion, be carefully scrutinized to ensure that the effect is not to expand rather than decrease township activity.

CHAIR: Let me ask you to comment also on the recent attempts in your state to set up substate regional bodies. Revenue sharing has not only reinforced old forms, it has discouraged new forms.

FARBER: That is correct. In 1970, South Dakota divided the state into substate regions, the primary purpose of which was to help set up units to help local governments plan and to develop grant applications. These substate planning districts were embarked on a statewide program of trying to get local units to work together, and they were making substantial progress. We also passed a constitutional amendment in 1972 abolishing the rigid constitutional statutes of county officers and providing home rule for counties. We were just getting into these reforms when revenue sharing began. What we have had in the last three or four years is, in effect, a suspension of these kinds of cooperative efforts.

As revenues decline in the future, these efforts may be revived, but I feel that if we are talking about the structural reform impact of revenue sharing in South Dakota, the program, as it currently operates, has been an impediment in many ways to structural reform.

CHAIR: As I understand it, the essence of why you believe revenue sharing has slowed structural reform efforts is that substate regions are not eligible for revenue sharing funds and the component governments are fiscally relieved by revenue sharing.

FARBER: Yes, especially if we assume that the $6 billion per year appropriated by the federal government for revenue sharing would instead have gone into categorical grants distributed on the basis of grant applications, some of which might have come to or through these substate districts.

CHAIR: One of the things that stands out in the data for the second round is that revenue sharing has in a much larger number of instances than I would have expected caused county governments to expand their role into new functional areas. Is this evident in South Dakota?

FARBER: I would like to approach that question from a rural point of view. I was interested this morning in the wide variety of effects revenue sharing has. South Dakota county officials are in frequent contact with one another, and a strategy begins to emerge for both municipal and county officials as to how they should approach revenue sharing. One thing the counties have decided is that the Congress wants uses other than just existing programs and old purposes supported out of these funds. At their meetings they talk about the importance of innovation in their uses of revenue sharing funds. As a result we had something of a breakthrough, in the beginning at least, in terms of revenue sharing expenditures for new types of purposes at the county level. County officials understand this to be the new game plan and that they'd better play or they will lose their revenue sharing money.

This has proved to be a unifying issue for both county and municipal governments in South Dakota. Their organizations have spent a good deal of money to propagandize the success of revenue sharing. Their spokesmen have made trips to Washington. All of our Congressmen have been visited by delegations. Senator Abourezk, who opposes revenue sharing, is a particular villain in this piece. There is not a week goes by that we don't have delegations going in to see him. They cannot persuade the Senator to see the light, yet in a way his opposition to revenue sharing has been a unifying political force among the counties and the cities. They really want revenue sharing continued.

CHAIR: Thank you. Next we will hear about county government in South Carolina.

C. BLEASE GRAHAM: My basic themes are quite similar to those for South Dakota. In short, we are talking about the limited municipalization of heretofore rural counties. If you look at it from a traditional point of view, county governments in South Carolina were really neighborhood state houses that were basically within horseback riding distance. That was the traditional measure for deciding on the places where state business would be conducted.

Our state was unique in that budgets for counties used to be passed at a special legislative session of the state general assembly. This, coupled with the fact that each county had one senator, meant that the senator was pretty much the king of the county. He could dominate the old road commission and by means of that arrangement dole out enough favors to keep getting reelected. Reapportionment broke that apart. County councils were established around 1970; there was also a change in the constitution in 1973 that allowed the state legislature to assign municipal types of functions to county governments.

At any rate, largely as a result of the suburbanization of the state in the common doughnut-around-the-hole pattern, county governments have been restructured to be able to provide municipal-type services on a countywide basis. In one case, that of sanitary landfill, this function was recently transferred from municipalities to counties. Many counties across the state have used revenue sharing to finance this new function and to improve garbage collection.

Another thing is that county councils in South Carolina are taking themselves much more seriously. The word "policy" is no longer alien to county councils, many of which have been set up in the last five years. There has been a fairly dramatic growth in the number of professional administrators and managers employed by county governments. This reflects an internal administrative restructuring along lines of the integrated executive model, rather than the pluralistic executive model.

Considering our state and a couple of counties I have looked at in Deil Wright's state (North Carolina), our general area validates your thesis that the role of counties has been expanding. New functions include basic kinds of municipal services like police and sanitary landfill, not so much yet in water, and relatively little in human services.

JOHN DE GROVE: Could you expand on that? How important was revenue sharing in this process?

GRAHAM: Very important. Newly recruited managers had extra money because of general revenue sharing. Counties in South Carolina have had all kinds of special-district governments. They couldn't be in the recreation business; they couldn't be in the fire business, and still can't for many functions. The county may have levied 150 mills but only directly used 10 mills of that; the rest was a pass-through, disbursed to special-district governments within the county. So general revenue sharing funds for a county government may represent 25 or 30 percent of its direct expenditures.

DE GROVE: What kinds of new programs are involved?

GRAHAM: We now have professionalized public works departments without raising taxes.

DEIL WRIGHT: Did you say that general revenue sharing was in some instances 25 percent of the total budget?

GRAHAM: Twenty-five percent in relation to the approximately 10 mills of own-raised funds that county governments directly expend.

CHAIR: We have heard in the discussion so far that many township governments have been propped up and are holding on more than they perhaps otherwise would as a consequence of revenue sharing. County government is apparently strengthened and the role of county government has been broadened in many areas in part as a result of the revenue sharing program. One area that the members of this panel have touched on, but that we have not gotten into yet, is the impact of revenue sharing on special districts. Does this strengthening of counties discourage setting up and relying on special districts because they are not eligible recipients?

Next is Arkansas.

GEORGE E. CAMPBELL: It will help if we first discuss certain facts about the operation of the city government of Little Rock and of municipalities generally in the state of Arkansas. This will help explain Little Rock's recent decision to annex approximately fifty-five square miles, almost doubling the area of the city, a decision that was significantly influenced by the revenue sharing program.

Our state constitution, like many of the southern Reconstruction and post-Reconstruction period, does not deal in great detail with municipal government. It is quite restrictive. The situation in terms of the ability to levy local taxes has not improved much since the basic Arkansas constitution was adopted 102 years ago. The property tax is at its constitutional ceiling in Little Rock and has been as long as anyone can remember. In the state as a whole, the property tax generates perhaps 10 or 12 percent—maybe a little more in smaller communities—of the total revenue of city general funds. You may ask where cities get the rest of their revenue, and that's the problem.

A substantial part of it comes from revenue sharing; therefore, the visibility of revenue sharing has been material. The situation in terms of the role of cities versus counties has been much like that just described for South Carolina. The county is not looked upon to perform services, other than to be an agent of the state in administering the court and taxation systems, and so forth. Neither the city nor the county has been looked to as a provider of health services, for example. The county basically provides police, fire, and sanitation services. Now the county role is growing, partly as a result of revenue sharing.

Little Rock is a fairly old city by all except eastern seaboard standards. It was established prior to 1820 before Arkansas became a state; it has been a governmental center for 150 years. In 1870, there were only four cities in Arkansas that had a population in excess of 2,500. Little Rock had about ten or twelve thousand at that time and has experienced steady growth since then. The Little Rock SMSA is currently about 320,000; Little Rock's population is 135,000.

A 20 percent increase in population, some 30,000 or so, would result from the annexation of the 55 square miles. Because of the relatively weak government of Pulaski County, which overlies Little Rock, and its lack of any zoning control, and because of the growth of the area—particularly because of the migration from rural areas as farm population decreased and even the small urban areas began to decline materially in population— there has been a spreading of developing residential areas around Little Rock but without the scope or quality of the public services available within the city. As a consequence, residential subdividers will arrange to annex forty acres here and forty acres there as they create residential subdivisions. They are required to provide certain minimal services and facilities—storm drainage, water and sewerage lines that tie in with the city system. The city has no authority to exercise zoning control beyond its municipal limits. It has general planning authority and can limit certain land uses, or if a person decides to subdivide land for residential purposes, the city can control that to a certain degree, but it could not exercise effective zoning.

Little Rock is bounded on the north by the Arkansas River and on the east by a natural boundary, bauxite pits and granite mines. This means expansion has to be almost totally to the south and west of the city into either low-lying or hilly areas that present significant problems in providing drainage, sewerage and water service. The need to exercise greater control over this outlying southwestern area was evident for a long time. As was noted in *Monitoring Revenue Sharing,* we had a fairly aggressive city manager who wanted to deal with this matter. When the talk about revenue sharing began, our congressman, Wilbur Mills, opposed it, but then he became converted. When that happened, the city fathers realized that there was going to be revenue sharing. They began to plan how to utilize it, and one of the things they very much wanted to do was to finance this annexation project.

There was, and still is today, $2 million set aside, approximately one year's shared revenue, to be used for capital improvements in the annexation area, primarily for fire stations and also for other purposes, such as a police substation and some road improvements. That $2 million was the carrot they put out in front of the residents of this area to have them go along with the annexation.

Annexation in our state, when a municipality proposes it, requires an election by those in the area to be annexed and in the city doing the annexing. The total vote applies, with no distinction made between voters inside and outside the city. Thus the system is usually weighted in favor of the municipality if you can generate a turnout. But a lot of people are lethargic about getting to the polls on issues that don't affect them directly.

The taxes to be collected from the annexed area, after the first couple of years of start-up costs, were estimated to equal the cost of the new projects and services that would be required initially. But the city clearly could not have committed itself to these initial services and capital investments if it had not been for revenue sharing.

As a footnote, annexation has not yet occurred, even though the election was held in May 1973 and the annexation plan carried. It was challenged in the courts under the Arkansas annexation statute that as of 1973, prohibited the annexation of land used for agricultural purposes. Even if agricultural purposes were not their highest and best use, if they were used for agricultural purposes at all, they were not subject to annexation. The city admitted that substantial areas in the annexation area were used for agriculture, although their highest and best use, of course, is their liquidative value for urban development. On this basis the Arkansas State Supreme Court turned down the annexation. However, in 1975 the state annexation statute was amended as a result of the efforts of the city of Little Rock to revise this land-use standard. The law now provides that if the fair-market value of annexed land, or if the highest and best use of the land, is for residential purposes and not for agricultural purposes, then it may be annexed. A subsequent election was held in 1975 after the new legislation became effective. The issue again passed and it is again being challenged in the courts. It is likely the annexation will be upheld this time.

CHAIR: The final person on this panel, Arthur R. Thiel, will focus on the state level.

ARTHUR R. THIEL: Revenue sharing, as far as Louisiana is concerned, came at a time when the state was flush. This is kind of unusual these days. In our case, it is because the state is heavily dependent on revenue derived from extractive taxes on its natural resources and is blessed with extensive natural resources. The energy crisis resulted in a pretty substantial increase in oil and gas prices. Furthermore, the state recently received windfall revenues from the federal government because of a recent court decision.

One of the main things the governor did with revenue sharing was to put it into highway construction. Revenue sharing gave the governor about $40 million a year that he could use for more roads. Because the state was in good financial condition, there was not much interest in the official reports in the news media about the use of these funds. Shared revenue was simply merged into the state construction budget; it was listed separately but not pulled out and discussed separately.

There was no controversy about revenue sharing. When the state received its first entitlement, it devised an accounting strategy so that it was able to use federal revenue sharing funds to obtain other federal money on a matching basis, although they did this only once.

The governor of Louisiana is very strong, not by law, but by practice. Legislators knew if they won the favor of the governor they could get roads in their area. (As an aside, the legislature passed a new law, in my opinion an excellent one, which becomes effective in the next fiscal year, outlining new procedures to be followed in allocating money for the construction of state highways.)

The financial good fortune of Louisiana is not expected to continue. It looks as if in the next couple of years or so we will face financial problems. This year's budget may be the first one where there will be some cutting back. However, as far as revenue sharing is concerned, it initially came at a time when the state was in good financial condition.

The other subject I want to discuss is special districts. Not many years ago, textbooks on government talked about the demise of the county as a unit of government. That is no longer the case. More people are looking to the county—in Louisiana, we call it a parish—as a basic unit of government because it covers a broad geographical area.

We have been promoting parish government in Louisiana. In most parishes, the governing body is the police jury, which is the same as the board of supervisors in most places. We are encouraging police juries to take on a more active role in providing services to stem the tide of new incorporations by small communities. When a group of people are living together and they need some particular service, unless they can get it from the parish, they have to incorporate. We don't think we help ourselves by having a lot of incorporated municipalities; in Louisiana, we use the special district to discourage such incorporations.

Under our constitution, the governing body of the parish is the governing body of all special districts that it creates. You get away from the problem of having a large number of separate boards or commissions this way. Some special districts have advisory boards, but the parish governing body is the actual governing body of the special district. It is a very useful device. I live in Baton Rouge. Baton Rouge Parish has a population of about 300,000; about two-thirds live within the city-parish limits and the other third live outside. There are several large groupings of people in the outlying area, and they use the special-district concept for the collection of garbage, for fire protection, and so forth. In other parishes they use the special-district device for drainage purposes or street lighting. Taxes are levied on that district to provide that particular service. When the basic needs of the people are met, in many cases there is no longer the desire or need to incorporate as a separate municipality. This is an efficient way to provide a given service and it keeps the governing body of the parish involved. The more we try to provide services on a special-district basis like this, I think the better off we are going to be. Special districts, as we know them in Louisiana, have not run into the problems found in some other areas.

CHAIR: If there are two adjoining fire special districts, does the parish have any kind of administrative arrangement whereby there are joint functions or joint services between them?

THIEL: Yes, that can be done, for example, on garbage collection. There really are not many advantages in living within or without the city of Baton Rouge. If you live within it, you pay the city millage. If you live outside, there are several areas surrounding the city that are heavily populated and have garbage districts. The special district contracts with the city to pick up the garbage and the people in the special district pay so many mills in property taxes, and that in turn is paid to the city.

The laws of the state permit governments to enter into contractual agreements to provide services to one another. I think you can appreciate the need for a special district because there are many areas that are rural, where you can drive for miles and see only a few houses. It is not feasible to run a garbage truck way out there to stop at one or two places on a ten or fifteen mile stretch, nor can you provide adequate fire protection. That is why many of these services are not applicable on a parishwide basis, but they are applicable on a special-district basis. The only purpose of the special district is to provide the money to pay for the special service involved. It does not mean that they have to buy garbage trucks or buy special equipment and so forth; they can contract for that service.

SCHOEPLEIN: In Illinois, for the last three years, just counting the number of special districts (I'm not talking about changes in the size of their budget), there has been no significant net change in the number of special districts other than school districts. There has, in fact, been a modest decrease in the number of special districts as a result of the consolidation of special districts rather than the absorption of their responsibilities by the county in, for example, rural counties with a declining population where road districts or fire districts are consolidated. On the other hand, there has been an offsetting modest increase in special districts adjacent to municipalities where they are formed to contract with the municipality for services, such as fire protection, thereby, so they believe, avoiding the other burdens of being a municipality as under annexation.

CAMPBELL: We use special districts quite widely in Arkansas, primarily for capital-improvement projects, sewer and water line construction to areas outside municipalities, or, in some instances, even inside municipalities. With a couple of exceptions that I can think of—for example, for fire protection districts—they have not been utilized to provide services. This kind of a role traces to constitutional limitations on the indebtedness of municipalities for capital purposes as well as the need for revenue-bond financing for bigger projects.

There has been perpetual "poor-mouthing," and with considerable justification, on the part of our municipalities for a long time about capital improvements. If anybody is outside the city or wants to subdivide, he must provide sewer, water, streets, gutters, storm drainage, and so forth before he is permitted to create a subdivision. The city does not like having to finance those kinds of projects.

I would like to make another point in line with what has been happening in South Carolina and perhaps Louisiana. We recently adopted a constitutional amendment in Arkansas that formally creates—I won't go into the history of why we call it this—Boards of Port, which is what county councils are called in Arkansas. Now these boards are being elected by district. For the first time in the memory of anyone who can talk about it, we will have county legislative bodies identifiable and responsible for making budget decisions that heretofore had been made by a single county administrator or county judge. I think we will find our counties expanding into new areas, particularly in the central part of the state where we have a substantial urban population. The availability of revenue sharing will encourage that because sometimes it amounts to as much as a 75 percent increase in available funds (that is, in relation to the own-raised revenue of the county used for its own direct expenditures).

FARBER: I haven't noticed much change as far as special districts are concerned in the areas with which I am acquainted. There are 133 special districts in the state of South Dakota, although in the last two or three years, the creation of these units seems to have slowed up (though I do not have proof of that).

CHAIR: Perhaps the main point of this discussion is that there are a lot of factors that explain why people set up special districts. In general, this suggests that we should question the simplistic orthodox view that special districts are the bad guys of state-local government.

CAMPBELL: One footnote: in my experience, the formation of special districts is related to the availability of federal funds to contribute to the cost of public improvement projects. We often form them, for example, to get Farmers Home Administration loans in rural areas.

GRAHAM: South Carolina had an explosion of special districts in the early 1970s. I think it has definitely slowed down now. In our state there's a tight relationship between cities, counties, and substate regional governments. The councils of governments in many cases are contract planners, and in this role significantly influence decisions about the creation and role of special districts.

CHAIR: I thank the members of this panel and all of the discussants.

B Background and Summary Fiscal Effects Data on the Sixty-five Sample Jurisdictions Monitored by the Brookings Field Associates

Table B-1. Background Information on the Sample Jurisdictions

Jurisdiction[a]	Population[b] (thousands)	Fiscal[e] pressure	Revenue sharing[c] Per capita[d] (dollars)	As a percent of own-source general revenue	Per capita income, 1972 (dollars)	Per capita taxes[f] (dollars)
Local governments						
Arizona-West						
Maricopa County	1,127.5	L	5.48	10.1	4,107	54
Phoenix	639.3	L	14.95	11.3	4,118	105
Scottsdale	73.8	N	10.00	8.6	4,865	105
Tempe	83.1	L	10.38	10.8	4,209	78
Arkansas-South						
Pulaski County	306.8	L	5.00	29.8	3,493	14
Little Rock	137.9	M	23.72	18.9	3,915	71
North Little Rock	65.3	L	12.01	16.2	3,506	26
Saline County	40.7	L	7.96	11.4	2,910	17
California-West						
Los Angeles County	6,928.1	M	13.06	7.9	4,486	148
Los Angeles	2,747.4	M	13.50	6.4	4,545	175
Carson	78.8	L	5.38	13.0	3,473	112
Colorado-West						
Longmont	29.6	M	11.29	9.2	3,891	92
Florida-South						
Jacksonville	517.3	M	18.85	11.7	3,686	100
Orange County	394.0	N	7.77	13.0	3,837	70
Orlando	109.7	L	20.91	9.3	3,921	140
Seminole County	119.4	L	6.06	17.6	3,592	53
Louisiana-South						
Baton Rouge	287.2	L	27.47	18.5	3,480	149

Maine-Northeast						
Bangor	33.4	M	36.53	8.2	3,097	145
Maryland-South						
Baltimore County	630.6	N	17.12	4.8	4,819	141
Baltimore	877.7	E	30.59	8.0	3,595	178
Carroll County	76.6	L	10.37	2.9	3,635	93
Harford County	130.0	L	8.99	4.3	3,985	45
Massachusetts-Northeast						
Worcester	174.3	E	25.74	6.0	3,763	321
Holden Town	13.1	L	9.48	2.2	4,363	149
Missouri-North Central						
St. Louis	554.0	E	27.29	9.7	3,292	259
New Jersey-Northeast						
Essex County	907.6	N	8.80	7.3	4,515	102
Newark	364.5	E	24.66	6.5	2,964	181
West Orange	43.1	N	5.70	4.4	5,716	194
Livingston Township	30.4	N	11.43	9.3	6,646	99
New York-Northeast						
Monroe County	710.7	L	7.85	4.5	4,532	105
Rochester	276.9	E	13.67	4.5	3,716	210
Greece Town	75.7	N	5.01	8.2	4,718	53
Irondequoit Town	62.5	L	5.23	7.4	5,266	53
New York City	7,664.2	E	33.39	5.0	4,309	477
North Carolina-South						
Orange County	65.0	M	4.06	3.5	3,737	30
Ohio-North Central						
Bulter County	238.7	L	1.44	7.8	3,703	23
Hamilton County	918.8	N	6.41	11.4	4,018	45
Hamilton	66.6	M	15.58	13.7	3,635	95
Cincinnati	428.5	M	23.55	4.9	3,657	199

Table B-1 *(continued)*

Jurisdiction[a]	Population[b] (thousands)	Fiscal[e] pressure	Revenue sharing[c]			Per capita income, 1972 (dollars)	Per capita[f] taxes (dollars)
			Per capita[d] (dollars)	As a percent of own-source general revenue			
Oregon-West							
Lane County	230.3	L	4.12	16.9	3,737	18
Cottage Grove	6.4	M	23.47	25.0	3,359	52
Eugene	87.1	M	22.92	11.2	4,085	102
Springfield	31.1	M	20.18	25.0	3,515	75
South Carolina-South							
Fairfield County	19.9	M	19.53	35.7	2,068	27
Winnsboro	3.1	L	35.08	43.4	2,660	40
Kershaw County	36.0	L	14.02	14.7	3,023	26
Camden	8.7	L	24.47	33.8	4,096	47
South Dakota-North Central							
Minnehaha County	98.3	L	5.17	15.3	3,405	29
Sioux Falls	74.2	L	16.45	11.4	3,594	124
Tripp County	8.3	L	15.48	13.6	3,297	85
Turner County	9.7	L	17.29	27.5	3,732	51
Wisconsin-North Central							
Dodge County	71.0	M	11.56	15.2	3,438	46
Beaver Dam	14.3	M	11.85	13.7	3,893	59
Mayville	4.2	M	6.37	7.2	3,682	48
Lowell Town	1.3	M	12.87	23.5	2,600	20
Theresa Town	1.1	M	5.25	23.1	2,905	19
Indian Reservation							
South Dakota-North Central							
Rosebud	7.2	E	18.68	n.a.	n.a.	8

State governments

California	21,185	10.19	M	2.6	4,264	752
Colorado	2,534	8.61	N	2.5	4,006	578
Illinois	11,144	9.29	M	2.5	4,220	698
Louisiana	3,793	12.24	L	3.0	2,876	492
Maine	1,059	11.91	L	3.4	3,030	543
Massachusetts	5,828	11.13	M	2.7	4,052	763
New York	18,120	12.69	L	2.4	4,248	952
North Carolina	5,451	9.59	N	2.7	3,196	454

Sources: Columns 1, 3, 5, 6: Office of Revenue Sharing, *State and Local Data Elements, Entitlement Period 7 and Entitlement Period 8* (GPO, 1977); idem, *Payment Summary, Entitlement Periods 1 through 5 with Entitlement Period 6 Estimate* (GPO, 1975). Column 2: field research data. Column 4: own-source general revenue, U.S. Bureau of the Census, *City Government Finances in 1972–73* (GPO, 1974), table 5; idem, *Government Finances in 1972–73* (GPO, 1974), table 17; and unpublished data from the Census Bureau.

n.a. Not available.

a. By state, with official Census Bureau region. Local governments are municipalities unless otherwise designated.

b. Popular estimates as of 1973 for local governments, 1975 for state governments.

c. An averaging of fiscal pressure ratings reported in the first- and second-round field reports, where E = extreme fiscal pressure, M = moderate, L = light, and N = none. See chapter 2 for more information about these ratings.

d. Computed on the basis of payments for entitlement period 5 (July 1, 1974 to June 30, 1975).

e. Computed as the ratio of revenue sharing payments in fiscal 1975 to own-source general revenue in fiscal 1973.

f. Per capita taxes for local governments are for fiscal 1975, and are computed on the basis of total taxes minus taxes for schools and other educational purposes. For states, per capita taxes are based on total state and local taxes (including school taxes) for fiscal 1974.

Table B-2. Summary Information on the Fiscal Effects of Revenue Sharing for the Sample Jurisdictions

Jurisdiction[a]	Cumulative[b] entitlement (thousands of dollars)	Cumulative[c] allocation		Uses of shared revenue as a percent of cumulative allocation					
		Amount (thousands of dollars)	As a percent of entitlement	New[d] spending	Maintained[e] spending	Revenue[f] stabilization	Tax reduction	Increased fund balances	Other[g]
Local governments									
Arizona-West									
Maricopa County	20,158.6	19,675.2	98	42.8	0	57.2	0	0	0
Phoenix	31,172.0	31,683.3	102	91.1	8.9	0	0	0	0
Scottsdale	2,281.6	2,116.8	93	77.2	0	22.8	0	0	0
Tempe	2,526.8	2,539.5	101	100.0	0	0	0	0	0
Arkansas-South									
Pulaski County	5,319.0	3,335.0	63	100.0	0	0	0	0	0
Little Rock	10,753.9	6,405.9	60	61.7	18.8	0	0	19.5	0
North Little Rock	2,536.7	2,246.5	89	67.3	32.7	0	0	0	0
Saline County	1,069.5	801.7	75	76.3	23.7	0	0	0	0
California-West									
Los Angeles County	320,687.0	332,687.0	104	62.4	1.3	20.1	13.4	3.0	0
Los Angeles	122,313.1	116,368.7	95	22.2	63.4	14.4	0	0	0
Carson	1,239.3	1,138.3	92	42.8	57.2	0	0	0	0
Colorado-West									
Longmont	1,030.7	1,233.7	120	88.0	12.0	0	0	0	0
Florida-South									
Jacksonville	31,654.7	21,917.1	69	27.4	45.2	27.4	0	0	0
Orange County	8,676.1	8,935.5	103	4.6	1.6	93.8	0	0	0
Orlando	6,482.5	4,212.8	65	100.0	0	0	0	0	0
Seminole County	1,836.3	1,755.3	96	80.9	17.3	0	0	0	1.8
Louisiana-South									
Baton Rouge	26,271.4	26,768.9	102	60.4	1.6	36.5	0	0	.4

Maine-Northeast								
Bangor	3,972.2	3,226.2	81	6.4	7.9	53.0	0	32.7	0
Maryland-South								
Baltimore County	38,348.0	36,200.0	94	0	0	34.5	47.8	17.7	0
Baltimore	90,158.3	86,880.0	96	3.1	12.0	58.2	1.3	0	25.5
Carroll County	2,928.1	2,700.0	92	82.8	0	0	0	0	17.2
Harford County	4,558.7	4,579.2	100	81.4	0	0	18.6	0	0
Massachusetts-Northeast								
Worcester	15,785.4	16,081.4	102	10.9	49.2	35.0	0	5.0	0
Holden Town	343.1	329.3	96	62.5	34.0	3.5	0	0	0
Missouri-North Central								
St. Louis	49,175.8	46,758.9	95	29.0	71.0	0	0	0	0
New Jersey-Northeast								
Essex County	27,176.7	27,195.0	100	0	0	96.3	3.7	0	0
Newark	31,562.6	31,583.1	100	0	0	81.0	19.0	0	0
West Orange	871.7	872.2	100	5.6	2.9	91.5	0	0	0
Livingston	1,036.0	1,036.8	100	72.5	0	27.5	0	0	0
New York-Northeast								
Monroe County	18,342.4	18,220.2	99	47.0	1.4	34.7	13.2	3.8	0
Rochester	11,766.9	11,766.9	100	0	0	100.0	0	0	0
Greece Town	1,421.2	1,341.4	94	22.4	3.8	27.9	36.4	9.5	0
Irondequoit Town	1,079.2	1,079.5	100	60.1	0	31.0	8.8	0	0
New York City	842,873.2	587,559.5	70	0	0	54.3	0	0	45.7
North Carolina-South								
Orange County	775.7	787.0	102	96.1	3.8	0	0	0	0
Ohio-North Central								
Butler County	2,248.1	1,989.2	89	2.7	0	94.7	0	0	2.6
Hamilton County	19,295.6	5,908.3	31	66.1	0	0	0	0	33.9
Hamilton	3,390.3	1,756.5	52	51.6	37.4	0	0	0	11.0
Cincinnati	32,545.9	24,710.5	76	10.9	89.1	0	0	0	0

Table B-2 (continued)

Jurisdiction[a]	Cumulative[b] entitlement (thousands of dollars)	Cumulative[c] allocation		Uses of shared revenue as a percent of cumulative allocation					
		Amount (thousands of dollars)	As a percent of entitlement	New[d] spending	Maintained[e] spending	Revenue[f] stabilization	Tax reduction	Increased fund balances	Other[g]
Oregon-West									
Lane County	2,876.6	2,693.3	94	87.4	9.7	0	0	3.0	0
Cottage Grove	508.1	479.8	94	80.1	0	0	19.3	.5	0
Eugene	6,821.5	5,736.2	84	50.4	49.6	0	0	0	0
Springfield	2,152.6	2,032.0	94	52.1	46.5	0	0	0	0
South Carolina-South									
Fairfield County	1,083.8	1,001.3	92	94.8	0	5.2	0	0	0
Winnsboro	355.9	356.1	100	100.0	0	0	0	0	0
Kershaw County	1,801.8	1,160.0	64	75.7	23.2	0	0	1.1	0
Camden	759.1	765.2	101	80.1	6.5	5.3	0	8.2	0
South Dakota-North Central									
Minnehaha County	1,756.7	1,123.2	64	18.7	4.7	76.6	0	0	0
Sioux Falls	4,112.8	2,835.4	69	71.3	1.9	26.4	.4	0	0
Tripp County	507.9	347.4	68	62.4	16.8	13.5	7.2	0	0
Turner County	652.3	55.2	9	4.9	58.1	0	0	0	0
Wisconsin-North Central									
Dodge County	2,535.4	935.3	37	20.7	0	0	59.0	20.3	0
Beaver Dam	484.4	198.1	41	0	0	52.5	0	47.5	0
Maryville	75.0	31.1	40	0	0	100.0	0	0	0
Lowell Town	36.3	33.1	91	100.0	0	0	0	0	0
Theresa Town	20.1	15.0	75	100.0	0	0	0	0	0
Indian reservation									
South Dakota-North Central									
Central Rosebud	488.0	128.0	26	100.0	0	0	0	0	0

State governments

	Column 1	2	3	4	5	6	7	8	9
California (West)	724,821.8	495,000.0	68	0	0	0	86.9	13.1	0
Colorado (West)	71,381.5	58,397.6	82	10.6	58.1	0	0	0	31.3
Illinois (North Central)	347,216.6	110,150.0	32	0	0	0	0	0	100.0
Louisiana (South)	158,085.5	139,010.7	88	100.0	0	0	0	0	0
Maine (Northeast)	41,465.1	40,161.0	97	72.7	0	24.9	0	1.2	1.2
Massachusetts (Northeast)	214,648.6	214,572.6	100	0	39.5	60.5	0	0	0
New York (Northeast)	758,349.8	658,000.0	87	21.0	15.6	7.1	7.6	22.8	25.9
North Carolina (South)	174,220.7	162,200.0	93	94.1	2.8	0	3.0	0	0

Sources: Column 1: Office of Revenue Sharing, *Payment Summary, Entitlement Periods 1 through 5 with Entitlement Period 6 Estimate* (GPO, 1975). Columns 2–9: field research data.

a. By state, with official Census Bureau region. Local governments are municipalities unless otherwise designated.
b. Cumulative revenue sharing entitlements for the period December 1972 through June 1975 (entitlement periods 1 through 5).
c. Cumulative allocations reported by the field associates for the period December 1972 through June 1974. As explained in chapter 2, allocations refer to revenue sharing received and anticipated (and in some cases including interest earned on trust fund accounts) about which the recipient government has made some "quite firm" decision concerning its use.
d. The sum of new capital, new or expanded operations, and increased pay and benefit uses.
e. The sum of program maintenance and federal aid restoration uses.
f. The sum of tax stabilization and borrowing avoidance uses.
g. Uses of shared revenue not traceable to specific net effect categories.

C *Text of Title I of the State and Local Fiscal Assistance Amendments of 1976*

The following thirty-four pages contain a facsimile reproduction of the official text of Title I of Public Law 92-512 (86 Stat. 919), the "State and Local Fiscal Assistance Act of 1972," as amended by Public Law 94-488 (90 Stat. 2341), the "State and Local Fiscal Assistance Amendments of 1976" (U.S.C. 1221, et seq.). This text was compiled by the Chief Counsel for Revenue Sharing, Office of the General Counsel, Department of the Treasury.

TITLE I—FISCAL ASSISTANCE TO STATE AND LOCAL GOVERNMENTS

Subtitle A—Allocation and Payment of Funds

SEC. 101. SHORT TITLE.

This title may be cited as the "State and Local Fiscal Assistance Act of 1972" as amended by the "State and Local Fiscal Assistance Amendments of 1976"

SEC. 102. PAYMENTS TO STATE AND LOCAL GOVERNMENTS.

(a) IN GENERAL.—Except as otherwise provided in this title, the Secretary shall, for each entitlement period, pay out of the Trust Fund to—

(1) each State government a total amount equal to the entitlement of such State government determined under section 107 for such period, and

(2) each unit of local government a total amount equal to the entitlement of such unit determined under section 108 for such period.

In the case of entitlement periods ending after the date of the enactment of this Act, such payments shall be made in installments, but not less often than once for each quarter, and, in the case of quarters ending after September 30, 1972, shall be paid not later than 5 days after the close of each quarter. Such payments for any entitlement period may be initially made on the basis of estimates. Proper adjustment shall be made in the amount of any payment to a State government or a unit of local government to the extent that the payments previously made to such government under this subtitle were in excess of or less than the amounts required to be paid.

(b) LIMITATIONS ON ADJUSTMENTS.—No adjustment shall be made to increase or decrease a payment made for any entitlement period beginning after December 31, 1976, to a State government or a unit of local government, unless a demand therefor shall have been made by such government or the Secretary within 1 year of the end of the entitlement period with respect to which the payment was made.

(c) RESERVES FOR ADJUSTMENTS.—The Secretary may reserve such percentage (not exceeding 0.5 percent) of the total entitlement payment for any entitlement period with respect to any State government and all units of local government within such State as he deems

223

necessary to insure that there will be sufficient funds available to pay adjustments due after the final allocation of funds among such governments.

RECOVERY OF CERTAIN OVERPAYMENTS.—In the case of an adjustment to decrease a payment made for an entitlement period ending before January 1, 1977, under title I of the State and Local Fiscal Assistance Act of 1972 to a unit of local government (as defined in section 108(d)(1) of that Act), the amount of such adjustment shall be withheld from the reserves for adjustments established by the Secretary under section 102(c) of such Act for the State within which such units of local government are located. Amounts withheld under this subsection shall be covered into the State and Local Government Fiscal Assistance Trust Fund.

SEC. 103. THE REQUIREMENT THAT LOCAL GOVERNMENTS USE REVENUE SHARING FUNDS ONLY FOR PRIORITY EXPENDITURES IS REPEALED.

SEC. 104. THE PROHIBITION ON USE OF REVENUE SHARING FUNDS AS MATCHING FUNDS IS REPEALED.

SEC. 105. CREATION OF TRUST FUND; APPROPRIATIONS; AUTHORIZATIONS FOR ENTITLEMENTS.

(a) TRUST FUND.—

(1) IN GENERAL.—There is hereby established on the books of the Treasury of the United States a trust fund to be known as the "State and Local Government Fiscal Assistance Trust Fund" (referred to in this subtitle as the "Trust Fund"). The Trust Fund shall remain available without fiscal year limitation and shall consist of such amounts as may be appropriated to it and deposited in it as provided in subsection (b) or (c). Except as provided in this title, amounts in the Trust Fund may be used only for the payments to State and local governments provided by this subtitle.

(2) TRUSTEE.—The Secretary of the Treasury shall be the trustee of the Trust Fund and shall report to the Congress not later than March 1 of each year on the operation and status of the Trust Fund during the preceding fiscal year.

(b) APPROPRIATIONS.—

(1) IN GENERAL.—There is appropriated to the Trust Fund, out of amounts in the general fund of the Treasury attributable to the collections of the Federal individual income taxes not otherwise appropriated—

(A) for the period beginning January 1, 1972, and ending June 30, 1972, $2,650,000,000;

(B) for the period beginning July 1, 1972, and ending December 31, 1972, $2,650,000,000;

(C) for the period beginning January 1, 1973, and ending June 30, 1973, $2,987,500,000;

(D) for the fiscal year beginning July 1, 1973, $6,050,000,000;

(E) for the fiscal year beginning July 1, 1974, $6,-200,000,000;

(F) for the fiscal year beginning July 1, 1975, $6,350,000,000; and

(G) for the period beginning July 1, 1976, and ending December 31, 1976, $3,325,000,000.

(2) NONCONTIGUOUS STATES ADJUSTMENT AMOUNTS.—There is appropriated to the Trust Fund, out of amounts in the general fund of the Treasury attributable to the collections of the Federal individual income taxes not otherwise appropriated—

(A) for the period beginning January 1, 1972, and ending June 30, 1972, $2,390,000;

(B) for the period beginning July 1, 1972, and ending December 31, 1972, $2,390,000;

(C) for the period beginning January 1, 1973, and ending June 30, 1973, $2,390,000;

(D) for each of the fiscal years beginning July 1, 1973, July 1, 1974, and July 1, 1975, $4,780,000; and

(E) for the period beginning July 1, 1976, and ending December 31, 1976, $2,390,000.

(3) DEPOSITS.—Amounts appropriated by paragraph (1) or (2) for any fiscal year or other period shall be deposited in the Trust Fund on the later of (A) the first day of such year or period, or (B) the day after the date of enactment of this Act.

(c) AUTHORIZATION OF APPROPRIATIONS FOR ENTITLEMENTS.—

(1) IN GENERAL.—In the case of any entitlement period described in paragraph (3), there are authorized to be appropriated to the Trust Fund to pay the entitlements hereinafter provided for such entitlement period an amount equal to $6,650,000,000 times a fraction—

(A) the numerator of which is the amount of the Federal individual income taxes collected in the last calendar year ending more than one year before the end of such entitlement period, and

(B) the denominator of which is the amount of the Federal individual income taxes collected in the calendar year 1975.

The amount determined under this paragraph is not to exceed $6,850,000,000.

(2) NONCONTIGUOUS STATES ADJUSTMENT AMOUNTS.—In the case of any entitlement period described in paragraph (3), there are authorized to be appropriated to the Trust Fund to pay the entitlements hereinafter provided for such entitlement period an amount equal to $4,780,000 times a fraction—

(A) the numerator of which is the amount of the Federal individual income taxes collected in the last calendar year ending more than one year before the end of such entitlement period, and

(B) the denominator of which is the amount of the Federal individual income taxes collected in the calendar year 1975.

The amount determined under this paragraph is not to exceed $4,923,759.

(3) ENTITLEMENT PERIODS.—The following entitlement periods are described in this paragraph:

(A) The entitlement period beginning January 1, 1977, and ending September 30, 1977;

(B) The entitlement period beginning October 1, 1977, and ending September 30, 1978;

(C) The entitlement period beginning October 1, 1978, and ending September 30, 1979; and

(D) The entitlement period beginning October 1, 1979, and ending September 30, 1980.

(4) SHORT ENTITLEMENT PERIOD.—In the case of an entitlement period of 9 months which follows an entitlement period of 6 months—

(A) the amount determined under paragraph (1) for such 9-month period shall be reduced by one-half the amount appropriated for such 6-month period under subsection (b)(1), and

(B) the amount determined under paragraph (2) for such entitlement period shall be reduced by one-half the amount appropriated for such 6-month entitlement period under subsection (b)(2).

(d) TRANSFERS FROM TRUST FUND TO GENERAL FUND.—The Secretary shall from time to time transfer from the Trust Fund to the general fund of the Treasury any moneys in the Trust Fund which he determines will not be needed to make payments to State governments and units of local government under this subtitle.

SEC. 106. ALLOCATION AMONG STATES.

(a) IN GENERAL.—There shall be allocated an entitlement to each State—

(1) for each entitlement period beginning before December 31, 1976, out of amounts appropriated under section 105(b)(1) for that entitlement period, an amount which bears the same ratio to the amount appropriated under that section for that period as the amount allocable to that State under subsection (b) bears to the sum of the amounts allocable to all States under subsection (b); and

(2) for each entitlement period beginning on or after January 1, 1977, out of amounts authorized under section 105(c)(1) for that entitlement period, an amount which bears the same ratio to the amount authorized under that section for that period as the amount allocable to that State under subsection (b) bears to the sum of the amounts allocable to all States under subsection (b).

(b) DETERMINATION OF ALLOCABLE AMOUNT.—

(1) IN GENERAL.—For purposes of subsection (a), the amount allocable to a State under this subsection for any entitlement period shall be determined under paragraph (2), except that such amount shall be determined under paragraph (3) if—

(A) in the case of an entitlement period beginning before December 31, 1976, the amount allocable to such State under paragraph (3) is greater than the sum of the amounts allocable to such State under paragraph (2) and subsection (c); and

(B) in the case of an entitlement period beginning on or after January 1, 1977, the amount allocable to such State under paragraph (3) is greater than the amount allocable to such State under paragraph (2).

(2) THREE FACTOR FORMULA.—For purposes of paragraph (1), the amount allocable to a State under this paragraph for any entitlement period is the amount which bears the same ratio to $5,300,000,000 as—

(A) the population of that State, multiplied by the general tax effort factor of that State, multiplied by the relative income factor of that State, bears to

(B) the sum of the products determined under subparagraph (A) for all States.

(3) FIVE FACTOR FORMULA.—For purposes of paragraph (1), the amount allocable to a State under this paragraph for any entitlement period is the amount to which that State would be entitled if—

(A) ⅓ of $3,500,000,000 were allocated among the States on the basis of population,

(B) ⅓ of $3,500,000,000 were allocated among the States on the basis of urbanized population,

(C) ⅓ of $3,500,000,000 were allocated among the States on the basis of population inversely weighted for per capita income,

(D) ½ of $1,800,000,000 were allocated among the States on the basis of income tax collections, and

(E) ½ of $1,800,000,000 were allocated among the States on the basis of general tax effort.

(c) NONCONTIGUOUS STATES ADJUSTMENT.—

(1) IN GENERAL.—In addition to the amounts allocated to the States under subsection (a), there shall be allocated for each entitlement period an additional amount to any State in which civilian employees of the United States Government receive an allowance under section 5941 of title 5, United States Code—

(A) in the case of an entitlement period beginning before December 31, 1976, out of amounts appropriated under section 105(b)(2), if the allocation of such State under subsection (b) is determined by the formula set forth in paragraph

(2) of that subsection; and

(B) in the case of an entitlement period beginning on or after January 1, 1977, out of amounts authorized under section 105(c)(2)

(2) DETERMINATION OF AMOUNT.—The additional amount allocable to any State under this subsection for any entitlement period is an amount equal to a percentage of the amount allocable to that State under subsection (b) for that period which is the same as the percentage of basic pay received by such employees stationed in that State as an allowance under such section 5941. If the total amount appropriated under section 105(b)(2) for any entitlement period beginning before December 31, 1976, or authorized under section 105(c)(2) for any entitlement period beginning on or after January 1, 1977, is not sufficient to pay in full the additional amounts allocable under this subsection for that period, the Secretary shall reduce proportionately the amounts so allocable.

SEC. 107. ENTITLEMENTS OF STATE GOVERNEMNTS.

(a) DIVISION BETWEEN STATE AND LOCAL GOVERNMENTS.—The State government shall be entitled to receive one-third of the amount allocated to that State for each entitlement period. The remaining portion of each State's allocation shall be allocated among the units of local government of that State as provided in section 108.

(b) STATE MUST MAINTAIN TRANSFERS TO LOCAL GOVERNMENTS.—

(1) GENERAL RULE.—

(A) PRE-1977 ENTITLEMENT PERIODS.—The entitlement of any State government for any entitlement period beginning on or after July 1, 1973, and before December 31, 1976, shall be reduced by the amount (if any) by which—

(i) the average of the aggregate amounts transferred by the State government (out of its own sources) during such period and the preceding entitlement period to all units of local government in such State, is less than,

(ii) the similar aggregate amount for the one-year period beginning July 1, 1971.

(B) POST-1976 ENTITLEMENT PERIODS.—The entitlement of any State government for any entitlement period beginning on or after January 1, 1977, shall be reduced by the amount (if any) by which—

(i) one-half of the aggregate amounts transferred by the State government (out of its own sources) during the 24 month period ending on the last day of the last fiscal year of such State for which the relevant data are available (in accordance with regulations prescribed by the Secretary) on the first day of such entitlement period, to all units of local government in such State, is less than,

(ii) one-half of the similar aggregate amount for the 24 month period ending on the day before the start of the 24 month period described in clause (i).

(C) For purposes of subparagraphs (A)(i) and (B)(i), the amount of any reduction in the entitlement of a State government under this subsection for any entitlement period shall, for subsequent entitlement periods, be treated as an amount transferred by the State government (out of its own sources) during such period to units of local government in such State.

(2) ADJUSTMENT WHERE STATE ASSUMES RESPONSIBILITY FOR CATEGORY OF EXPENDITURES.—If the State government establishes to the satisfaction of the Secretary that since June 30, 1972, it has assumed responsibility for a category of expenditures which (before July 1, 1972) was the responsibility of local governments located in such State, then, under regulations prescribed by the Secretary, the aggregate amount taken into account under paragraph (1)(A)(ii) or (1)(B)(ii) shall be reduced to the extent that increased State government spending (out of its own sources) for such category has replaced corresponding amounts which for the period utilized for purposes of such paragraph it transferred to units of local government.

(3) ADJUSTMENT WHERE NEW TAXING POWERS ARE CONFERRED UPON LOCAL GOVERNMENTS.—If a State establishes to the satisfaction of the Secretary that since June 30, 1972, one or more units of local government within such State have had conferred upon them new taxing authority, then, under regulations prescribed by the Secretary, the aggregate amount taken into account under paragraph (1)(A)(ii) (in the case of an entitlement period beginning before December 31, 1976) or paragraph (1)(B)(ii) (in the case of an entitlement period beginning on or after January 1, 1977).

(4) SPECIAL RULE FOR PERIOD BEGINNING JULY 1, 1973.—In the case of the entitlement period beginning July 1, 1973, the preceding entitlement period for purposes of paragraph (1)(A) shall be treated as being the one-year period beginning July 1, 1972.

(5) SPECIAL RULE FOR PERIOD BEGINNING JULY 1, 1976.—In the case of the entitlement period beginning July 1, 1976, and ending December 31, 1976, the aggregate amount taken into account under paragraph (1)(A) for the preceding entitlement period and the aggregate amount taken into account under paragraph (1)(B) shall be one-half of the amounts which (but for this paragraph) would be taken into account.

(6) SPECIAL RULE FOR THE PERIOD BEGINNING JANUARY 1, 1977.—In the case of the entitlement period beginning January 1, 1977, and ending September 30, 1977, the aggregate amounts taken into account under clauses (i) and (ii) of paragraph (1)(B) shall be three-fourths of the amount which (but for this paragraph) would be taken into account.

(7) ADJUSTMENT WHERE FEDERAL GOVERNMENT ASSUMES RESPONSIBILITY FOR CATEGORY OF EXPENDITURES.—If, for an entitlement period beginning on or after January 1, 1977, a State government establishes to the satisfaction of the Secretary that during all or part of the period utilized for purposes of paragraph (1)(B)(i), the Federal Government has assumed responsibility for a category of expenditures for which such State government transferred amounts which (but for this paragraph) would be included in the aggregate amount taken into account under paragraph (1)(B)(ii) for the period utilized for purposes of such paragraph, then (under regulations prescribed by the Secretary) the aggregate amount taken into account under paragraph (1)(B)(ii) shall be reduced to the extent that increased Federal Government spending in that State for such category of expenditures has replaced corresponding amounts which such State government had transferred to units of local government during the period utilized for purposes of paragraph (1)(B)(ii).

(8) REDUCTION IN ENTITLEMENT.—If the Secretary has reason to believe that paragraph (1) requires a reduction in the entitlement of any State government for any entitlement period, he shall give reasonable notice and opportunity for hearing to the State. If, thereafter, he determines that paragraph (1) requires the reduction of such entitlement, he shall also determine the amount of such reduction and shall notify the Governor of such State of such determinations and shall withhold from subsequent payments to such State government under this subtitle an amount equal to such reduction.

(9) TRANSFER TO GENERAL FUND.—An amount equal to the reduction in the entitlement of any State government which results from the application of this subsection (after any judicial review under section 143) shall be transferred from the Trust Fund to the general fund of the Treasury on the day on which such reduction becomes final.

(c) CROSS REFERENCE.—For reduction of State government entitlement because of provision for separate law enforcement officers, see section 108(e).

SEC. 108. ENTITLEMENTS OF LOCAL GOVERNMENTS.

(a) ALLOCATION AMONG COUNTY AREAS.—The amount to be allocated to this units of local government within a State for any entitlement period shall be allocated among the county areas located in that State so that each county area will receive an amount which bears the same ratio to the total amount to be allocated to the units of local government within that State as—

(1) the population of that county area, multiplied by the general tax effort factor of that county area, multiplied by the relative income factor of that county area, bears to

(2) the sum of the products determined under paragraph (1) for all county areas within that State.

(b) ALLOCATION TO COUNTY GOVERNMENTS, MUNICIPALITIES, TOWNSHIPS, ETC.—

(1) COUNTY GOVERNMENTS.—The county government shall be allocated that portion of the amount allocated to the county area for the entitlement period under subsection (a) which bears the same ratio to such amount as the adjusted taxes of the county government bear to the adjusted taxes of the county government and all other units of local government located in the county area.

(2) OTHER UNITS OF LOCAL GOVERNMENT.—The amount remaining for allocation within a county area after the application of paragraph (1) shall be allocated among the units of local government (other than the county government and other than township governments) located in that county area so that each unit of local government will receive an amount which bears the same ratio to the total amount to be allocated to all such units as—

(A) the population of that local government, multiplied by the general tax effort factor of that local government, multiplied by the relative income factor of that local government, bears to

(B) the sum of the products determined under subparagraph (A) for all such units.

(3) TOWNSHIP GOVERNMENTS.—If the county area includes one or more township governments, then before applying paragraph (2)—

(A) there shall be set aside for allocation under subparagraph (B) to such township governments that portion of the amount allocated to the county area for the entitlement period which bears the same ratio to such amount as the sum of the adjusted taxes of all such township governments bears to the aggregate adjusted taxes of the county government, such township governments, and all other units of local government located in the county area, and

(B) that portion of each amount set aside under subparagraph (A) shall be allocated to each township government on the same basis as amounts are allocated to units of local government under paragraph (2).

If this paragraph applies with respect to any county area for any entitlement period, the remaining portion allocated under paragraph (2) to the units of local government located in the county area (other than the county government and the township governments) shall be appropriately reduced to reflect the amounts set aside under subparagraph (A).

(4) INDIAN TRIBES AND ALASKAN NATIVE VILLAGES.—If within a county area there is an Indian tribe or Alaskan native village which has a recognized governing body which performs substantial governmental functions, then before applying paragraph (1) there shall be allocated to such tribe or village a portion of the amount allocated to the county area for the entitlement period

which bears the same ratio to such amount as the population of that tribe or village within that county area bears to the population of that county area. If this paragraph applies with respect to any county area for any entitlement period, the amount to be allocated under paragraph (1) shall be appropriately reduced to reflect the amount allocated under the preceding sentence.

(5) RULE FOR SMALL UNITS OF GOVERNMENT.—If the Secretary determines that in any county area the data available for any entitlement period are not adequate for the application of the formulas set forth in paragraphs (2) and (3)(B) with respect to units of local government (other than a county government) with a population below a number (not more than 500) prescribed for that county area by the Secretary, he may apply paragraph (2) or (3)(B) by allocating for such entitlement period to each such unit located in that county area an amount which bears the same ratio to the total amount to be allocated under paragraph (2) or (3)(B) for such entitlement period as the population of such unit bears to the population of all units of local government in that county area to which allocations are made under such paragraph. If the preceding sentence applies with respect to any county area, the total amount to be allocated under paragraph (2) or (3)(B) to other units of local government in that county area for the entitlement period shall be appropriately reduced to reflect the amounts allocated under the preceding sentence.

(6) ENTITLEMENT.—

(A) IN GENERAL.—Except as otherwise provided in this paragraph, the entitlement of any unit of local government for any entitlement period shall be the amount allocated to such unit under this subsection (after taking into account any applicable modification under subsection (c)).

(B) MAXIMUM AND MINIMUM PER CAPITA ENTITLEMENT.— Subject to the provision of subparagraphs (C) and (D), the per capita amount allocated to any county area or any unit of local government (other than a county government) within a State under this section for any entitlement period shall not be less than 20 percent, nor more than 145 percent, of two-thirds of the amount allocated to the State under section 106, divided by the population of that State.

(C) LIMITATION.—The amount allocated to any unit of local government under this section for any entitlement period shall not exceed 50 percent of the sum of (i) such government's adjusted taxes, and (ii) the intergovernmental transfers of revenue to such government (other than transfers to such government under this subtitle).

(D) ENTITLEMENT LESS THAN $200, OR GOVERNING BODY WAIVES ENTITLEMENT.—If (but for this subparagraph) the entitlement of any unit of local government below the level of the county government—

(i) would be less than $200 for any entitlement period ($100 for an entitlement period of 6 months, $150 for an entitlement period of 9 months), or

(ii) is waived for any entitlement period by the governing body of such unit, then the amount of such entitlement for such period shall (in lieu of being paid to such unit) be added to, and shall become a part of, the entitlement for such period of the county government of the county area in which such unit is located. If the entitlement of an Indian tribe or Alaskan native village is waived for any entitlement period by the governing body of that tribe or village, then the amount of such entitlement for such period shall (in lieu of being paid to such tribe or village) be added to, and shall become a part of, the entitlement for such period of the county government of the county area in which such tribe or village is located.

(7) ADJUSTMENT OF ENTITLEMENT.—

(A) IN GENERAL.—In adjusting the allocation of any county area or unit of local government, the Secretary shall make any adjustment required under paragraph (6)(B) first, any adjustment required under paragraph (6)(C) next, any adjustment required under paragraph (6)(D) next, and any adjustment required under subsection (e) last.

(B) ADJUSTMENT FOR APPLICATION OF MAXIMUM OR MINIMUM PER CAPITA ENTITLEMENT.—The Secretary shall adjust the allocations made under this section to county areas or to units of local government in any State in order to bring those allocations into compliance with the provisions of paragraph (6)(B). In making such adjustments he shall make any necessary adjustments with respect to county areas before making any necessary adjustments with respect to units of local government.

(C) ADJUSTMENT FOR APPLICATION OF LIMITATION.—In any case in which the amount allocated to a unit of local government is reduced under paragraph (6)(C) by the Secretary, the amount of that reduction—

(i) in the case of a unit of local government (other than a county government), shall be added to and increase the allocation of the county government of the county area in which it is located, unless (on account of the application of paragraph (6)) that county government may not receive it, in which case the amount of the reduction shall be added to and increase the entitlement of the State government of the State in which that unit of local government is located; and

(ii) in the case of a county government, shall be added

to and increase the entitlement of the State government of the State in which it is located.

(c) SPECIAL ALLOCATION RULES.—

(1) OPTIONAL FORMULA.—A State may by law provide for the allocation of funds among county areas, or among units of local government (other than county governments), on the basis of the population multiplied by the general tax effort factors of such areas or units of local government, on the basis of the population multiplied by the relative income factors of such areas or units of local government, or on the basis of a combination of those two factors. Any State which provides by law for such a variation in the allocation formula provided by subsection (a), or by paragraphs (2) and (3) of subsection (b), shall notify the Secretary of such law not later than 30 days before the beginning of the first entitlement period to which such law is to apply. Any such law shall—

(A) provide for allocating 100 percent of the aggregate amount to be allocated under subsection (a), or under paragraphs (2) and (3) of subsection (b);

(B) apply uniformly throughout the State; and

(C) apply during the period beginning on the first day of the first entitlement period to which it applies and ending September 30, 1980.

(2) CERTIFICATION.—Paragraph (1) shall apply within a State only if the Secretary certifies that the State law complies with the requirements of such paragraph. The Secretary shall not certify any such law with respect to which he receives notification later than 30 days prior to the first entitlement period during which it is to apply.

(d) GOVERNMENTAL DEFINITIONS AND RELATED RULES.—For purposes of this title—

(1) UNITS OF LOCAL GOVERNMENT.—The term "unit of local government" means the government of a county, municipality, or township, which is a unit of general government below the state (determined on the basis of the same principles as are used by the Bureau of the Census for general statistical purposes). Such term also means, except for purposes of paragraphs (1), (2), (3), (5), (6)(C), and (6)(D) of subsection (b), and, except for purposes of subsection (c), the recognized governing body of an Indian tribe or Alaskan native village which performs substantial governmental functions. Such term also means (but only for purposes of subtitles B and C) the office of the separate law enforcement officer to which subsection (e)(1) applies.

(2) CERTAIN AREAS TREATED AS COUNTIES.—In any State in which any unit of local government (other than a county government) constitutes the next level of government below the State government level, then, except as provided in the next sentence, the geographic area of such unit of government shall be treated

as a county area (and such unit of government shall be treated as a county government) with respect to that portion of the State's geographic area. In any State in which any county area is not governed by a county government but contains two or more units of local government, such units shall not be treated as county governments and the geographic areas of such units shall not be treated as county areas.

(3) TOWNSHIPS.—The term "township" includes equivalent subdivisions of government having different designations (such as "towns"), and shall be determined on the basis of the same principles as are used by the Bureau of the Census for general statistical purposes.

(4) UNITS OF LOCAL GOVERNMENT LOCATED IN LARGER ENTITY.—A unit of local government shall be treated as located in a larger entity if part or all of its geographic area is located in the larger entity.

(5) ONLY PART OF UNIT LOCATED IN LARGER ENTITY.—If only part of a unit of local government is located in a larger entity, such part shall be treated for allocation purposes as a separate unit of local government, and all computations shall, except as otherwise provided in regulations, be made on the basis of the ratio which the estimated population of such part bears to the population of the entirety of such unit.

(6) BOUNDARY CHANGES, GOVERNMENTAL REORGANIZATION, ETC.—If, by reason of boundary line changes, by reason of State statutory or constitutional changes, by reason of annexations or other governmental reorganizations, or by reason of other circumstances, the application of any provision of this section to units of local government does not carry out the purposes of this subtitle, the application of such provision shall be made, under regulations prescribed by the Secretary, in a manner which is consistent with such purposes.

(e) SEPARATE LAW ENFORCEMENT OFFICERS.—

(1) ENTITLEMENT OF SEPARATE LAW ENFORCEMENT OFFICERS.—The office of the separate law enforcement officer for any county area in the State of Louisiana, other than the parish of East Baton Rouge, shall be entitled to receive for each entitlement period beginning on or after January 1, 1977, an amount equal to 15 percent of the amount which would (but for the provisions of this subsection) be the entitlement of the government of such county area. The office of the separate law enforcement officer for the parish of East Baton Rouge shall be entitled to receive for each entitlement period beginning on or after January 1, 1977, an amount equal to 7.5 percent of the sum of the amount which would (but for the provisions of this subsection) be the entitlements of the governments of Baton Rouge, Baker, and Zachary, Louisiana, for each such entitlement period.

(2) REDUCTION OF ENTITLEMENT OF COUNTY GOVERNMENT.— The entitlement of the government of a county area for an enti-

tlement period shall be reduced by an amount equal to one half of the entitlement for the separate law enforcement officer for such county area for such entitlement period. For the purpose of applying this paragraph to the parish of East Baton Rouge, Louisiana, the entitlements of the governments of Baton Rouge, Baker, and Zachary, Louisiana, for each entitlement period shall each be reduced by an amount equal to 3.75 percent of the amount which would (but for the provisions of this paragraph) be the entitlement of each such government.

(3) REDUCTION OF ENTITLEMENT OF STATE GOVERNMENT.— The entitlement of the State government of Louisiana for an entitlement period shall be reduced by an amount equal to the sum of the reductions provided under paragraph (2) for governments of county areas in such State for such entitlement period. For purposes of this paragraph—

    (A) the reductions provided under paragraph (2) for the governments of Baton Rouge, Baker, and Zachary, Louisiana, shall be considered as reductions of entitlements of governments of county areas, and

    (B) the entitlement of the parish of Orleans for an entitlement period shall be considered to have been reduced by an amount equal to the additional amount provided for such parish for that entitlement period under paragraph (4).

(4) ENTITLEMENT OF PARISH OF ORLEANS.—In the case of the parish of Orleans, Louisiana, paragraphs (1) and (2) shall not apply, and such parish shall be entitled to receive, for each entitlement period beginning after December 31, 1976, an additional amount equal to 7.5 percent of the amount which would otherwise be the entitlement of such parish.

SEC. 109. DEFINITIONS AND SPECIAL RULES FOR APPLICATION OF ALLOCATION FORMULAS.

  (a) IN GENERAL.—For purposes of this subtitle—

    (1) POPULATION.—Population shall be determined on the same basis as resident population is determined by the Bureau of the Census for general statistical purposes.

    (2) URBANIZED POPULATION.—Unbanized population means the population of any area consisting of a central city or cities of 50,000 or more inhabitants (and of the surrounding closely settled territory for such city or cities) which is treated as an urbanized area by the Bureau of the Census for general statistical purposes.

    (3) INCOME.—Income means total money income received from all sources, as determined by the Bureau of the Census for general statistical purposes.

    (4) PERSONAL INCOME.—Personal income means the income of individuals, as determined by the Department of Commerce for national income accounts purposes.

    (5) DATES FOR DETERMINING ALLOCATIONS AND ENTITLEMENTS.—Except as provided in regulations, the determination

of allocations and entitlements for any entitlement period shall be made as of the first day of the third month immediately preceding the beginning of such period.

(6) INTERGOVERNMENTAL TRANSFERS.—The intergovernmental transfers of revenue to any government are the amounts of revenue received by that government from other governments as a share in financing (or as reimbursement for) the performance of governmental functions, as determined by the Bureau of the Census for general statistical purposes.

(7) DATA USED; UNIFORMITY OF DATA.—

(A) GENERAL RULE.—Except as provided in subparagraph (B) or (C), the data used shall be the most recently available data provided by the Bureau of the Census or the Department of Commerce, as the case may be.

(B) USE OF ESTIMATES, ETC.—Where the Secretary determines that the data referred to in subparagraph (A) are not current enough or are not comprehensive enough to provide for equitable allocations, he may use such additional data (including data based on estimates) as may be provided for in regulations.

(C) TAX COLLECTIONS.—Data with respect to tax collections for a period more recent than the most recent reporting year for an entitlement period (as defined in subsection (c)(2)(B)) shall not be used in the determination of entitlements for such period.

(b) INCOME TAX AMOUNT OF STATES.—For purposes of this subtitle—

(1) IN GENERAL.—The income tax amount of any State for any entitlement period is the income tax amount of such State as determined under paragraphs (2) and (3).

(2) INCOME TAX AMOUNT.—The income tax amount of any State for any entitlement period is 15 percent of the net amount collected from the State individual income tax of such State during 1972 or (if later) during the last calendar year ending before the beginning of such entitlement period.

(3) CEILING AND FLOOR.—The income tax amount of any State for any entitlement period—

(A) shall not exceed 6 percent, and

(B) shall not be less than 1 percent,

of the Federal individual income tax liabilities attributed to such State for taxable years ending during 1971 or (if later) during the last calendar year ending before the beginning of such entitlement period.

(4) STATE INDIVIDUAL INCOME TAX.—The individual income tax of any State is the tax imposed upon the income of individuals by such State and described as a State income tax under section 164(a)(3) of the Internal Revenue Code of 1954.

(5) FEDERAL INDIVIDUAL INCOME TAX LIABILITIES.—Federal individual income tax liabilities attributed to any State for any

period shall be determined on the same basis as such liabilities are determined for such period by the Internal Revenue Service for general statistical purposes.

(c) GENERAL TAX EFFORT OF STATES.—

    (1) IN GENERAL.—For purposes of this subtitle—

        (A) GENERAL TAX EFFORT FACTOR.—The general tax effort factor of any State for any entitlement period is (i) the net amount collected from the State and local taxes of such State during the most recent reporting year, divided by (ii) the aggregate personal income (as defined in paragraph (4) of subsection (a)) attributed to such State for the same period.

        (B) GENERAL TAX EFFORT AMOUNT.—The general tax effort amount of any State for any entitlement period is the amount determined by multiplying—

            (i) the net amount collected from the State and local taxes of such State during the most recent reporting year by

            (ii) the general tax effort factor of that State.

    (2) STATE AND LOCAL TAXES.—

        (A) TAXES TAKEN INTO ACCOUNT.—The State and local taxes taken into account under paragraph (1) are the compulsory contributions exacted by the State (or by any unit of local government or other political subdivision of the State) for public purposes (other than employee and employer assessments and contributions to finance retirement and social insurance systems, and other than special assessments for capital outlay), as such contributions are determined by the Bureau of the Census for general statistical purposes.

        (B) MOST RECENT REPORTING YEAR.—The most recent reporting year with respect to any entitlement period consists of the years taken into account by the Bureau of the Census in its most recent general determination of State and local taxes made before the beginning of such period.

(d) GENERAL TAX EFFORT FACTOR OF COUNTY AREA.—For purposes of this subtitle, the general tax effort factor of any county area for any entitlement period is—

    (1) the adjusted taxes of the county government plus the adjusted taxes of each other unit of local government within that county area, divided by

    (2) the aggregate income (as defined in paragraph (3) of subsection (a)) attributed to that county area.

(e) GENERAL TAX EFFORT FACTOR OF UNIT OF LOCAL GOVERNMENT.—For purposes of this subtitle—

    (1) IN GENERAL.—The general tax effort factor of any unit of local government for any entitlement period is—

        (A) the adjusted taxes of that unit of local government, divided by

        (B) the aggregate income (as defined in paragraph (3) of subsection (a)) attributed to that unit of local government.

(2) ADJUSTED TAXES.—

(A) IN GENERAL.—The adjusted taxes of any unit of local government are—

(i) the compulsory contributions exacted by such government for public purposes (other than employee and employer assessments and contributions to finance retirement and social insurance systems, and other than special assessments for capital outlay), as such contributions are determined by the Bureau of the Census for general statistical purposes,

(ii) adjusted (under regulations prescribed by the Secretary) by excluding an amount equal to that portion of such compulsory contributions which is properly allocable to expenses for education.

(B) CERTAIN SALES TAXES COLLECTED BY COUNTIES.—In any case where—

(i) a county government exacts sales taxes within the geographic area of a unit of local government and transfers part or all of such taxes to such unit without specifying the purposes for which such unit may spend the revenues, and

(ii) the Governor of the State notifies the Secretary that the requirements of this subparagraph have been met with respect to such taxes,

then the taxes so transferred shall be treated as the taxes of the unit of local government (and not the taxes of the county government).

(f) RELATIVE INCOME FACTOR.—For purposes of this subtitle, the relative income factor is a fraction—

(1) in the case of a State, the numerator of which is the per capita income of the United States and the denominator of which is the per capita income of that State;

(2) in the case of a county area, the numerator of which is the per capita income of the State in which it is located and the denominator of which is the per capita income of that county area; and

(3) in the case of a unit of local government, the numerator of which is the per capita income of the county area in which it is located and the denominator of which is the per capita income of the geographic area of that unit of local government.

For purposes of this subsection, per capita income shall be determined on the basis of income as defined in paragraph (3) of subsection (a).

(g) ALLOCATION RULES FOR FIVE FACTOR FORMULA.—For purposes of section 106(b)(3)—

(1) ALLOCATION ON BASIS OF POPULATION.—Any allocation among the States on the basis of population shall be made by allocating to each State an amount which bears the same ratio to

the total amount to be allocated as the population of such State bears to the population of all the States.

(2) ALLOCATION ON BASIS OF URBANIZED POPULATION.—Any allocation among the States on the basis of urbanized population shall be made by allocating to each State an amount which bears the same ratio to the total amount to be allocated as the urbanized population of such State bears to the urbanized population of all the States.

(3) ALLOCATION ON BASIS OF POPULATION INVERSELY WEIGHTED FOR PER CAPITA INCOME.—Any allocation among the States on the basis of population inversely weighted for per capita income shall be made by allocating to each State an amount which bears the same ratio to the total amount to be allocated as—

(A) the population of such State, multiplied by a fraction the numerator of which is the per capita income of all the States and the denominator of which is the per capita income of such State, bears to

(B) the sum of the products determined under subparagraph (A) for all the States.

(4) ALLOCATION ON BASIS OF INCOME TAX COLLECTIONS.—Any allocation among the States on the basis of income tax collections shall be made by allocating to each State an amount which bears the same ratio to the total amount to be allocated as the income tax amount of such State bears to the sum of the income tax amounts of all the States.

(5) ALLOCATION ON BASIS OF GENERAL TAX EFFORT.—Any allocation among the States on the basis of general tax effort shall be made by allocating to each State an amount which bears the same ratio to the total amount to be allocated as the general tax effort amount of such State bears to the sum of the general tax effort amounts of all the States.

Subtitle B—Administrative Provisions
SEC. 121. REPORT ON USE OF FUNDS: PUBLICATION AND PUBLIC HEARINGS.

(a) REPORTS ON USE OF FUNDS.—Each State government and unit of local government which receives funds under subtitle A shall, after the close of each fiscal year, submit a report to the Secretary (which report shall be available to the public for inspection) setting forth the amounts and purposes for which funds received under subtitle A have been appropriated, spent, or obligated during such period and showing the relationship of those funds to the relevant functional items in the government's budget. Such report shall identify differences between the actual use of funds received and the proposed use of such funds. Such reports shall be in such form and detail and shall be submitted at such time as the Secretary may prescribe.

(b) PUBLIC HEARINGS REQUIRED.—

(1) HEARING ON PROPOSED USE.—Not less than 7 calendar days before its budget is presented to the governmental body responsi-

ble for enacting the budget, each State government or unit of local government which expends funds received under subtitle A in any fiscal period, the budget for which is to be enacted on or after January 1, 1977, shall, after adequate public notice, have at least one public hearing at which citizens shall have the opportunity to provide written and oral comment on the possible uses of such funds before the governmental authority responsible for presenting the proposed budget to such body.

(2) BUDGET HEARING.—Each State government or unit of local government which expends fund received under subtitle A in any fiscal period, the budget for which is to be enacted on or after January 1, 1977, shall have at least one public hearing on the proposed use of such funds in relation to its entire budget. At such hearing, citizens shall have the opportunity to provide written and oral comment to the body responsible for enacting the budget, and to ask questions concerning the entire budget and the relation thereto of funds made available under subtitle A. Such hearing shall be at a place and time that permits and encourages public attendance and participation.

(3) WAIVER.—The provisions of paragraph (1) may be waived in whole or in part in accordance with regulations of the Secretary if the cost of such a requirement would be unreasonably burdensome in relation to the entitlement of such State government or unit of local government to funds made available under subtitle A. The provisions of paragraph (2) may be waived in whole or in part in accordance with regulations of the Secretary if the budget processes required under applicable State or local laws or charter provisions assure the opportunity for public attendance and participation contemplated by the provisions of this subsection and a portion of such process includes a hearing on the proposed use of funds made available under subtitle A in relation to its entire budget.

(c) NOTIFICATION AND PUBLICITY OF PUBLIC HEARINGS: ACCESS TO BUDGET SUMMARY AND PROPOSED USE OF FUNDS.—

(1) IN GENERAL.—Each State government and unit of local government which expends funds received under subtitle A in any fiscal period, the budget for which is to be enacted on or after January 1, 1977, shall—

(A) at least 10 days prior to the public hearing required by subsection (b)(2)—

(i) publish, in at least one newspaper of general circulation, the proposed uses of funds made available under subtitle A together with a summary of its proposed budget and a notice of the time and place of such public hearing; and

(ii) make available for inspection by the public at the principal office of such State government or unit of local government a statement of the proposed use of funds, together with a summary of its proposed budget; and

(B) within 30 days after adoption of its budget as provided for under State or local law—

(i) make a summary of the adopted budget, including the proposed use of funds made available under subtitle A, available for inspection by the public at the principal office of such State government or unit of local government; and

(ii) publish in at least one newspaper of general circulation a notice of the availability for inspection of the information referred to in clause (i).

(2) WAIVER.—The provisions of paragraph (1) may be waived, in whole or in part, with respect to publication of the proposed use of funds and the summaries, in accordance with regulations of the Secretary, where the cost of such publication would be unreasonably burdensome in relation to the entitlement of such State government or unit of local government to funds made available under subtitle A, or where such publication is otherwise impractical or infeasible. In addition, the 10-day provisions of paragraph (1)(A) may be modified to the maximum extent necessary to comply with applicable State and local law if the Secretary is satisfied that the citizens of such State or local government will receive adequate notification of the proposed use of funds consistent with the intent of this section.

(d) REPORT SUBMITTED TO THE GOVERNOR.—The Secretary shall furnish to the Governor of the State in which any unit of local government which receives funds under subtitle A is located, a copy of each report filed with the Secretary as required under subsection (a), in such manner and form as the Secretary may prescribe by regulation.

(e) BUDGETS.—The Secretary shall promulgate regulations for the application of this section to circumstances under which the State government or unit of local government does not adopt a budget.

(f) REPORT OF THE SECRETARY.—The Secretary shall include with the report required under section 105(a)(2) a report to the Congress on the implementation and administration of this Act during the preceding fiscal year. Such report shall include, but not be limited to, a comprehensive and detailed analysis of—

(1) the measures taken to comply with section 122, including a description of the nature and extent of a y noncompliance and the status of all pending complaints;

(2) the extent to which recipient jurisdictions have complied with section 123, including a description of the nature and extent of any noncompliance and of measures taken to ensure the independence of audits conducted pursuant to subsection (c) of such section;

(3) the manner in which funds distributed under subtitle A have been distributed in recipient jurisdictions; and

(4) any significant problems arising in the administration of the Act and the proposals to remedy such problems through appropriate legislation.

(g) PARTICIPATION BY SENIOR CITIZENS.—In conducting any hearing required under this section, or under its own budget processes, a State or unit of local government shall endeavor to provide senior citizens and their organizations with an opportunity to be heard prior to the final allocation of any funds provided under the Act pursuant to such a hearing.

SEC. 122. NONDISCRIMINATION PROVISIONS.

(a) PROHIBITION.—

(1) IN GENERAL.—No person in the United States shall, on the ground of race, color, national origin, or sex, be excluded from participation in, be denied the benefits of, or be subjected to discrimination under any program or activity of a State government or unit of local government, which government or unit receives funds made available under subtitle A. Any prohibition against discrimination on the basis of age under the Age Discrimination Act of 1975 or with respect to an otherwise qualified handicapped individual as provided in section 504 of the Rehabilitation Act of 1973 shall also apply to any such program or activity. Any prohibition against discrimination on the basis of religion, or any exemption from such prohibition, as provided in the Civil Rights Act of 1964 or title VIII of the Act of April 11, 1968, hereafter referred to as Civil Rights Act of 1968, shall also apply to any such program or activity.

(2) EXCEPTIONS.—

(A) FUNDING.—The provisions of paragraph (1) of this subsection shall not apply where any State government or unit of local government demonstrates, by clear and convincing evidence, that the program or activity with respect to which the allegation of discrimination has been made is not funded in whole or in part with funds made available under subtitle A.

(B) CONSTRUCTION PROJECTS IN PROGRESS.—The provisions of paragraph (1), relating to discrimination on the basis of handicapped status, shall not apply with respect to construction projects commenced prior to January 1, 1977.

(b) DETERMINATION BY THE SECRETARY.—

(1) NOTICE OF NONCOMPLIANCE.—Within 10 days after the Secretary has received a holding described in subsection (c)(1) or has made a finding described in subsection (c)(4), with respect to a State government or a unit of local government, he shall send a notice of noncompliance to such government setting forth the basis of such holding or finding.

(2) PROCEDURE BEFORE SECRETARY; SUSPENSION OF PAYMENT OF REVENUE SHARING FUNDS.—Within 30 days after a notice of non-compliance has been sent to a State government or a unit of

local government in accordance with paragraph (1), such government may informally present evidence to the Secretary regarding the issues of—

(A) (except in the case of a holding described in subsection (c)(1)) whether there has been exclusion, denial, or discrimination on account of race, color, national origin, or sex, or a violation of any prohibition against discrimination on the basis of age under the Age Discriminiation Act of 1975, or with respect to an "otherwise qualified handicapped individual", as provided in section 504 of the Rehabilitation Act of 1973, or a violation of any prohibition against discrimination on the basis of religion as provided in the Civil Rights Act of 1964 or title VIII of the Civil Rights Act of 1968, and

(B) whether the program or activity in connection with which such exclusion, denial, discrimination, or violation is charged has been funded in whole or in part with funds made available under subtitle A.

Before the end of such 30-day period, unless a compliance agreement is entered into with such government, the Secretary shall issue a determination as to whether such government failed to comply with subsection (a). If the Secretary determines that such government has failed to comply with subsection (a), the Secretary shall suspend the payment of funds under subtitle A to such government unless such government within the 10 day period following such determination enters into a compliance agreement or requests a hearing with respect to such determination.

(3) HEARINGS BEFORE ADMINISTRATIVE LAW JUDGE; SUSPENSION OR TERMINATION OF PAYMENT OF REVENUE SHARING FUNDS.—

(A) Hearings requested by a State government or a unit of local government pursuant to paragraph (2) shall begin before an administrative law judge within 30 days after the Secretary receives the request for the hearing.

(B) Within 30 days after the beginning of the hearing provided under subparagraph (A), the administrative law judge conducting the hearing shall, on the record then before him, issue a preliminary finding (which shall be consistent with subsection (c)(2)) as to whether such government has failed to comply with subsection (a). If the administrative law judge issues a preliminary finding that such government is not likely to prevail, on the basis of the evidence presented, in demonstrating compliance with subsection (a), then the Secretary shall suspend the payment of funds under subtitle A to such government. No such preliminary finding shall be issued in any case where a determination has previously been issued under subparagraph (C).

(C) If, after the completion of such hearing, the administrative law judge issues a determination (consistently with subsection (c)(2)) that such government has failed to comply with subsection (a), then, unless such government enters into a compliance agreement before the 31st day after such issuance, the Secretary, subject to the provisions of subparagraph (D), shall suspend the payment of funds under subtitle A to such government; if a suspension in accordance with subparagraph (B) is still in effect, then, subject to the provisions of subparagraph (D), that suspension is to be continued.

(D) In the event of a determination described in subparagraph (C), the administrative law judge may, in his discretion, order the termination of payment of funds under subtitle A to such government or unit.

(E) If, after the completion of such hearing, the administrative law judge issues a determination (consistently with subsection (c)(2)) that there has not been a failure to comply with subsection (a), and a suspension is in effect in accordance with subparagraph (B), such suspension shall be promptly discontinued.

(c) HOLDING BY COURT OR GOVERNMENTAL AGENCY; FINDING BY SECRETARY.—

(1) DESCRIPTION.—A holding is described in this paragraph if it is a holding by a Federal Court, a State Court, or a Federal administrative law judge, with respect to a State government or a unit of local government which expends funds received under subtitle A that such government has, in the case of a person in the United States, excluded such person from participation in, denied such person the benefits of, or subjected such person to discrimination under any program or activity on the ground of race, color, national origin, or sex, or violated any prohibition against discrimination (A) on the basis of age under the Age Discrimination Act of 1975 or (B) with respect to an "otherwise qualified handicapped individual", as provided in section 504 of the Rehabilitation Act of 1973 or (C) on the basis of religion as provided in the Civil Rights Act of 1964 or title VIII of the Civil Rights Act of 1968, in connection with any such program or activity.

(2) EFFECT ON PROCEEDINGS OR HEARING.—If there has been a holding described in paragraph (1) with respect to a State government or a unit of local government, then, in the case of proceedings by the Secretary pursuant to subsection (b)(2) or a hearing pursuant to subsection (b)(3) with respect to such government, such proceedings or such hearing shall relate only to the question of whether the program or activity in which the exclusion, denial, discrimination, or violation occurred is funded in whole or in part with funds made available under subtitle A. In such proceedings or hearing, the holding described in paragraph (1), to the effect that there has been exclusion, denial, or discrimination on

account of race, color, national origin, or sex, or a violation of any prohibition against discrimination (A) on the basis of age under the Age Discrimination Act of 1975, (B) with respect to an "otherwise qualified handicapped individual", as provided in section 504 of the Rehabilitation Act of 1973, (C) on the basis of religion as provided in the Civil Rights Act of 1964 or title VIII of the Civil Rights Act of 1968, shall be treated as conclusive.

(3) EFFECT OF REVERSAL.—If a holding described in paragraph (1) is reversed by an appellate tribunal, then proceedings under subsection (b) which are dependent upon such holding shall be discontinued; any suspension or termination of payments resulting from such proceedings shall also be discontinued.

(4) FINDING BY SECRETARY.—A finding is described in this paragraph if it is a finding by the Secretary with respect to a complaint referred to in section 124(d), a determination by a State or local administrative agency, or other information (pursuant to procedures provided in regulations prescribed by the Secretary) that it is more likely than not that a State government or unit of local government has failed to comply with subsection (a).

(d) COMPLIANCE AGREEMENT.—For purposes of this section and section 124, a compliance agreement is an agreement between—

(1) the governmental office or agency responsible for prosecuting the claim or complaint which is the basis of the holding described in subsection (c)(1) and the chief executive officer of the State government or the unit of local government that has failed to comply with subsection (a), if such agreement is approved by the Secretary, or

(2) the Secretary and such chief executive officer, setting forth the terms and conditions with which such government or unit has agreed to comply that would satisfy the obligations of such government under subsection (a). Such agreement shall cover all the matters which had been determined or would constitute failures to comply with subsection (a), and may consist of a series of agreements which, in the aggregate, dispose of all such matters. Within 15 days after the execution of such agreement (or, in the case of an agreement under paragraph (1), the approval of such agreement by the Secretary, if later), the Secretary shall send a copy of such agreement to each person who has filed a complaint referred to in section 124(d) with respect to such failure to comply with subsection (a), or, in the case of an agreement under paragraph (1), to each person who has filed a complaint with the governmental office or agency (described in such paragraph) with respect to such failure to comply with subsection (a).

(e) RESUMPTION OF SUSPENDED PAYMENTS.—If payment to a State government or a unit of local government of funds made available under subtitle A has been suspended under subsection (b)(2) or (b)(3), payment of such funds shall be resumed only if—

(1) such government enters into a compliance agreement (but only at the times and under the circumstances set forth in such

agreement, or, in the case of any agreement under subsection (d)(1), only at the times and under the circumstances set forth in the Secretary's approval of such agreement);

(2) such government complies fully with the holding of a Federal or State court, or Federal administrative law judge, if that holding covers all the matters raised by the Secretary in the notice pursuant to subsection (b)(1), or if such government is found to be in compliance with subsection (a) by such court or Federal administrative law judge;

(3) in the case of a hearing before an administrative law judge under subsection (b)(3), the judge determines that such government is in compliance with subsection (a); or

(4) the provisions of subsection (c)(3) (relating to reversal of holding of discrimination) require such suspension of payment to be discontinued.

For purposes of this section, compliance by a government may include the satisfying of a requirement of the payment of restitution to persons injured by the failure of such government to comply with subsection (a).

(f) RESUMPTION OF TERMINATED PAYMENTS.—If payment to a State government or unit of local government of funds made available under subtitle A has been terminated under subsection (b)(3)(D), payment of such funds shall be resumed only if the determination resulting in such termination is reversed by an appellate tribunal.

(g) AUTHORITY OF ATTORNEY GENERAL.—Whenever the Attorney General has reason to believe that a State government or a unit of local government has engaged or is engaging in a pattern or practice in violation of the provisions of this section, the Attorney General may bring a civil action in an appropriate United States district court. Such court may grant as relief any temporary restraining order, preliminary or permanent injunction, or other order, as necessary or appropriate to insure the full enjoyment of the rights described in this section, including the suspension, termination, or repayment of funds made available under subtitle A, or placing any further payments under subtitle A in escrow pending the outcome of the litigation.

(h) AGREEMENTS BETWEEN AGENCIES.—The Secretary shall endeavor to enter into agreements with State agencies and with other Federal agencies authorizing such agencies to investigate noncompliance with subsection (a). The agreements shall describe the cooperative efforts to be undertaken (including the sharing of civil rights enforcement personnel and resources) to secure compliance with this section, and shall provide for the immediate notification of the Secretary of any actions instituted by such agencies against a State government or a unit of local government alleging a violation of any Federal civil rights statute or regulations issued thereunder.

SEC. 123. MISCELLANEOUS PROVISIONS.

(a) ASSURANCES TO THE SECRETARY.—In order to qualify for any payment under subtitle A for any entitlement period beginning on or after January 1, 1973, a State government or unit of local government must establish (in accordance with regulations prescribed by the Secretary, and, with respect to a unit of local government, after an opportunity for review and comment by the Governor of the State in which such unit is located) to the satisfaction of the Secretary that—

(1) it will establish a trust fund in which it will deposit all payments it receives under subtitle A;

(2) it will use amounts in such trust fund (including any interest earned thereon while in such trust fund) during such reasonable period or periods as may be provided in such regulations;

(3) The assurance relating to matching is repealed; (see Section 104.).

(4) it will provide for the expenditure of amounts received under subtitle A only in accordance with the laws and procedures applicable to the expenditure of its own revenues;

(5) it will—

(A) use fiscal, accounting, and audit procedures which conform to guidelines established therefor by the Secretary (after consultation with the Comptroller General of the United States),

(B) provide to the Secretary (and to the Comptroller General of the United States), on reasonable notice, access to, and the right to examine, such books, documents, papers or records as the Secretary may reasonably require for purposes of reviewing compliance with this title (or, in the case of the Comptroller General, as the Comptroller General may reasonably require for purposes of reviewing compliance and operations under subsection (c)(2)), and

(C) make such annual and interim reports (other than reports required by section 121) to the Secretary as he may reasonably require;

(6) all laborers and mechanics employed by contractors or subcontractors in the performance of work on any construction project, 25 percent or more of the costs of which project are paid out of its trust fund established under paragraph (1), will be paid wages at rates not less than those prevailing on similar construction in the locality as determined by the Secretary of Labor in accordance with the Davis-Bacon Act, as amended (40 U.S.C. 276a-276a-5), and that with respect to the labor standards specified in this paragraph the Secretary of Labor shall act in accordance with Reorganization Plan Numbered 14 of 1950 (15 F.R. 3176; 64 Stat. 1267) and section 2 of the Act of June 13, 1934, as amended (40 U.S.C. 276c);

(7) individuals employed by it whose wages are paid in whole or in part out of its trust fund established under paragraph (1) will be paid wages which are not lower than the prevailing rates of pay for persons employed in similar public occupations by the same employer; and

(8) in the case of a unit of local government as defined in the second sentence of section 108(d)(1) (relating to governments of Indian

tribes and Alaskan native villages), it will expend funds received by it under subtitle A for the benefit of members of the tribe or village residing in the county area from the allocation of which funds are allocated to it under section 108(b)(4).

Paragraph (7) shall apply with respect to employees in any category only if 25 percent or more of the wages of all employees of the State government or unit of local government in such category are paid from the trust fund established by it under paragraph (1).

(b) WITHHOLDING OF PAYMENTS.—If the Secretary determines that a State government or unit of local government has failed to comply substantially with any provision of subsection (a) or any regulations prescribed thereunder, after giving reasonable notice and opportunity for a hearing to the Governor of the State or the chief executive officer of the unit of local government, he shall notify the State government or unit of local government that if it fails to take corrective action within 60 days from the date of receipt of such notification further payments to it will be withheld for the remainder of the entitlement period and for any subsequent entitlement period until such time as the Secretary is satisfied that appropriate corrective action has been taken and that there will no longer be any failure to comply. Until he is satisfied, the Secretary shall make no further payments of such amounts.

(c) ACCOUNTING, AUDITING, AND EVALUATION.—

(1) INDEPENDENT AUDITS.—Each State government and unit of local government which expects to receive funds under subtitle A for any entitlement period beginning on or after January 1, 1977 (other than a government to which an election under paragraph (2) applies with respect to such entitlement period), shall have an independent audit of its financial statements conducted for the purpose of determining compliance with this title, in accordance with generally accepted auditing standards, not less often than once every 3 years.

(2) ELECTION.—Paragraph (1) shall not apply to any State or unit of local government whose financial statements are audited by independent auditors under State or local law not less often than every 3 years, if (A) such government makes an election under this paragraph that the provisions of paragraph (1) shall not apply, and (B) such government certifies that such audits under state or local law will be conducted in accordance with generally accepted auditing standards. Such election shall include a brief description of the auditing standards to be applied. Such election shall apply to audits of funds received under subtitle A for such entitlement periods as are specified in such election and as to which such State or local law auditing provisions are applicable.

(3) SERIES OF AUDITS.—If a series of audits conducted over a period not exceeding 3 fiscal years covers, in the aggregate, all of the funds of accounts in the financial activity of such a government, then such series of audits shall be treated as a single audit for purposes of paragraph (1) and paragraph (2).

(4) ENTITLEMENTS UNDER $25,000.—

(A) The requirements of paragraph (1) shall not apply to a State government or unit of local government for any fiscal period in which such government receives less than $25,000 of funds made available under subtitle A, unless subparagraph (B) applies for such fiscal period.

(B) In the case of a fiscal period which is described in subparagraph (A), if State or local law requires an audit of such government's financial statements, then the conducting of such audit shall constitute compliance with the requirements of paragraph (1).

(5) WAIVER.—The Secretary may waive the requirements of paragraph (1) or paragraph (2), in whole or in part, with respect to any State government or unit of local government for any fiscal period as to which he finds (in accordance with regulations prescribed by the Secretary) (A) that the financial accounts of such governments for such period are not auditable, and (B) that such government demonstrates substantial progress toward making such financial accounts auditable.

(6) COORDINATION WITH OTHER FEDERALLY REQUIRED AUDITS.—An audit of the financial statements of a State government or unit of local government for a fiscal period, conducted in accordance with the provisions of any Federal law other than this title, shall be accepted as an audit which satisfies the requirements of paragraph (1) with respect to the fiscal period for which such audit is conducted, if such audit substantially complies with the requirements for audits conducted under paragraph (1).

(7) AUDIT OPINIONS.—Any opinions rendered with respect to audits made pursuant to this subsection shall be provided to the Secretary, in such form and at such times as he may require.

(8) COMPTROLLER GENERAL SHALL REVIEW COMPLIANCE.—The Comptroller General of the United States shall make such reviews of the work as done by the Secretary, the State governments and the units of local government as may be necessary for the Congress to evaluate compliance and operations under this title.

(e) PROHIBITION OF USE FOR LOBBYING PURPOSES.—No State government or unit of local government may use any part of the funds it receives under subtitle A for the purpose of lobbying or other activities intended to influence any legislation regarding the provisions of this Act. For the purpose of this subsection, dues paid to National or State associations shall be deemed not to have been paid from funds received under subtitle A.

SEC. 124. PRIVATE CIVIL ACTIONS.

(a) STANDING.—Whenever a State government or a unit of local government, or any officer or employee thereof acting in an official capacity, has engaged or is engaging in any act or practice prohibited by this Act, upon exhaustion of administrative remedies, a civil action may be instituted by the person aggrieved in an appropriate United States district court or in a State court of general jurisdiction.

(b) RELIEF.—The court may grant as relief to the plaintiff any temporary restraining order, preliminary or permanent injunction or other order, including the suspension, termination, or repayment of funds, or placing any further payments under this title in escrow pending the outcome of the litigation.

(c) INTERVENTION BY ATTORNEY GENERAL.—In any action instituted under this section to enforce compliance with section 122(a), the Attorney General, or a specially designated assistant for or in the name of the United States, may intervene upon timely application if he certifies that the action is of general public importance. In such action the United States shall be entitled to the same relief as if it had instituted the action.

(d) EXHAUSTION OF ADMINISTRATIVE REMEDIES.—As used in this section, administrative remedies shall be deemed to be exhausted upon the expiration of 90 days after the date the administrative complaints were filed with the Secretary or with an Agency with which the Secretary has an agreement under section 122(h) if, within such period, the Secretary or such Agency—

(1) issues a determination that such Government or unit has not failed to comply with this Act; or
(2) fails to issue a determination on such complaint.

(e) ATTORNEY FEES.—In any action under this section to enforce section 122(a), the court, in its discretion, may allow to the prevailing party, other than the United States, reasonable attorney fees, and the United States shall be liable for fees and costs the same as a private person.

SEC. 125.INVESTIGATIONS AND COMPLIANCE REVIEWS.

By March 31, 1977, the Secretary shall promulgate regulations establishing—

(1) reasonable and specific time limits (in no event to exceed 90 days) for the Secretary to conduct an investigation and make a finding after receiving a complaint (described in section 124(d)), a determination by a State or local administrative agency, or other information relating to the possible violation of the provisions of this Act;
(2) reasonable and specific time limits for the Secretary to conduct audits and reviews (including investigations of allegations) relating to possible violations of the provisions of this Act.

The regulations promulgated pursuant to paragraphs (1) and (2) shall also establish reasonable and specific time limits for the Secretary to advise any complainant of the status of his investigation, audit, or review of any allegation of violation of section 122(a) or any other provision of this Act.

Subtitle C—General Provisions

SEC. 141. DEFINITIONS AND SPECIAL RULES.

(a) SECRETARY.—For purposes of this title, the term "Secretary" means the Secretary of the Treasury or his delegate. The term "Secretary of the Treasury" means the Secretary of the Treasury personally, not including any delegate.

(b) ENTITLEMENT PERIOD.—For purposes of this title, the term "entitlement period" means—

(1) The period beginning January 1, 1972, and ending June 30, 1972.

(2) The period beginning July 1, 1972, and ending December 31, 1972.

(3) The period beginning January 1, 1973, and ending June 30, 1973

(4) The one-year periods beginning on July 1 of 1973, 1974, and 1975.

(5) The period beginning July 1, 1976, and ending December 31, 1976.

(6) The period beginning January 1, 1977, and ending September 30, 1977.

(7) The one-year periods beginning October 1 of 1977, 1978, and 1979.

(c) DISTRICT OF COLUMBIA.—

(1) TREATMENT AS STATE AND LOCAL GOVERNMENT.—For purposes of this title, the District of Columbia shall be treated both—

(A) as a State (and any reference to the Governor of a State shall, in the case of the District of Columbia, be treated as a reference to the Commissioner of the District of Columbia), and

(B) as a county area which has no units of local government (other than itself) within its geographic area.

(2) REDUCTION IN CASE OF INCOME TAX ON NONRESIDENT INDIVIDUALS.—If there is hereafter enacted a law imposing a tax on income earned in the District of Columbia by individuals who are not residents of the District of Columbia, then the entitlement of the District of Columbia under subtitle A for any entitlement period shall be reduced by an amount equal to the net collections from such tax during such entitlement period attributable to individuals who are not residents of the District of Columbia. The preceding sentence shall not apply if—

(A) the District of Columbia and Maryland enter into an agreement under which each State agrees to impose a tax on income earned in that State by individuals who are residents of the other State, and the District of Columbia and Virginia enter into an agreement under which each State agrees to impose a tax on income earned in that State by individuals who are residents of the other State, or

(B) the Congress enacts a law directly imposing a tax on income earned in the District of Columbia by individuals who are not residents of the District of Columbia.

SEC. 142. REGULATIONS.

(a) GENERAL RULE.—The Secretary shall prescribe such regulations as may be necessary or appropriate to carry out the provisions of this title.

(b) ADMINISTRATIVE PROCEDURE ACT TO APPLY.—The rulemaking provisions of subchapter II of chapter 5 of title 5 of the United States Code shall apply to the regulations prescribed under this title for entitlement periods beginning on or after January 1, 1973.

SEC. 143. JUDICIAL REVIEW.

(a) PETITIONS FOR REVIEW.—Any State which receives a notice of reduction in entitlement under section 107(b), and any State or unit of local government which receives a notice of withholding of payments under section 123(b) a determination under section 122(b)(3)(C) that payments be suspended, or a determination under section 122(b)(3)(D) that payments be terminated, may, within 60 days after receiving such notice, file with the United States court of appeals for the circuit in which such State or unit of local government is located a petition for review of the action of the Secretary. A copy of the petition shall forthwith be transmitted to the Secretary; a copy shall also forthwith be transmitted to the Attorney General.

(b) RECORD.—The Secretary shall file in the court the record of the proceeding on which he based his action, as provided in section 2112 of title 28, United States Code. No objection to the action of the Secretary shall be considered by the court unless such objection has been urged before the Secretary.

(c) JURISDICTION OF COURT.—The court shall have jurisdiction to affirm or modify the action of the Secretary or to set it aside in whole or in part. The findings of fact by the Secretary, if supported by substantial evidence contained in the record, shall be conclusive. However, if any finding is not supported by substantial evidence contained in the record, the court may remand the case the the Secretary to take further evidence, and the Secretary may thereupon make new or modified findings of fact and may modify his previous actions. He shall certify to the court the record of any further proceedings. Such new or modified findings of fact shall likewise be conclusive if supported by substantial evidence contained in the record.

(d) REVIEW BY SUPREME COURT.—The judgment of the court shall be subject to review by the Supreme Court of the United States upon certiorari or certification, as provided in section 1254 of title 28, United States Code.

SEC. 144. AUTHORITY TO REQUIRE INFORMATION ON INCOME TAX RETURNS.

(a) GENERAL RULE.—

(1) INFORMATION WITH RESPECT TO PLACE OF RESIDENCE.—
Subpart B of part II of subchapter A of chapter 61 of the Internal

Revenue Code of 1954 (relating to income tax returns) is amended by adding at the end thereof the following new section:

SEC. 6017A. PLACE OF RESIDENCE.

In the case of an individual, the information required on any return with respect to the taxes imposed by chapter 1 for any period shall include information as to the State, county, municipality, and any other unit of local government in which the taxpayer (and any other individual with respect to whom an exemption is claimed on such return) resided on one or more dates (determined in the manner provided by regulations prescribed by the Secretary or his delegate) during such period.

(2) CLERICAL AMENDMENT.—The table of sections for such subpart B is amended by adding at the end thereof the following:

Sec. 6017A. Place of residence.

(b) CIVIL PENALTY.—

(1) IN GENERAL.—Subchapter B of chapter 68 of the Internal Revenue Code of 1954 is amended by adding at the end thereof the following new section:

SEC. 6687. FAILURE TO SUPPLY INFORMATION WITH RESPECT TO PLACE OF RESIDENCE.

(a) CIVIL PENALTY.—If any person fails to include on his return any information required under section 6017A with respect to his place of residence, he shall pay a penalty of $5 for each such failure, unless it is shown that such failure is due to reasonable cause.

(b) DEFICIENCY PROCEDURES NOT TO APPLY.—Subchapter B of chapter 63 (relating to deficiency procedures for income, estate, gift, and chapter 42 taxes) shall not apply in respect of the assessment or collection of any penalty imposed by subsection (a).

(2) CLERICAL AMENDMENT.—The table of sections for such subchapter B is amended by adding at the end thereof the following:

Sec. 6687. Failure to supply information with respect to place of residence.

SEC. 145. ENTITLEMENT FACTORS AFFECTED BY MAJOR DISASTERS.*

(a) In the administration of this title the Secretary shall disregard any change in data used in determining the entitlement of a State government or a unit of local government for a period of 60 months if that change—

(1) results from a major disaster determined by the President under section 301 of the Disaster Relief Act of 1974, and

(2) reduces the amount of the entitlement of that State government or unit of local government

(b) The amendment made by this section takes effect on April 1, 1974.

SEC. 145. STUDY OF REVENUE SHARING AND FEDERALISM.*

(a) STUDY.—The Advisory Commission on Intergovernmental Relations shall study and evaluate the American Federal fiscal system in terms of the allocation and coordination of public resources among

Federal, State, and local governments including, but not limited to, a study and evaluation of—

(1) the allocation and coordination of taxing and spending authorities between levels of government, including a comparison of other Federal Government systems;

(2) State and local governmental organization from both legal and operational viewpoints to determine how general local governments do and ought to relate to each other, to special districts, and to State governments in terms of service and financing responsibilities, as well as annexation and incorporation responsibilities;

(3) the effectiveness of Federal Government stabilization policies on State and local areas and the effects of State and local fiscal decisions on aggregate economic activity;

(4) the legal and operational aspects of citizen participation in Federal, State, and local governmental fiscal decisions;

(5) forces likely to affect the nature of the American Federal system in the short-term and long-term future and possible adjustments to such system, if any, which may be desirable, in light of future developments.

(b) COOPERATION OF OTHER FEDERAL AGENCIES.—

(1) Each department, agency, and instrumentality of the Federal Government is authorized and directed to furnish to the Commission, upon request made by the Chairman, and to the extent permitted by law and within the limits of available funds, such data, reports, and other information as the Commission deems necessary to carry out its functions under this section.

(2) The head of each department or agency of the Federal Government is authorized to provide to the Commission such services as the Commission requests on such basis, reimbursable and otherwise, as may be agreed between the department or agency and the Chairman of the Commission. All such requests shall be made by the Chairman of the Commission.

(3) The Administrator of General Services shall provide to the Commission, on a reimbursable basis, such administrative support services as the Commission may request.

(c) REPORTS.—The Commission shall submit to the President and the Congress such interim reports as it deems advisable, and not later than three years after the day on which the first appropriation is made available under subsection (d), a final report containing a detailed statement of the findings and conclusions of the Commission, together with such recommendations for legislation as it deems advisable.

(d) AUTHORIZATION OF APPROPRIATIONS.—There are authorized to be appropriated to the Commission, effective with the fiscal year beginning October 1, 1977, such sums as may be necessary to carry out the provisions of this section.

MISCELLANEOUS PROVISIONS.

(a) BUDGET ACT.—In accordance with section 401(d)(2) of the Congressional Budget Act of 1974 (31 U.S.C. 1351(d)(2); 88 Stat. 297,

318), subsections (a) and (b) of section 401 of such Act shall not apply to this Act.

EFFECTIVE DATES.

(a) Except as otherwise provided in this Act, the amendments made by the State and Local Fiscal Assistance Amendments of 1976 shall apply to entitlement periods beginning on or after January 1, 1977.

(b) The amendment made by section 145 regarding study of the Advisory Commission on Intergovernmental Relations takes effect on February 1, 1977.

*Note: Due to error in numbering there are two Sections 145.

☆U.S. GOVERNMENT PRINTING OFFICE:1977   723-044/93   1-3

Bibliography

This bibliography does not constitute a full listing of all publications relevant to revenue sharing, but it is a reasonably representative list of major, especially recent, sources on this subject.

Aaron, Henry. "The Honest Citizen's Guide to Revenue Sharing," *Tax Review*, vol. 32 (October 1971).

American Enterprise Institute for Public Policy Research. *General Revenue Sharing Proposals, Legislative Analysis*. Legislative Analysis 7. Washington: AEI, June 1971.

Angrick, William P. "General Revenue Sharing and Environmental Quality," *The Annals*, vol. 419 (May 1975).

Banfield, Edward C. "Revenue Sharing in Theory and Practice," *Public Interest*, no. 23 (Spring 1971).

Beer, Samuel H., "The Adoption of General Revenue Sharing: A Case Study in Public Sector Politics," *Public Policy*, vol. 24 (Spring 1976).

Blair, Patricia W. *General Revenue Sharing in American Cities: First Impressions*. Washington: National Clearinghouse on Revenue Sharing, December 1974.

Bradford, David F., and Wallace E. Oates. "The Analysis of Revenue Sharing in a New Approach to Collective Fiscal Decisions," *Quarterly Journal of Economics*, vol. 85 (August 1971).

Break, George F. "Revenue Sharing: Its Implications for Present and Future Intergovernmental Fiscal Systems: The Case For," *National Tax Journal*, vol. 24 (September 1971).

————. "Revenue Sharing: Priorities and Policy Instruments," *The Journal of Finance*, vol. 23 (May 1968).

Byrnes, John W. "Federal Action to Strengthen State and Local Revenue Capabilities," *National Tax Journal*, vol. 24 (September 1971).

Cantor, Arnold. "Revenue Sharing: Passing the Buck," *American Federationist*, vol. 77 (November 1970).

Caputo, David A. "General Revenue Sharing and American Federalism: Towards the Year 2000," *The Annals*, vol. 419 (May 1975).

————, and Richard L. Cole. *Urban Politics and Decentralization: The Case of General Revenue Sharing*. Boston: D. C. Heath, 1974.

Cole, Richard L. "Revenue Sharing: Citizen Participation and Social Service Aspects," *The Annals*, vol. 419 (May 1975).

Comptroller General of the United States. *Revenue Sharing: Its Use by and Impact on Local Governments*. Report to the Congress. Washington: U.S. General Accounting Office, April 25, 1974.

257

————. *Revenue Sharing: Its Use by and Impact on State Governments."* Report to the Congress. Washington: U.S. General Accounting Office, August 2, 1973.

————. *Revenue Sharing and Local Government Modernization: A Conference Report."* Washington: Government Printing Office, April 17, 1975.

Corman, James C. "Grave Doubts about Revenue Sharing," *Georgetown Law Journal,* vol. 60 (October 1971).

Dommel, Paul R. *The Politics of Revenue Sharing.* Bloomington: Indiana University Press, 1974.

Elazar, Daniel J. "The Dilemmas of Revenue Sharing," *Ripon Forum* (May 1972).

Ford, President Gerald R. *Renewal of General Revenue Sharing.* Message to Congress, April 25, 1975. Washington: Government Printing Office, 1975.

Frankel, Max. "Revenue Sharing Is a Counter-Revolution," *New York Times Magazine,* April 25, 1971.

Griffiths, Martha W. "Revenue Sharing and Its Alternatives: What Future for Fiscal Federalism?" *Tax Review,* vol. 28 (December 1967).

Heilbroner, Robert L. "The Share-the-Tax Revenue Plan," *New York Times Magazine,* December 27, 1965.

Heller, Walter W. *New Dimensions of Political Economy.* Godkin Lectures Series. Cambridge: Harvard University Press, 1966.

————, and Joseph A. Pechman. *Questions and Answers on Revenue Sharing.* Washington: Brookings Institution, 1967.

————, and others. *Revenue Sharing and the City.* Baltimore: published for Resources for the Future by The Johns Hopkins Press, 1968.

McBreen, Maureen. "History of Federal Revenue Sharing Proposals and Enactment of the State and Local Fiscal Assistance Act of 1972 (Public Law 92-512)." Congressional Research Service Report 72-243E. Washington: Library of Congress, November 16, 1972.

Mills, Wilbur D. "A Federal Legislator's Viewpoint on Fiscal Federalism," *National Tax Journal,* vol. 24 (September 1971).

Musgrave, Richard A., and A. Mitchell Polinsky. "Revenue Sharing: A Critical View," *Harvard Journal of Legislation,* vol. 8 (January 1971).

Myers, Will S., Jr. "Fiscal Balance in the American Federal System," *State Government,* vol. 41 (Winter 1968).

————. "A Legislative History of Revenue Sharing," *The Annals,* vol. 419 (May 1975).

Nathan, Richard P., Allen D. Manvel, and Susannah E. Calkins. *Monitoring Revenue Sharing.* Washington: Brookings Institution, 1975.

National Science Foundation, Research Applied to National Needs. *General Revenue Sharing, Research Utilization Project.* 5 vols. Washington: Government Printing Office, 1975.

Otten, Alan L., and Charles B. Seib. "No Strings Aid for the States," *Reporter,* January 28, 1965.

Pechman, Joseph. "Fiscal Federalism for the 1970's," *National Tax Journal,* vol. 24 (September 1971).

Raven-Hansen, Peter. "The Revenue Sharing Act of 1972: Untied and Untraceable Dollars from Washington," *Harvard Journal of Legislation*, vol. 10 (February 1973).

Reagan, Michael D. "The Pro and Con Arguments," *The Annals*, vol. 419 (May 1975).

Reischauer, Robert D., "General Revenue Sharing: The Program's Incentives," in Wallace E. Oates, ed., *Financing the New Federalism: Revenue Sharing, Conditional Grants, and Taxation*. Baltimore: Johns Hopkins University Press, 1975.

Reuss, Congressman Henry S. *Revenue Sharing: Crutch or Catalyst for State and Local Governments?* New York: Praeger Publishers, 1970.

―――. "Should We Abandon Revenue Sharing?" *The Annals*, vol. 419 (May 1975).

Revenue Sharing Advisory Service. *Revenue Sharing Bulletin*, published monthly by the Revenue Sharing Advisory Service, Washington, D.C.

―――. *Revenue Sharing Handbook*. Washington: RSAS, July 1973.

Robinson, William H. "Revenue Sharing and Creative Federalism—Some Perspectives," in *Federal-State-Local Fiscal Relationships: A Symposium*. Princeton: Tax Institute of America, 1968.

Rockefeller, Nelson A. "Revenue Sharing: A View from the Statehouse," *Georgetown Law Journal*, vol. 60 (October 1971).

Schultze, Charles L., and others. *Setting National Priorities: The 1972 Budget*. Washington: Brookings Institution, 1971.

Shannon, John. "Federal Tax Sharing: The Key to Balanced Fiscal Federalism," in National Tax Association, *Proceedings of Sixty-Second Annual Conference*. Boston: NTA, 1969.

―――. "Federal Revenue Sharing: Time for Renewal?" *National Tax Journal*, vol. 27 (December 1974).

Sklar, Morton H. *Civil Rights under General Revenue Sharing*. Washington: Center for National Policy Review, Catholic University Law School, July 1975.

Stenberg, Carl W. "Revenue Sharing and Governmental Reform," *The Annals*, vol. 419 (May 1975).

Thompson, Richard E. *Revenue Sharing: A New Era in Federalism?* Washington: Revenue Sharing Advisory Service, 1973.

Ulmer, Melville J. "The Limitations of Revenue Sharing," *Annals of the American Academy of Political and Social Science*, vol. 397 (September 1971).

U.S. Advisory Commission on Intergovernmental Relations. *General Revenue Sharing: An ACIR Re-evaluation*. Washington: ACIR, October 1974.

―――. *Revenue Sharing: An Idea Whose Time Has Come*. Information Report M-54. Washington: Government Printing Office, December 1970.

U.S. Congress. House. Committee on Ways and Means. *General Revenue Sharing*. Hearing. 92:1. Washington: Government Printing Office, 1971.

U.S. Congress. Joint Committee on Internal Revenue Taxation. *General Explanation of the State and Local Fiscal Assistance Act and the Federal-State*

Tax Collection Act of 1972. Washington: Government Printing Office, 1973.

―――. *Digest of Testimony on General Revenue Sharing and Alternative Methods of Providing Fiscal Aid to State and Local Governments at Public Hearings held by the Committee on Ways and Means, June 2 to June 28, 1971.* 92:1. Washington: Government Printing Office, 1971.

―――. *Summary of Testimony on General Revenue Sharing at Public Hearings, June 2 to 28, 1971, held by the Committee on Ways and Means, July 7, 1971.* 92:1. Washington: Government Printing Office, 1971.

U.S. Congress. Joint Economic Committee. *Revenue Sharing and Its Alternatives: What Future for Fiscal Federalism?* 3 vols. Washington: Government Printing Office, 1967.

―――. *Revenue Sharing and Its Alternatives: What Future for Fiscal Federalism?* Hearing. 90:1. Washington: Government Printing Office, 1967.

U.S. Congress. Senate. Committee on Finance. *Revenue Sharing.* Hearings on H.R. 14370. 92:2. Washington: Government Printing Office, 1972.

―――. Subcommittee on Revenue Sharing. *General Revenue Sharing.* Hearing. 94:1. Washington: Government Printing Office, 1975.

―――. Committee on Government Operations. Subcommittee on Intergovernmental Relations. *Intergovernmental Revenue Act of 1969 and Related Legislation.* Hearing. 91:2. Washington: Government Printing Office, 1970.

―――. *Revenue Sharing.* Hearing. 93:2. Washington: Government Printing Office, 1974.

―――. *Revenue Sharing: A Selection of Recent Research.* Washington: Government Printing Office, March 1975.

Watt, Graham W. "The Goals and Objectives of General Revenue Sharing," *The Annals,* vol. 419 (May 1975).

Weidenbaum, Murray L. *Potential Impacts of Revenue Sharing.* Reprint 26. Washington: American Enterprise Institute for Public Policy Research, October 1974.

―――, and Robert L. Joss. "Alternative Approaches to Revenue Sharing: A Description and Framework for Evaluation," *National Tax Journal,* vol. 23, no. 1 (March 1970).

Wright, Deil S. "Revenue Sharing and Structural Features of American Federalism," *The Annals,* vol. 419 (May 1975).

Index